jQuery UI 1.7

The User Interface Library for jQuery

Build highly interactive web applications with
ready-to-use widgets from the jQuery User
Interface library

Dan Wellman

BIRMINGHAM - MUMBAI

jQuery UI 1.7
The User Interface Library for jQuery

First published: November 2009

Production Reference: 1021109

Published by Packt Publishing Ltd.
32 Lincoln Road
Olton
Birmingham, B27 6PA, UK.

ISBN 978-1-847199-72-0

www.packtpub.com

Cover Image by Vinayak Chittar (vinayak.chittar@gmail.com)

Credits

Author
Dan Wellman

Reviewers
Marc Grabanski

Akash Mehta

Jörn Zaefferer

Acquisition Editor
Douglas Paterson

Development Editor
Nikhil Bangera

Technical Editors
Vinodhan Nair

Gagandeep Singh

Indexer
Rekha Nair

Editorial Team Leader
Gagandeep Singh

Project Team Leader
Priya Mukherji

Proofreader
Claire Cresswell-Lane

Graphics
Nilesh Mohite

Production Coordinator
Shantanu Zagade

Cover Work
Shantanu Zagade

About the Author

Dan Wellman lives with his wife and three children in his home town of Southampton on the south coast of England. By day his mild-mannered alter-ego works for a small yet accomplished e-commerce production agency. By night he battles the forces of darkness and fights for truth, justice, and less intrusive JavaScript.

He has been writing computer-related articles, tutorials, and reviews for around five years and is rarely very far from a keyboard of some description. This is his third book.

I'd like to thank the Packt editorial team, all of the technical reviewers and the jQuery UI team, without whom this book would not have been possible. Special thanks go to Jörn Zaefferer who provided essential feedback and was always happy to answer my late-night, niggling questions.

Thanks also to my fantastic friends, in no particular order; Steve Bishop, Eamon O' Donoghue, James Zabiela, Andrew Herman, Aaron Matheson, Dan Goodall, Mike Woodford, Mike Newth, John Adams, Jon Field and Vicky Hammond and all the rest of the guys and girls.

About the Reviewers

Marc Grabanski got involved early on with jQuery by authoring what would become the jQuery UI Datepicker. He works, arguably too much, building user interfaces and web software all the day long with his company MJG International.

> If I were to thank anyone it would be Jesus Christ for transforming me from a video game addict into something useful to society and the people around me.

Akash Mehta is a web application developer and technical author based in Australia. His area of work covers e-learning solutions, information systems, and developer training. He regularly writes web development articles for Adobe, CNet, the APC Magazine, and other publications in print and online. He is a regular speaker at IT conferences, user groups, and BarCamps. Currently, Akash provides web development, technical writing, consulting, and training services through his website, `http://bitmeta.org/`.

> I would like to thank my parents, for their constant support and encouragement, and Sophie, for her enduring patience and amazing inspiration.

Jörn Zaefferer is a professional software developer from Cologne, Germany. He creates application programming interfaces (APIs), graphical user interfaces (GUIs), software architectures, and designs databases, for both web and desktop applications.

His work focuses on the Java-platform, while clientside-scripting evolves around jQuery. He started contributing to jQuery in mid-2006, and has since co-created and maintained QUnit, jQuery's unit testing framework; released and maintained a half-dozen of very popular jQuery plugins, and contributed to jQuery books as both author and tech-reviewer. He also is a lead developer for jQuery UI.

This book is dedicated to my eternally patient and understanding wife Tammy and my beautiful kids Bethany, Matthew, James, and Jessica. Shining supernovas that light up my life.

Table of Contents

Preface

Modern web application user interface design requires rapid development and proven results. jQuery UI, a trusted suite of official plugins for the jQuery JavaScript library, gives you a solid platform on which to build rich and engaging interfaces with maximum compatibility, stability, and a minimum of time and effort.

jQuery UI has a series of ready-made, great looking user interface widgets, and a comprehensive set of core interaction helpers designed to be implemented in a consistent and developer-friendly way. With all this, the amount of code that you need to write personally to take a project from conception to completion is drastically reduced.

Specially revised for version 1.7 of jQuery, this book has been written to maximize your experience with the library by breaking down each component and walking you through examples that progressively build upon your knowledge, taking you from beginner to advanced usage in a series of easy-to-follow steps.

In this book, you'll learn how each component can be initialized in a basic default implementation and then see how easy it is to customize its appearance and configure its behavior to tailor it to the requirements of your application. You'll look at the configuration options and the methods exposed by each component's API to see how these can be used to bring out the best of the library.

Events play a key role in any modern web application if it is to meet the expected minimum requirements of interactivity and responsiveness, and each chapter will show you the custom events fired by the component covered and how these events can be intercepted and acted upon.

What this book covers

Chapter 1, *Introducing jQuery UI*, gives a general overview and introduction to jQuery UI. You find out exactly what the library is, where it can be downloaded from, and where resources for it can be found. We look at the freedom the license gives you to use the library and how the API has been simplified to give the components a consistent and easy to use programming model.

In Chapter 2, *The CSS Framework*, we look in details at the extensive CSS framework that provides a rich environment for integrated theming via ThemeRoller, or allows developers to easily supply their own custom themes or skins.

In Chapter 3, *Tabs*, we look at the tabs component; a simple but effective means of presenting structured content in an engaging and interactive widget.

Chapter 4, *The Accordion Widget*, looks at the accordion widget, another component dedicated to the effective display of content. Highly engaging and interactive, the accordion makes a valuable addition to any web page and its API is exposed in full to show exactly how it can be used.

In Chapter 5, *The Dialog*, we focus on the dialog widget. The dialog behaves in the same way as a standard browser alert, but it does so in a much less intrusive and more visitor-friendly manner. We look at how it can be configured and controlled to provide maximum benefit and appeal.

Chapter 6, *Slider*, looks at the slider widget that provides a less commonly used, but no less valuable user interface tool for collecting input from your visitors. We look closely at its API throughout this chapter to see the variety of ways that in which it can be implemented.

In Chapter 7, *Datepicker*, we look at the datepicker. This component packs a huge amount of functionality into an attractive and highly usable tool, allowing your visitors to effortlessly select dates. We look at the wide range of configurations that its API makes possible as well as seeing how easy common tasks such as skinning and localization are made.

In Chapter 8, *Progressbar*, we look at the new progressbar widget; examining its compact API and seeing a number of ways in which it can be put to good use in our web applications.

In Chapter 9, *Drag and Drop*, we begin looking at the low-level interaction helpers, tackling first the related drag-and-droppable components. We look at how they can be implemented individually and how they can be used together for maximum effect.

Chapter 10, *Resizing*, looks at the resizing component and how it is used with the dialog widget from earlier in the book. We see how it can be applied to any element on the page to allow it be resized in a smooth and attractive way.

In Chapter 11, *Selecting*, we look at the selectable component, which allows us add behavior to elements on the page and allow them be selected individually or as a group. We see that this is one component that really brings the desktop and the browser together as application platforms.

Chapter 12, *Sorting*, looks at the final interaction helper — the sortable component. This is an especially effective component that allows you to create lists on a page that can be reordered by dragging items to a new position on the list. This is another component that can really help you to add a high level of professionalism and interactivity to your site with a minimum of effort.

Chapter 13, *UI Effects*, is dedicated solely to the special effects that are included with the library. We look at an array of different effects that allow you to show, hide, move, and jiggle elements in a variety of attractive and appealing animations. There is no 'fun with' section at the end of this chapter; the whole chapter is a 'fun with' section.

What you need for this book

- A copy of the latest jQuery UI full build (1.7.2 at the time of writing)
- A code or text editor
- A browser
- The code download for the book

Who this book is for

This book is for developers who want to quickly and easily build engaging, highly interactive interfaces for their web applications, or less commonly, for embedded applications.

Nokia was the first mobile phone company to announce that they were adopting jQuery to power parts of their cell phone operating system. I'm sure that by the time this book is published there will be more companies adapting the library for their own needs, and wherever jQuery goes, jQuery UI can follow.

People who are comfortable with HTML, JavaScript, and CSS along with having at least some experience with jQuery itself will get the most benefit from what this book has to offer. However, no prior knowledge of the UI library itself is required.

Consider the following code:

```
$("#myEl").click(function() {
  $("<p>").attr("id", "new").css({
    color:"#000000"
  }).appendTo("#target");
)};
```

If you cannot immediately see, and completely understand, what this simple code snippet does, you would probably get more from this book after first learning about jQuery itself. Consider reading Karl Swedberg and Jonathan Chaffer's excellent *Learning jQuery 1.3*, also by Packt Publishing, or visit http://www.learningjquery. com for an excellent foundation in jQuery, and then come back to this book.

Each jQuery UI specific method or property that we work with will be fully covered in the explanatory text that accompanies each code example, and where it is practical, some of the standard jQuery code will also be discussed. CSS and HTML will take a back seat and be covered very briefly, if at all, unless it is completely central to the discussion at hand.

Basic concepts of using jQuery itself won't be covered. Therefore, you should already be familiar with advanced DOM traversal and manipulation, attribute and style getting and setting, and making and handling AJAX calls. You should be comfortable with the programming constructs exposed by jQuery such as method chaining, using JavaScript objects, and working with callback functions.

Conventions

In this book, you will find a number of styles of text that distinguish between different kinds of information. Here are some examples of these styles, and an explanation of their meaning.

Code words in text are shown as follows: "We can include other contexts through the use of the `include` directive."

A block of code is set as follows:

```
[default]
var pickerOpts = {
  changeMonth: true,
  changeYear: true,
  yearRange: "-25:+25"
};
```

When we wish to draw your attention to a particular part of a code block, the relevant lines or items are set in bold:

```
[default]
var pickerOpts = {
  minDate: new Date(),
  maxDate: "+10"
};
```

New terms and **important words** are shown in bold. Words that you see on the screen, in menus or dialog boxes for example, appear in the text like this: "clicking the **Next** button moves you to the next screen".

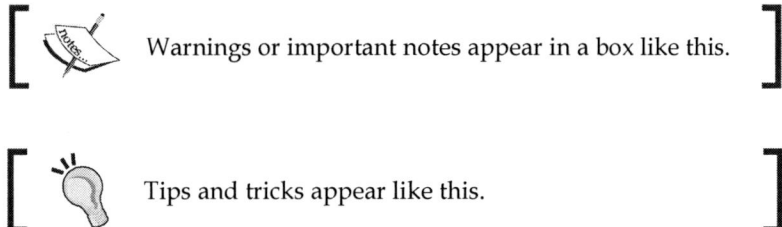

Warnings or important notes appear in a box like this.

Tips and tricks appear like this.

Reader feedback

Feedback from our readers is always welcome. Let us know what you think about this book—what you liked or may have disliked. Reader feedback is important for us to develop titles that you really get the most out of.

To send us general feedback, simply send an email to feedback@packtpub.com, and mention the book title via the subject of your message.

If there is a book that you need and would like to see us publish, please send us a note in the **SUGGEST A TITLE** form on www.packtpub.com or email suggest@packtpub.com.

If there is a topic that you have expertise in and you are interested in either writing or contributing to a book on, see our author guide on www.packtpub.com/authors.

Customer support

Now that you are the proud owner of a Packt book, we have a number of things to help you to get the most from your purchase.

> **Downloading the example code for the book**
> Visit http://www.packtpub.com/files/code/9720_Code.zip to directly download the example code.
> The downloadable files contain instructions on how to use them.

Errata

Although we have taken every care to ensure the accuracy of our content, mistakes do happen. If you find a mistake in one of our books—maybe a mistake in the text or the code—we would be grateful if you would report this to us. By doing so, you can save other readers from frustration, and help us to improve subsequent versions of this book. If you find any errata, please report them by visiting http://www.packtpub.com/support, selecting your book, clicking on the **let us know** link, and entering the details of your errata. Once your errata are verified, your submission will be accepted and the errata added to any list of existing errata. Any existing errata can be viewed by selecting your title from http://www.packtpub.com/support.

Piracy

Piracy of copyright material on the Internet is an ongoing problem across all media. At Packt, we take the protection of our copyright and licenses very seriously. If you come across any illegal copies of our works, in any form, on the Internet, please provide us with the location address or web site name immediately so that we can pursue a remedy.

Please contact us at copyright@packtpub.com with a link to the suspected pirated material.

We appreciate your help in protecting our authors, and our ability to bring you valuable content.

Questions

You can contact us at questions@packtpub.com if you are having a problem with any aspect of the book, and we will do our best to address it.

1
Introducing jQuery UI

Welcome to jQuery UI 1.7: The User Interface Library for jQuery. This resource aims to take you from your first steps to an advanced usage of the JavaScript library of UI widgets and interaction helpers built on top of the hugely popular and easy-to-use jQuery.

jQuery UI extends the underlying jQuery library to provide a suite of rich and interactive widgets along with code-saving interaction helpers, built to enhance the user interfaces of your websites and web applications. It's the official UI library for jQuery and although it is not the only library built on top of jQuery, in my opinion it is without a doubt the best.

jQuery has quickly become one of the most popular JavaScript libraries in use today and jQuery UI will definitely become the extension library of choice, thanks to its ever-growing range of common UI widgets, high levels of configurability, and its exceptional ease of implementation.

jQuery UI runs on top of jQuery and hence the syntax used to initialize, configure, and manipulate the different components is in the same comfortable, easy-to-use style as jQuery. We automatically get all of the great jQuery functionality at our disposal as well. The library is also supported by a range of incredibly useful tools, such as the CSS framework that provides a range of helper CSS classes, and the excellent ThemeRoller application that allows us to visually create our own custom themes for the widgets.

Over the course of this book we'll look at each of the existing components that make up the library. We will also be looking at their configuration options and trying out their methods in order to fully understand how they work and what they are capable of. By the end of the book, you'll be an expert in its implementation.

We already have a basic working knowledge of the components when we add a new component because of the consistency in how we implement the different components that make up the library. Therefore, we only need to learn any widget-specific functionality.

This chapter will cover the following topics:

- How to obtain a copy of the library
- How to set up a development environment
- The structure of the library
- ThemeRoller
- The format of the API
- Browser support
- How the library is licensed

Downloading the library

To obtain a copy of the library, we should visit the download builder at `http://jqueryui.com/download`, which gives us a range of different options for building a download package that is tailored for our particular implementational requirements. The following screenshot shows the download builder:

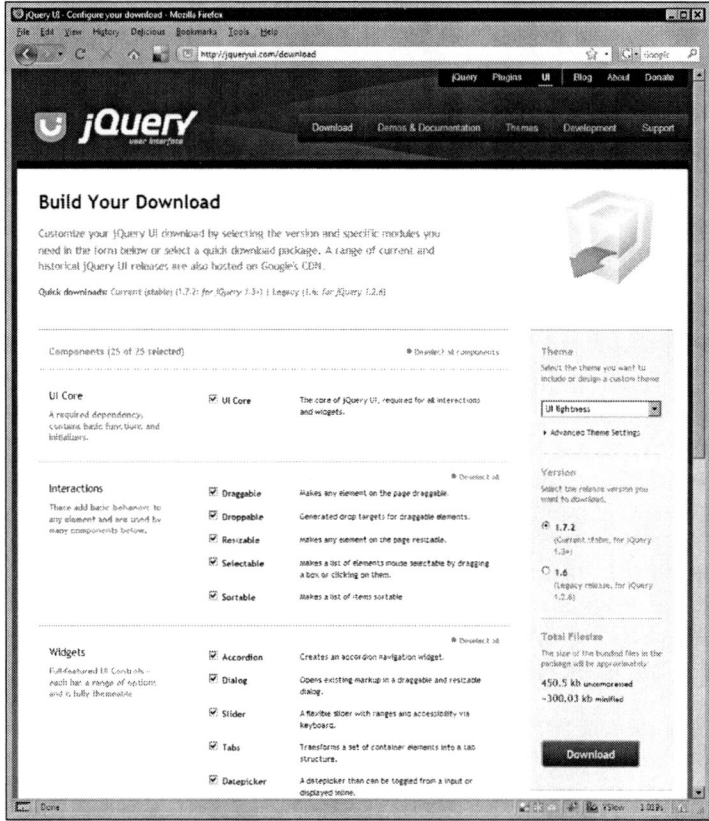

We can either download the complete current release of the library, or a complete package of the legacy 1.6 version, or we can select the components that we want and download a custom package.

 This book is specifically tailored towards version 1.7 of jQuery UI (at the time of writing the current stable release is 1.7.2) and is not compatible with legacy versions of the library. jQuery UI 1.7 requires jQuery 1.3.

The page is laid out in a really friendly and easy-to-use way. It lists all of the different components in their respective groupings (core, interaction helpers, and widgets) and allows us to choose from one of 25 different predesigned themes along with providing information about the package (including both its compressed and uncompressed size).

We'll look at the different files found within the library in just a moment, but for now we should download the complete library. It will contain everything we need, including the JavaScript and CSS files, as well as any images from the current theme that different components rely on. It even contains the latest version of jQuery itself, so we don't need to worry about downloading this separately.

For now, just use the **Current (stable)** link at the top of the page. This will give us the default theme that is called **smoothness**. We'll look at downloading and using other themes in the next chapter.

Hosted Files

In reality, we don't even need to download the library in order to implement it in a production web application. Both jQuery and jQuery UI are hosted on Google's **content delivery network (CDN)**, so we can include <script> elements that link to these files instead of using local versions. Only the complete library (not individual components) is available, although there are a range of different releases.

On a live site that receives a lot of international traffic, using a CDN will help ensure that the library files are downloaded to a visitor's computer from a server that is geographically close to them. This helps in making the response quicker for them and saving our own bandwidth. This is not recommended for local development however.

Setting up a development environment

We'll need a location to unpack the jQuery UI library in order to easily access the different parts of it within our own files. We should first create a project folder, into which all of our example files, as well as all of the library and other associated resources can be saved.

Create a new directory on your **C:** drive, or in your home directory, and call it jqueryui. This will be the root folder of our project and will be the location where we store all of the example files from the code download.

To unpack the library, open it in a compression program, such as the open source **7zip**, and choose the extract or unzip command. When prompted for a location to unpack the archive to, choose the jqueryui folder that we just created.

The code examples that we'll be looking at use other resources, mostly images, but occasionally some PHP files too. The accompanying code download available on Packt's website contains all of the images that we'll be using. You should download this now if you can, visit: http://www.packtpub.com/support/book/user-interface-library-for-jquery. You'll need to create a new folder within the jqueryui project folder and call it img, then unpack all of the subdirectories within the img folder in the archive to this new folder.

The code download also contains all the examples files as well as the library itself. It would be incredibly easy to unpack the entire code download to a local directory and run each of the examples as they are.

These files are provided in the hope that they will be used for reference purposes only! I'd urge you to follow the examples in the book on the fly, manually creating each file as it is shown instead of just referring to the files in the code download. The best way to learn code is to code.

This is all we need to do, no additional platforms or applications need to be installed and nothing needs to be configured or set up. As long as you have a browser and some kind of code or text editor then everything is in place to begin developing with the library.

The structure of the library

Let's take a moment to look at the structure of the unpacked library. This will give us a feel for its composition and structure. Open up the `jqueryui` folder where we unpacked the library. The contents of this folder should be as follows:

- A `css` directory
- A `development-bundle` directory
- A `js` directory
- An `index` file

The `css` folder is used to store the complete CSS framework that comes with the library. Within this folder will be a directory that has the name of the theme we chose when building the download package. Inside this is single file that contains all of the CSS, and a folder that holds all the images used by the theme. We can also store the CSS files we'll be creating in the `css` directory.

The `js` folder contains minified versions of jQuery and the complete jQuery UI library, with all components rolled into this one file. In a live project, it is the `js` and `css` folders that we'd want to drop into our site.

The `index` is an HTML file that gives a brief introduction to the library and displays all of the widgets along with some of the CSS classes. If this is the first time you've ever used the library, you can take a look to see some of the things that we'll be working with throughout the course of this book.

The `development-bundle` directory contains a series of resources to help us develop with the library and contains the following subdirectories:

- A `demos` folder
- A `docs` folder
- An `external` folder
- A `themes` folder
- A `ui` folder

Also present in the directory are the license files, documents showing the version of the library and its main contributors. An uncompressed version of jQuery is also present.

The `demos` folder contains a series of basic examples showing all of the different components in action. The `docs` folder contains API documents for each of the different components.

The `external` folder contains a set of tools that may be of use to developers. They are as follows:

- The `bgiframe` plugin
- The `cookie` plugin
- A JavaScript implementation of the diff algorithm `jsDiff`
- The unit testing suite `qunit`
- The `simulate` plugin

The `bgiframe` plugin is used to fix the issue in IE6 where `<select>` elements appear above other content, regardless of z-index. This plugin is due to be removed in release 1.8 of jQuery UI and replaced with the stackfix utility. The `cookie` plugin makes it easy to use browser cookies. `jsDiff` is the JavaScript implementation of an algorithm that can be used to compare two strings and show the differences between them.

`qunit` is jQuery's unit testing suite and can be used to run unit tests on widgets and plugins that we may create. For more information on QUnit visit: `http://docs.jquery.com/QUnit`. The `simulate` plugin simulates mouse and keyboard events and allows the functionality of widgets or plugins to be tested automatically.

Other than the `cookie` plugin (which we use in Chapter 12), we won't be using any of these tools in the examples we'll look at.

The `themes` folder contains two different themes—the first is the **base** theme that is a neutral, minimal theme of grey tones. The second is the **smoothness** theme, which we chose when building our download. It is very similar to the base theme.

The `ui` folder contains the individual, uncompressed source files of each of the different components of the library.

ThemeRoller

ThemeRoller is a custom tool written with jQuery and PHP. It allows us to visually produce our own custom jQuery UI theme and package it up in a convenient, downloadable archive, which we can drop into our project with no further coding (other than using the stylesheet in a HTML `<link>` element of course).

ThemeRoller was created by **Filament Group, Inc.** and makes use of a number of jQuery plugins released into the open source community. It can be found at `http://ui.jquery.com/themeroller`.

ThemeRoller is certainly the most comprehensive tool available for creating your own jQuery UI themes. We can very quickly and easily create an entire theme comprised of all of the styles needed for targeting elements, including the images we'll need.

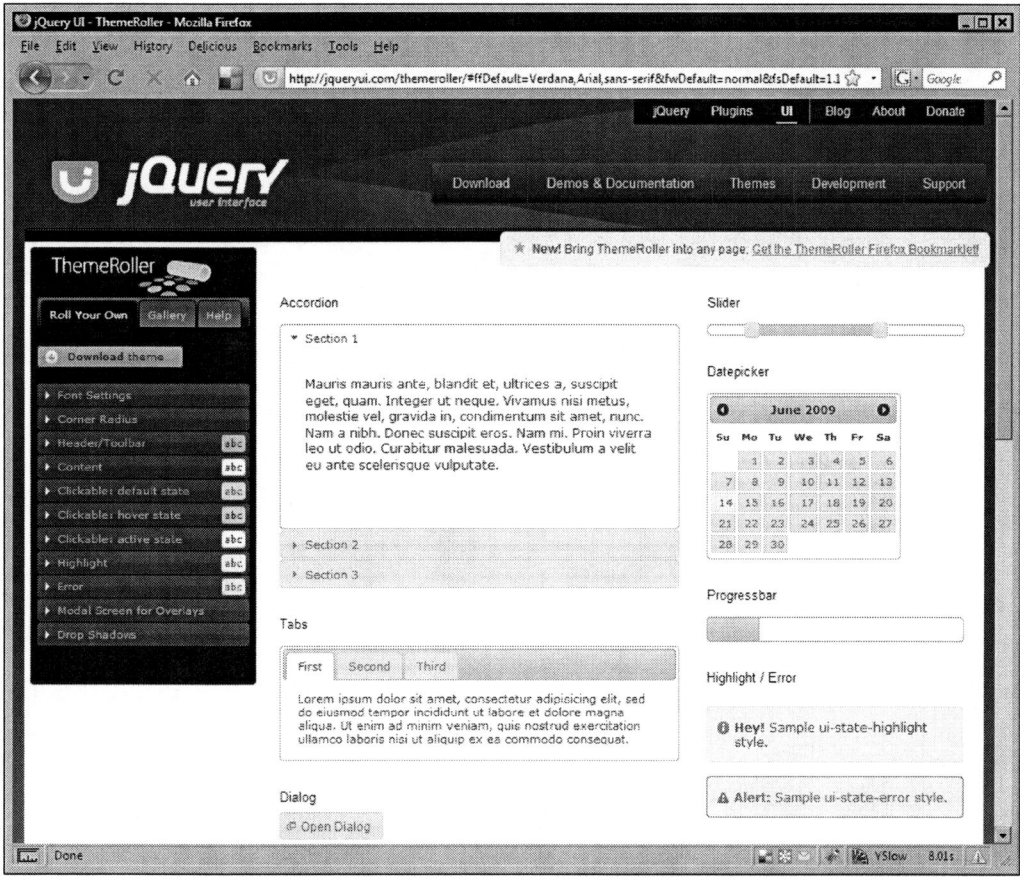

If you looked at the `index.html` file a little earlier on then the ThemeRoller landing page will instantly be familiar as it shows all of the UI widgets on the page, skinned with the default **smoothness** theme.

The page features an interactive menu on the left that is used to work with the application. Each item within the menu expands to give you access to the available style settings for each part of the widget, such as the content and the clickable elements.

Here we can create our custom theme with ease and see the changes instantly as they are applied to the different visible parts of each widget on the page:

When you're not feeling particularly inspired while creating a theme, there is also a gallery of preconfigured themes that you can instantly use to generate a fully configured theme. Aside from this convenience, the best thing about these preselected themes is that when you select one, it is loaded into the left menu. Therefore, you can easily make little tweaks as required:

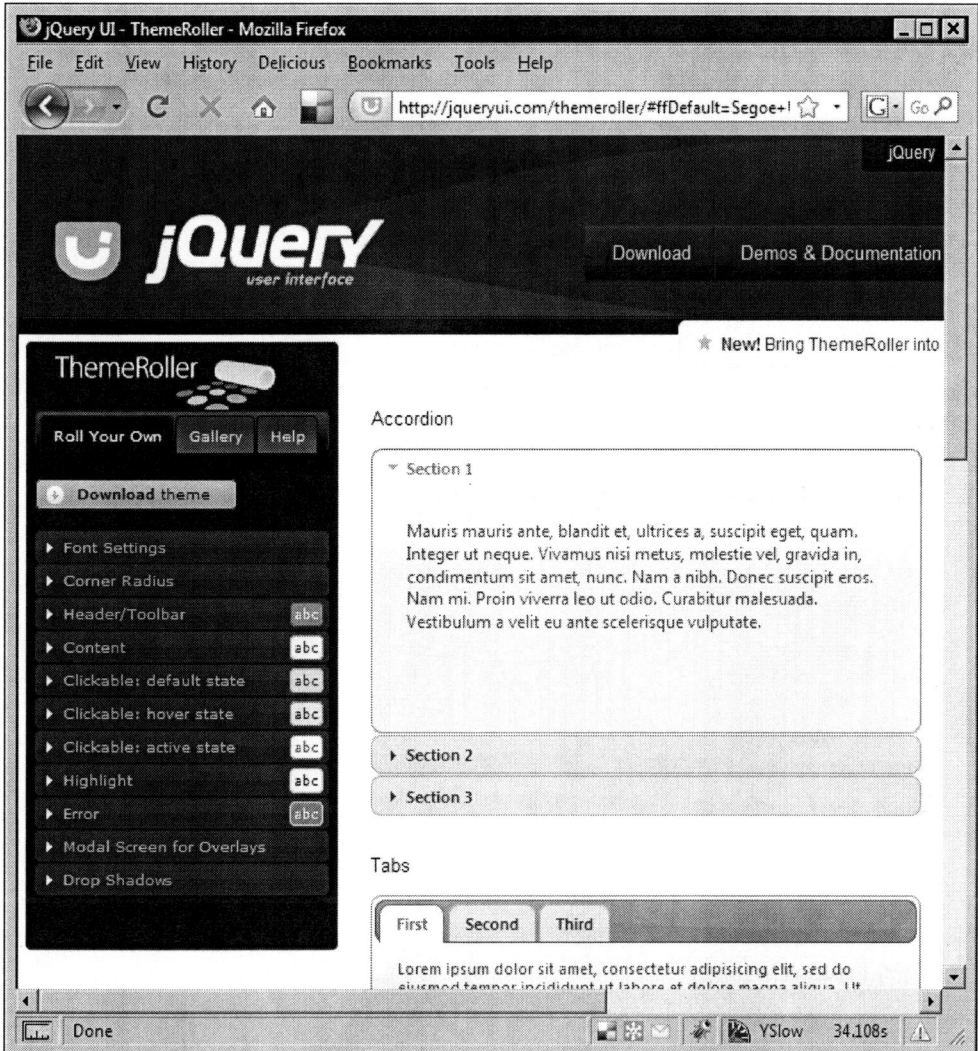

Without a doubt, this is the best way to create a visually appealing custom theme that matches the UI widgets to your existing site, and is the recommended method of creating custom skins.

Installing and using the new theme is as easy as selecting or creating it. The **Download theme** button in the above screenshot takes us back to the download builder, which has the CSS and images for the new theme integrated into the download package.

If it's just the new theme we want, we can deselect the actual components and just download the theme. Once downloaded the css folder within the downloaded archive will contain a folder that has the name of the theme. We can simply drag this folder into our own local css folder, and then link to the stylesheet from our own pages.

We won't be looking at this tool in much detail throughout the book. We'll be focusing instead on the style rules that we need to manually override in our own stylesheet to generate the desired look of the examples.

Component categories

There are two types of components found within the jQuery UI library—low-level interaction helpers that are designed to work primarily with mouse events, and there are the widgets that produce visible objects on the page, which are designed to perform a specific function.

The interaction helpers category includes the following components:

- Draggable
- Droppable
- Resizable
- Selectable
- Sortable

The higher-level widgets included (at the time of writing) are as follows:

- Accordion
- Datepicker
- Dialog
- Progressbar
- Slider
- Tabs

The `ui.core.js` file that is required by all other library components, comes under neither category, but could nevertheless be seen as the core component of the library. This file sets up the construct that all widgets use to function and adds some core functionality which is shared by all of the library components. This file isn't designed to be used standalone, and exposes no functionality that can be used outside of another component.

Apart from these components, there is also a series of UI effects that produce different animations or transitions on targeted elements on the page. These are excellent for adding flair and style to our pages, in addition to the strong functionality of the components. We'll be looking at these effects in the final chapter of the book.

I'd like to add here that the jQuery UI library is currently undergoing a rapid period of expansion and development. It is also constantly growing and evolving with bug fixes and feature enhancements continually being added. It would be impossible to keep entirely up-to-date with this aggressive expansion and cover components that are literally about to be released.

The great thing about jQuery UI's simplified API is that once you have learned to use all of the existing components (as this book will show you), you'll be able to pick up any new components very quickly. As this book is being written, there are already a number of new components nearing release, with many more in the pipeline and all of these components will automatically be ThemeRoller-ready.

Browser support

Like jQuery itself, jQuery UI supports all of the major browsers in use today including the following:

- IE6, IE7, and IE8
- Firefox 2 and Firefox 3
- Opera 9 and Opera 10
- Safari 3 and Safari 4
- Chrome 1, Chrome 2, and Chrome 3

This is by no means a comprehensive list, but I think that it includes the most common browsers currently in use, making jQuery UI very well supported.

The widgets are built from semantically correct HTML elements generated as needed by the components. Therefore, we won't see excessive or unnecessary elements being created or used.

Book examples

The library is as flexible as standard JavaScript, and by this I mean that there is often more than one way of doing the same thing, or achieving the same end. For example, the callback properties used in the configuration objects for different components, can usually take either references to functions or inline anonymous functions, and use them with equal ease and efficiency.

In practice, it is advisable to keep your code as minimal as possible (which jQuery really helps with anyway). But to make the examples more readable and understandable, we'll be separating as much of the code as possible into discrete modules. Therefore, callback functions and configuration objects will be defined separately from the code that calls or uses them.

To reduce the number of files that we have to create and work with, all of the JavaScript will go into the host HTML page on which it runs, as opposed to in separate files. Please keep in mind that this is not advisable for production websites. I'd also just like to make it clear that the main aim throughout the course of this book is to learn how to use the different components that make up jQuery UI. If an example seems a little convoluted, it may simply be that this is the easiest way to expose the functionality of a particular method or property, as opposed to a situation that we would find ourselves coding for in regular implementations.

Library licensing

Like jQuery, the jQuery UI library is dual licensed under the MIT and GPL open source licenses. These are both very unrestrictive licenses that allow the creators of the library to take credit for its production and retain intellectual rights over it, without preventing us as developers from using the library in any way that we like.

The MIT license explicitly states that users of the software (jQuery UI in this case) are free to use, copy, merge, modify, publish, distribute, sublicense, and sell. This lets us do pretty much whatever we want with the library.

The only requirement imposed by this license is that we must keep the original copyright and warranty statements intact.

This is an important point to make. You can take the library and do whatever you like with it. Build applications on top of the library and then sell those applications, or give them away for free. Put the library in embedded systems like cell phone OSs and sell those. But whatever you do, leave the original text file with John Resig's name in it present. You may also duplicate it word for word in the help files or documentation of your application.

The MIT license is very lenient, but because it is not copyrighted itself, we are free to change it. We could therefore demand that users of our software give attribution to us instead of the jQuery team, or pass off the code as our own.

The GPL license is copyrighted, and offers an additional layer of protection for the library's creators and the users of our software. jQuery is provided free and open source and the GPL license ensures that it will always remain free and open source, regardless of the environment it may end up in, and that the original creators of the library are given the credit they deserve. Again, the original GPL license file must be available within your application.

The licenses are not there to restrict us in any way and are not the same as the kind of license that comes with software you might install on your computer. In most cases, how the library is licensed will not be a consideration when using it.

API introduction

The version 1.5 release of jQuery UI was a milestone in the library's history. This was the release in which the API for each component was significantly simplified, making the library both easier to use and more powerful.

Once you've worked with one of the components from the library, you'll instantly feel at home when working with any of the other components since the methods of each component are called in exactly the same way.

The API for each component consists of a series of different methods. While these are all technically methods, it may be useful to categorize them based on their particular function.

The plugin method	This method is used to initialize the component and is simply the name of the component followed by parentheses. I will refer to this throughout the book as the plugin method or widget method.
Common methods	The destroy method can be used with any of the components to completely disable the widget being used and in most cases returns the underlying HTML to its original state. The option method is used by all components to get or set any configuration option after initialization. The enable and disable methods are used by most library components.
Specialized methods	Each component has one or more methods unique to that particular component that performs specialized functions.

Methods are consistently called throughout each of the different components by passing the method that we'd like to call as a simple string to the component's plugin method, with any arguments that the method accepts passed as strings after the method name.

For example, to call the `destroy` method of the accordion component, we would simply do as follows:

```
$("#someElement").accordion("destroy");
```

See how easy that was? Every single method exposed by all of the different components is called in this same simple way.

Some methods, like standard JavaScript functions, accept arguments that trigger different behavior in the component. If we wanted to call the `disable` method on a tab in the tabs widget for example, we would do the following:

```
$("#someElement").tabs("disable", 1);
```

The `disable` method, when used in conjunction with the tabs widget, accepts an integer which refers to the index of the individual tab within the widget.

Similarly, to enable the tab again we would use the `enable` method:

```
$("#someElement").tabs("enable", 1);
```

Again we supply an argument to modify how the method is used. Sometimes the arguments that are passed to the method vary between components. The accordion widget for example does not enable or disable individual accordion panels, only the whole widget, so no additional arguments following the method name are required.

The `option` method is slightly more complex than the other common methods, but it's also more powerful and is just as easy to use. The method is used to either get or set any configurable option after the component has been initialized.

To use the `option` method in getter mode to retrieve the current value of an option, we could use the following code:

```
$("#someElement").accordion("option", "navigation");
```

This code would return the current value of the `navigation` option of the accordion widget. So to trigger getter mode we just supply the option name that we'd like to retrieve.

In order to use the `option` method in setter mode instead, we can supply the option name and the new value as arguments:

```
$("#someElement").accordion("option", "navigation", "true");
```

This code would set the value of the `navigation` option to `true`. As you can see, although the `option` method gives us the power to both get and set configuration options, it still retains the same easy to use format of the other methods.

Using jQuery UI feels just like using jQuery and having built up confidence coding with jQuery, moving on to jQuery UI is the next logical step to take.

Events and callbacks

The API for each component also contains a rich event model that allows us to easily react to different interactions. Each component exposes its own set of unique custom events, yet the way in which these events are used is the same, regardless of which event is used.

We have two ways of working with events in jQuery UI. Each component allows us to add callback functions that are executed when the specified event is fired, as values for configuration options. For example, to use the `select` event of the tabs widget that is fired any time a tab is selected, we could use the following code:

```
var config = {
  select: function() {
  }
};
```

The name of the event is used as the `option` name and an anonymous function is used as the `option` value. We'll look at all of the individual events that are used with each component in later chapters.

The other way of working with events is to use jQuery's `bind()` method. To use events in this way, we simply specify the name of the component followed by the name of the event.

```
$("#someElement").bind("tabsselect", function() {
});
```

Usually, but not always, callback functions used with the `bind()` method are executed after the event has been fired, while callbacks specified using configuration options are executed directly before the event is fired.

The callback functions are called in the context of the DOMElement that triggers the event. For example, in a tabs widget with several tabs, the `select` event will be fired from the actual tab that is clicked, not the tabs widget as a whole. This is extremely useful to us as developers, because it allows us to associate the event with a particular tab.

Some of the custom events fired by jQuery UI components are cancellable and if stopped can be used to prevent certain actions taking place. The best example of this (which we'll look at later in the book) is preventing a dialog widget from closing by returning `false` in the callback function of the `beforeclose` event.

```
beforeclose: function() {
  if (readyToClose === false) {
    return false
  }
}
```

If the arbitrary condition in this example was not met, `false` would be returned by the callback function and the dialog would remain open. This is an excellent and powerful feature that can give us fine-grained control over the widget's behavior.

Callback arguments

Any anonymous functions that we supply as callback functions to the different events are automatically passed two objects, the original event object, and an object containing useful information about the widget. The information contained with the second object varies between components, we'll look at this in greater detail in later chapters.

To use these two objects we just specify them as arguments to the function.

```
var config = {
  select: function(e, ui) {
    e.target
    ui.index
  }
};
```

Every single component will automatically supply these objects to any callback functions we define.

Summary

jQuery UI removes the difficulty of building engaging and effective user interfaces. It provides a range of components that can quickly and easily be used out of the box with little configuration. They each expose a comprehensive set of properties and methods for integration with your pages or applications if a more complex configuration is required.

Each component is designed to be efficient, lightweight, and semantically correct along with making use of the latest object-oriented features of JavaScript. When combined with jQuery, it provides an awesome addition to any web developer's toolkit.

So far, we've seen how the library can be obtained, how your system can be set up to utilize it, and how the library is structured. We've also looked at how the different widgets can be themed or customized, how the API simply and consistently exposes the library's functionality, and the different categories of component.

We've covered some important topics during the course of this chapter, but now, thankfully, we can get on with using the components of jQuery UI and get down to some proper coding!

2
The CSS Framework

Version 1.7 of jQuery UI (the latest release at the time of writing) was an exciting release because it introduced the comprehensive new CSS framework. All widgets are effectively and consistently themed by the framework. There are many helper classes that we can use in our implementations, even if we aren't using any of the library components.

In this chapter we'll be covering the following subjects:

- The files that make up the framework
- How to use the classes exposed by the framework
- How to switch themes quickly and easily
- Customizing the framework

The files that make up the framework

There are two locations within the library's structure where the CSS files that make the framework reside. They are:

- The css folder

  This folder holds the complete CSS framework, including the theme that was selected when the download package was built. All the necessary CSS has been placed in a single, lean, and mean stylesheet to minimize HTTP requests in production environments.

  This version of the framework will contain styles for all the components that were selected in the download builder, so its size will vary depending on how much of the library is being used. The full version of each theme weighs in at 26.7 Kb and is not compressed.

- The themes folder

  Another version of the framework exists within the development-bundle\
  themes folder. Two themes are provided in this folder — the base theme and
  whichever theme was selected when the library was downloaded. The base
  theme is a grey, neutral theme identical to smoothness.

Within each of these theme folders are all the individual files that make up the
framework. Each of the different components of the framework are split into
their own respective files.

Component	Use
ui.all.css	All the required files for a theme can be linked by using this file in development. It consists of @import directives that pull in the ui.base.css and the ui.theme.css files.
ui.base.css	This file is used by ui.all.css. It also contains @import directives that pull in the ui.core.css file, as well as each of the widget CSS files. However, it contains none of the theme styles that control each widget's appearance.
ui.core.css	This file provides core framework styles such as the clear-fix helper and a generic overlay.
ui.accordion.css	These files are the individual source files that control the layout and basic appearance of each widget.
ui.datepicker.css	
ui.dialog.css	
ui.progressbar.css	
ui.resizable.css	
ui.slider.css	
ui.tabs.css	
ui.theme.css	This file contains the complete theme and targets of all the visual elements that make up each widget in the library.

Let's take a look at each of these files in more detail.

ui.all.css

The all file makes use of CSS imports using the @import rule to read in two
files — the ui.base.css file and the ui.theme.css file. This is all that is present in
the file and all that is needed to implement the complete framework and the selected
theme. From the two directives found in this file, we can see the separation between
the part of the framework that makes the widgets function and the theme that gives
them their visual appearance.

ui.base.css

This file also consists of only `@import` rules, and imports the `ui.core.css` file along with each of the individual widget files. At this point I should mention that the Resizable component has its own framework file, along with each of the widgets.

ui.core.css

The core file provides generic styles for the framework that are used by all components. It contains the following classes:

Class	Use
`.ui-helper-hidden`	Hides elements with `display:none`.
`.ui-helper-hidden-accessible`	Hides elements by positioning them offscreen so that they are still accessible to assistive technology.
`.ui-helper-reset`	This is the reset mechanism for jQuery UI (it doesn't use a separate reset stylesheet), which neutralizes the margins, padding, and other common default styles applied to common elements by browsers. For an introduction to see the importance of resetting default browser styling, visit: `http://sixrevisions.com/css/css-tips/css-tip-1-resetting-your-styles-with-css-reset/`
`.ui-helper-clearfix:after` `.ui-helper-clearfix` `* html .ui-helper-clearfix` `.ui-helper-clearfix`	These classes provide a cross-browser solution for automatically clearing floats. Whenever an element is floated, this class is added to its parent container to clear the float.
`.ui-helper-zfix`	The `.ui-helper-zfix` class provides rules that are applied to iframe elements in order to fix z-index issues when overlays are used.
`.ui-state-disabled`	This class sets the `cursor` to `default` for disabled elements and uses the `!important` directive to ensure that it is not overridden.
`.ui-icon`	This rule is the library's method of replacing the text content of an element with a background image. The responsibility of setting the background images for the different icons found in the library is delegated to the `ui.theme.css` file and not here.
`.ui-widget-overlay`	This class sets the basic style properties of the overlay that is applied to the page when dialogs and other modal pop ups are shown. As images are used by the overlay, some styles for this class are also found in the `theme` file.

The core file lays the ground for the rest of the framework. We can also give these class names to our own elements to clear floats or hide elements whenever we use the library.

The individual component framework files

Each widget in the library, as well as the Resizable interaction helper has a framework file that controls the CSS, which makes the widget function correctly. For example, the tab headings in the tabs widget must be floated left in order to display them as tabs. These framework files set this rule. These styles will need to be preserved when we are overriding the framework in a custom theme.

These files are brief, with each component using the smallest number of rules possible for it to function correctly. Generally the files are compact (usually not more than 20 style rules long). The dialog and datepicker source files are the exception, with each requiring a large number of rules to function correctly as pop ups.

ui.theme.css

This file will be customized to the theme that was selected or created with ThemeRoller and set's all of the visual properties (colors, images, and so on) for the different elements that make up each widget.

Within the ui.reset.css file, there are many comments that contain descriptive labels enclosed within curly braces. These are called **placeholders** and the CSS styles that precede them are updated by ThemeRoller when the theme is created.

This is the file that will be generated for the complete theme and contains styles for all the visible parts of each widget when creating or selecting a theme using ThemeRoller. When overriding the framework to create a custom theme, it is mostly rules in this file that will be overridden.

Each widget is constructed from a set of common elements. For example, the outer container of each widget has the class name ui-widget, while any content within the widget will be held in a container with the class name ui-widget-content. It is this consistent layout and classing convention, which makes the framework so effective.

This is the biggest stylesheet used by the framework and contains too many classes to list here in its entirety (but feel free to open it up at this point and take a look through it). The following table lists the different categories of classes:

Category	Use
Containers	Sets style properties for widget, heading, and content containers.
Interaction States	These classes set the default, hover, and active states for any clickable elements.
Interaction Cues	This category applies visual cues to elements including highlight, error, disabled, primary, and secondary styles.
States and images	These classes set the images used for icons displayed in the content and heading containers, as well as any clickable elements including default, hover, active, highlight, focus, and error states.
Image positioning	All of the icon images used by the theme are stored in a single file (known as a **sprite file**), and are displayed individually by manipulating the `background-position` properties of the sprite file. This category sets the background-positions for all individual icons.
Corner Radius	CSS3 is used to give rounded corners to supporting browsers (just Firefox 3+, Safari 3+ and Chrome 1+).
Overlays	The image used for the generic overlay defined in the core CSS file is set here, as is a class that implements a semi-transparent overlay over specified elements.

The jQuery UI documentation features an extensive overview of the theming API at:
`http://docs.jquery.com/UI/Theming/API`

Linking to the required framework files

For rapid theming of all jQuery UI widgets in a development environment we can just link to the `ui.all.css` file from our pages:

```
<link rel="stylesheet" type="text/css"
  href="development-bundle/themes/smoothness/ui.all.css">
```

To use each file individually, we would need to use the following `<link>` elements:

```
<link rel="stylesheet" type="text/css"
  href="development-bundle/themes/base/ui.core.css">
<link rel="stylesheet" type="text/css"
  href="development-bundle/themes/base/ui.tabs.css">
<link rel="stylesheet" type="text/css"
  href="development-bundle/themes/base/ui.theme.css">
```

The CSS resources, when linked to separately, should be added to the HTML page in the following order—`core.css`, the widget's CSS file, and the `theme.css` file. In a production environment of course, we'd use the super-efficient combined file to minimize HTTP requests for CSS.

```
<link rel="stylesheet" type="text/css"
  href="css/smoothness/jquery-ui-1.7.1.custom.css">
```

For easier coding and convenience, we'll be linking to the `ui.all.css` file in our examples, but it's useful to know what each of the different framework files do in order to better understand how the framework files work together.

Using the framework classes

Along with using the framework while we're implementing official jQuery UI widgets, we can also use it when we're deploying our own custom plugins or widgets that we have written ourselves.

Containers

Containers are recommended because it means that widgets or plugins that we write will be ThemeRoller ready and easier for end developers to theme and customize. Let's look at how easy it is to use the framework. In your text editor create a new file and add the following code:

```
<!DOCTYPE HTML PUBLIC "-//W3C//DTD HTML 4.01//EN"
  "http://www.w3.org/TR/html4/strict.dtd">
<html lang="en">
  <head>
    <link rel="stylesheet" type="text/css"
      href="development-bundle/themes/base/ui.theme.css">
    <meta http-equiv="Content-Type"
      content="text/html; charset=utf-8">
    <title>CSS Framework - Containers</title>
  </head>
  <body>
    <div class="ui-widget">
      <div class="ui-widget-header ui-corner-top">
        <h2>This is a ui-widget-header container</h2></div>
      <div class="ui-widget-content ui-corner-bottom">
        <p>This is a ui-widget-content container</p></div>
    </div>
  </body>
</html>
```

Save this page as `containers.html` within the `jqueryui` project folder that we created in the last chapter when we unpacked the library. We're linking to the `ui.theme.css` file from the `base` development theme in the library. If we were building a more complex widget we'd probably want to link to the `ui.core.css` file as well.

Working with this file when creating widgets or plugins is essential because it lets us verify that the class names we give our containers will pick up appropriate styling and reassures us that they will be ThemeRoller ready. Any style that we need to apply ourselves would go into a separate stylesheet like each widget from the library has their own custom stylesheets.

We use only a couple of elements in this example. Our outer container is given the class name `ui-widget`. If we were making a custom widget, we'd also want to put a custom class name on this element. For example, if we were making a content scroller, we might add the class `ui-widget-scroller` or similar.

Within the outer container we have two other containers — one is the `ui-widget-heading` container and one is the `ui-widget-content` container. We also give these elements variants of the corner-rounding classes — `ui-corner-top` and `ui-corner-bottom` respectively.

Inside the header and content containers we just have a couple of appropriate elements that we might want to put in, such as `<h2>` in the header and `<p>` in the content element. These elements will inherit some rules from their respective containers but are not styled directly by the theme file.

When we view this basic page in a browser, we should see that our two container elements pick up the styles from the `theme` file:

Interactions

Let's look at some more of the framework classes in action. Create the following new page:

```html
<!DOCTYPE HTML PUBLIC "-//W3C//DTD HTML 4.01//EN"
  "http://www.w3.org/TR/html4/strict.dtd">
<html lang="en">
  <head>
    <link rel="stylesheet" type="text/css"
      href="development-bundle/themes/base/ui.theme.css">
    <meta http-equiv="Content-Type"
      content="text/html; charset=utf-8">
    <title>CSS Framework - Interaction states</title>
  </head>
  <body>
    <div class="ui-widget">
      <div class="ui-state-default ui-state-active ui-corner-all">
        <a href="#">I am clickable and selected</a></div>
      <div class="ui-state-default ui-corner-all">
        <a href="#">I am clickable but not selected</a></div>
    </div>
  </body>
</html>
```

Save this file as `interactions.html` in the `jqueryui` project folder. We've defined two clickable elements in these examples, which are comprised of a container `<div>` and an `<a>` element. Both containers are given the classes `ui-state-default` and `ui-corner-all`, but the first is also given the selected state `ui-state-active`. This will give our clickable elements the following appearance:

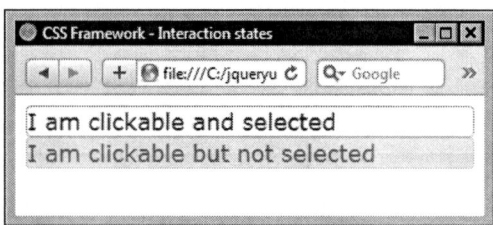

Both our containers are styled according to the rules found in the theme file we're linking to. The CSS framework doesn't provide styles on the :hover CSS pseudo-class, instead it applies a set of styles using a class name, which is added using JavaScript. To see this in action before the closing <body> tag, add the following code:

```
<script type="text/javascript"
  src="development-bundle/jquery-1.3.2.js"></script>
<script type="text/javascript">
  $(function() {
    $(".ui-state-default a").hover(function() {
      $(this).parent().addClass("ui-state-hover");
    }, function() {
      $(this).parent().removeClass("ui-state-hover");
    });
  });
</script>
```

This simple script adds the ui-state-hover class name to a clickable element when the mouse pointer moves on to it, and then removes it when the mouse pointer moves off it. When we run the page in a browser and hover over the second clickable element, we should see the ui-state-hover styles:

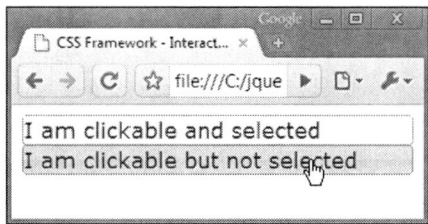

Icons

The framework provides a series of images that we can use of as icons. Change the contents of the ui-widget container in interactions.html so that it appears as follows (new code is shown in bold):

```
<div class="ui-widget">
  <div class="ui-state-default ui-state-active ui-corner-all">
    <div class="ui-icon ui-icon-circle-plus"></div>
      <a href="#">I am clickable and selected</a></div>
  <div class="ui-state-default ui-corner-all">
    <div class="ui-icon ui-icon-circle-plus"></div>
      <a href="#">I am clickable but not selected</a></div>
</div>
```

Save this as `icons.html` in the `jqueryui` directory. In this example, our nested `<div>` elements, which have the classes `ui-icon` and `ui-icon-circle-plus` are given the correct icon from a sprite file.

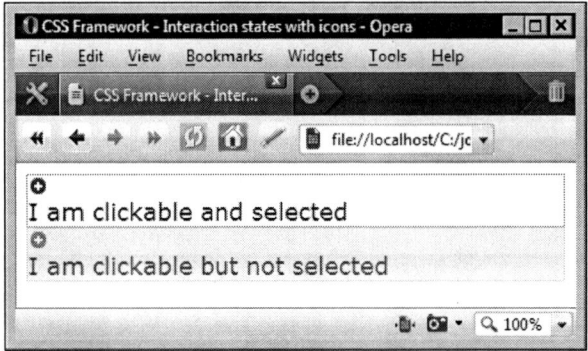

As you can see, the `ui-state-active` icon differs slightly from the `ui-state-default` icon. We haven't positioned the icons at all in this example because this would necessitate the creation of a new stylesheet. The point of this example is to see how the icons can be automatically added using the class names from the framework.

Interaction cues

Another set of classes we can use is the interaction cues. We will look at another example using these; in a new page in your text editor, add the following code:

```
<!DOCTYPE HTML PUBLIC "-//W3C//DTD HTML 4.01//EN"
  "http://www.w3.org/TR/html4/strict.dtd">
<html lang="en">
  <head>
    <link rel="stylesheet" type="text/css"
      href="development-bundle/themes/base/ui.core.css">
    <link rel="stylesheet" type="text/css"
      href="development-bundle/themes/base/ui.theme.css">
    <link rel="stylesheet" type="text/css"
      href="css/ui.form.css">
    <meta http-equiv="Content-Type"
      content="text/html; charset=utf-8">
    <title>CSS Framework - Interaction cues</title>
  </head>
  <body>
    <div class="ui-widget ui-form">
      <div class="ui-widget-header ui-corner-all">
```

```
        <h2>Login Form</h2></div>
      <div class="ui-widget-content ui-corner-all">
        <form action="#" class="ui-helper-clearfix">
          <label class="ui-helper-reset">Username</label>
          <div class="ui-state-error ui-corner-all">
            <input type="text">
            <div class="ui-icon ui-icon-alert"></div>
      <p class="ui-helper-reset ui-state-error-text">Required field</p>
          </div>
        </form>
      </div>
    </div>
  </body>
</html>
```

Save this file as cues.html in the jqueryui folder. This time we link to the ui.core.css file as well as the ui.theme.css file so that we can make use of some of the helper classes from the core file. We also link to a custom file ui.form.css that we'll create in a moment.

On the page we have the outer widget container, with the classes ui-form and ui-widget. The ui-form class will be used to pick up our custom styles from the ui.form.css stylesheet. Within the widget we have ui-widget-header and ui-widget-content containers.

Within the content section we've got a <form> with a single row of elements, a <label> element followed by a <div> element that has the ui-state-error and ui-corner-all classes hardcoded to it.

Within this <div> we have a standard <input>, a <div> with the ui-icon, and ui-icon-alert classes added along with a <p> element with the ui-state-error-text class name added to it. Because the <form> has child elements that are floated, we can make use of the ui-helper-clearfix class, which we add as a class name.

We should now create the custom ui.form.css stylesheet. In a new page in your text editor, add the following code:

```
.ui-form { width:470px; margin:0 auto; }
.ui-form .ui-widget-header h2 { margin:10px 0 10px 20px; }
.ui-form .ui-widget-content { padding:20px; }
.ui-form label, .ui-form input, .ui-form .ui-state-error,
.ui-form .ui-icon, .ui-form .ui-state-error p { float:left; }
.ui-form label, .ui-state-error p {
  font-size:12px; padding:10px 10px 0 0;
}
.ui-form .ui-state-error { padding:4px; }
```

```
.ui-form .ui-state-error p {
  font-weight:bold; padding-top:5px;
}
.ui-form .ui-state-error .ui-icon { margin:5px 3px 0 4px; }
```

Within our `jqueryui` project folder, there is a folder called `css` that is used (as I mentioned) to store the single-file production version of the framework. All of the CSS files we create throughout the book will also be saved in here for convenience. Save this file as `ui.form.css` in the `css` folder.

Imagine we have more form elements and a submit button. By adding the `ui-state-error` class to the `<div>` element we can use the error classes for form validation, which upon an unsuccessful submission would show the icon and text. Here's how the page should look:

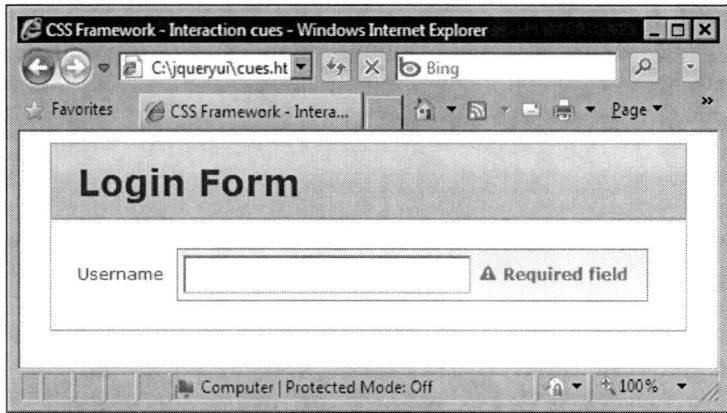

Switching themes quickly and easily

After developing a new widget using the base theme, we may decide that we want to switch to a fancier theme or one that fits in better with our site when we deploy it. People might want to use a different theme than the one we chose when downloading the library if we wrote and released a new plugin. Thankfully, the CSS framework makes switching themes a painless task. Looking at the previous example, all we need to do to change the skin of the widget is choose a new theme using ThemeRoller, and then download the new theme (we can download just the new theme by deselecting all of the components in the download builder).

Within the downloaded archive there would be a directory with the name of the chosen theme, such as dot-luv. We drag the theme folder out of the archive and into the development-bundle\themes folder and link the new theme file from our page, giving our form a completely new look as shown in the following figure:

The theme I used to obtain the previous screenshot is Dot Luv. We'll be using the **smoothness** theme or themes of our own creation for the remainder of the book.

Overriding the theme

Using the ThemeRoller gallery and customization tools we can generate an extraordinary number of unique themes. But there may be times when we need a deeper level of customization than we are able to reach using ThemeRoller; in this situation we have two options.

We can either create a complete theme file from scratch by ourselves, or we can create an additional stylesheet that overrides only those rules in the ui.theme.css file that we need it to. The latter is probably the easiest method and results in having to write less code.

We'll now take a look at this aspect of theming and resurrect our basic form example one last time. Switch back to the base theme in the `<head>` of cues.html if you changed it for the previous example. Save the page as cuesOverridden.html and then create the following new stylesheet:

```
.ui-corner-all { -moz-border-radius:0; -webkit-border-radius:0; }
.ui-widget-header { font-family:Georgia; background:#534741;
border:1px solid #362f2d; color:#c7b299; }
.ui-form .ui-widget-header h2 { margin:0; border:1px solid #998675;
padding:10px; font-style:italic; font-weight:normal; }
```

```
.ui-form .ui-widget-content { background:#c7b299; border:1px solid
#362f2d; border-top:0; padding:0; }
.ui-widget-content form { padding:20px; border:1px solid #f3eadf; }
.ui-widget-content .ui-state-error { border:1px solid #e7cc17;
background:#fbf5cd; }
.ui-widget-content .ui-state-error-text { color:#e7cc17; padding-
left:10px; }
.ui-state-error .ui-icon { display:none; }
```

Save this as `overrides.css` in the `css` folder. In this stylesheet we're mostly overriding rules from the `ui.theme.css` file. These are simple styles and we're just changing colors, backgrounds, and borders. Link to this stylesheet by adding the following line of code below the other stylesheets in `cuesOverridden.html`:

```
<link rel="stylesheet" type="text/css" href="css/overrides.css">
```

Our humble form should now appear as in the following screenshot:

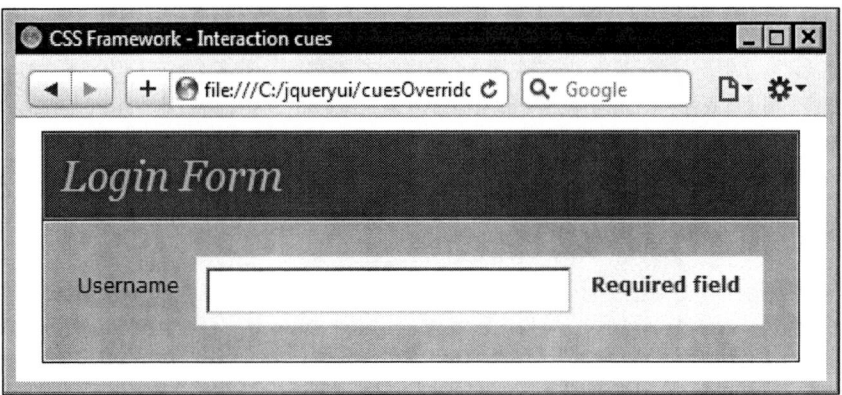

As long as we match or exceed the specificity of the selectors used in the `ui.theme. css` file, and as long as our stylesheet appears after the theme file, our rules will take precedence. A long discussion on CSS selector weight is beyond the scope of this book. However a brief explanation of specificity may be beneficial as it is the key to overriding the selected theme.

CSS specificity refers to how specific a CSS selector is—the more specific it is, the more weight it will have, and will subsequently override other rules that are applied to the element being targeted by other selectors. For example, consider the following selectors:

```
#myContainer .bodyText
.bodyText
```

The first selector is more specific than the second selector because it not only uses the class name of the element being targeted but also its parent container. It will therefore override the second selector, regardless of whether the second selector appears after it.

In this example, we have full control over the elements that we're skinning. But when working with any widgets from the library or with plugins authored by third parties, a lot of markup could be generated automatically, which we have no control over (without hacking the actual library files themselves). Therefore, we may need to rely on overriding styles in this way. All we need to do to find which styles to override is to open up the `ui.theme.css` file in a text editor and take a look at the selectors used there. Or failing to do that, we can use Firebug's CSS viewer to see the rules that we need to override.

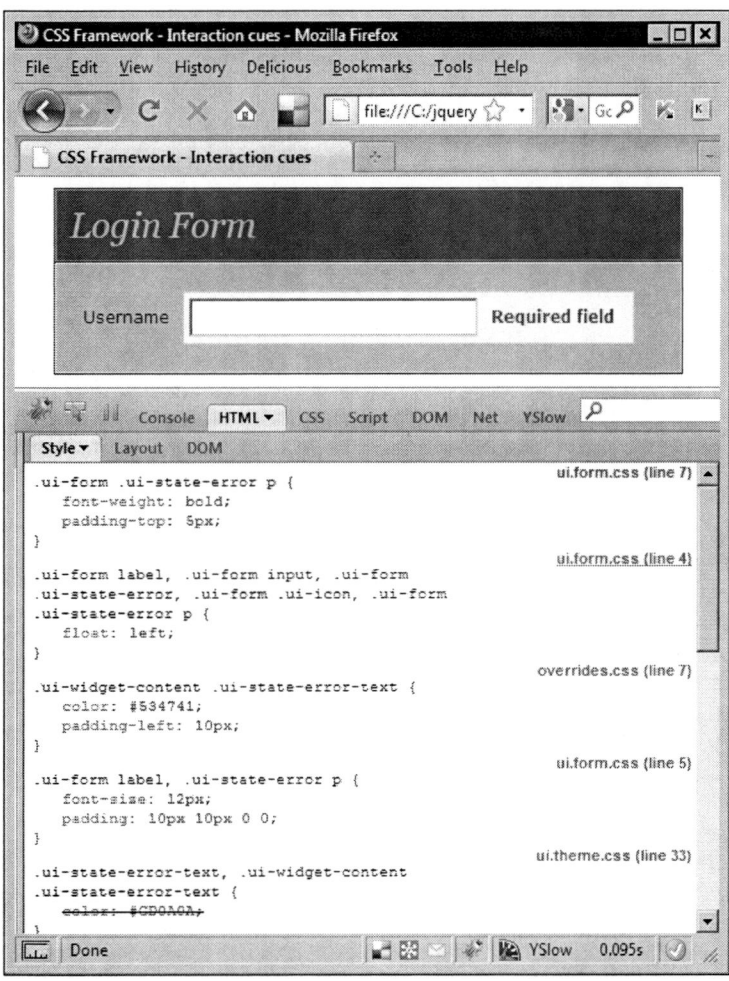

Summary

In this chapter we've seen how the CSS framework consistently styles each of the library components. We've looked at the files that make it and how they work together to provide the complete look and feel of the widgets. We also saw how tightly integrated the ThemeRoller application is with the framework.

We saw how easy it is to install or change a theme using ThemeRoller. We also looked at how we can override the theme file if we require a radical customization of a widget that we cannot obtain with ThemeRoller alone.

The chapter also covered building our own widgets or plugins in a way that is compatible with and can make use of the framework as well as to ensure that our creations are ThemeRoller ready. We can also make use of the helper classes provided by the framework, such as the `ui-helper-clearfix` class, to quickly implement common CSS solutions.

3
Tabs

Now that we've been formally introduced to the jQuery UI library and the CSS framework we can move on to begin looking at the components included in the library. Over the next six chapters, we'll be looking at the widgets. These are a set of visually engaging, highly configurable user interface widgets built on top of the foundation provided by the low-level interaction helpers.

The UI tabs widget is used to toggle visibility across a set of different elements, each element containing content that can be accessed by clicking on its heading which appears as an individual tab.

The tabs are structured so that they line up next to each other, whereas the content sections are layered on top of each other, with only the top one visible. Clicking a tab will highlight the tab and bring its associated content panel to the top of the stack. Only one content panel can be open at a time.

The following screenshot shows the different components of a set of UI tabs:

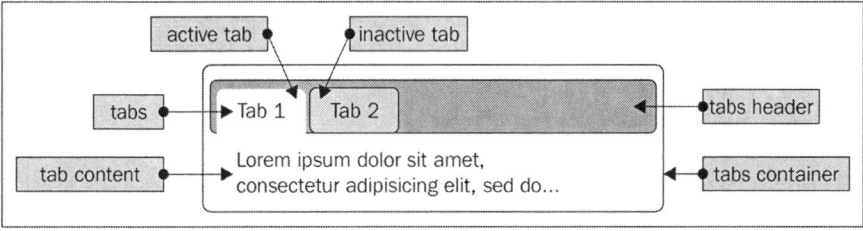

In this chapter, we will look at the following topics:

- The default implementation of the widget
- How the CSS framework targets tab widgets
- How to apply custom styles to a set of tabs

- Configuring tabs using their options
- Built-in transition effects for content panel changes
- Controlling tabs using their methods
- Custom events defined by tabs
- AJAX tabs

A basic tab implementation

The structure of the underlying HTML elements, on which tabs are based, is rigid and widgets require a certain number of elements for them to work.

The tabs must be created from a list element (ordered or unordered) and each list item must contain an <a> element. Each link will need to have a corresponding element with a specified id that it is associated with the link's href attribute. We'll clarify the exact structure of these elements after our first example.

In a new file in your text editor, create the following page:

```
<!DOCTYPE HTML PUBLIC "-//W3C//DTD HTML 4.01//EN"
  "http://www.w3.org/TR/html4/strict.dtd">
<html lang="en">
  <head>
    <link rel="stylesheet" type="text/css"
      href="development-bundle/themes/smoothness/ui.all.css">
    <meta http-equiv="Content-Type"
      content="text/html; charset=utf-8">
    <title>jQuery UI Tabs Example 1</title>
  </head>
  <body>
    <div id="myTabs">
      <ul>
        <li><a href="#a">Tab 1</a></li>
        <li><a href="#b">Tab 2</a></li>
      </ul>
      <div id="a">This is the content panel linked to the first tab,
        it is shown by default.</div>
      <div id="b">This content is linked to the second tab and will
        be shown when its tab is clicked.</div>
    </div>
    <script type="text/javascript"
      src="development-bundle/jquery-1.3.2.js"></script>
    <script type="text/javascript"
      src="development-bundle/ui/ui.core.js"></script>
    <script type="text/javascript"
```

```
      src="development-bundle/ui/ui.tabs.js"></script>
    <script type="text/javascript">
      $(function(){

        $("#myTabs").tabs();
      });
    </script>
  </body>
</html>
```

Save the code as `tabs1.html` in your `jqueryui` working folder. Let's review what was used. The following script and CSS resources are needed for the default tab widget instantiation:

- `ui.all.css`
- `jquery-1.3.2.js`
- `ui.core.js`
- `ui.tabs.js`

A tab widget consists of several standard HTML elements arranged in a specific manner (these can be either hardcoded into the page, or added dynamically, or can be a mixture of both depending on the requirements of your implementation).

- An outer container element, which the `tabs` method is called on
- A list element (`<ul>` or `<ol>`)
- An `<a>` element for each tab
- An element for the content of each tab

The first two elements within the outer container make the clickable tab headings, which are used to show the content section that is associated with the tab. Each tab should include a list item containing the link.

The `href` attribute of the link should be set as a fragment identifier, prefixed with #. It should match the `id` attribute of the `element` that forms the content section, with which it is associated. The content sections of each tab are created by the `<div>` elements. The `id` attribute is required and will be targeted by its corresponding `<a>` element. We've used `<div>` elements in this example as the content panels for each tab, but other elements, such as `<span>` elements can also be used.

The elements discussed so far, along with their required attributes, are the minimum that are required from the underlying markup.

We link to several `<script>` resources from the library at the bottom of the `<body>` before its closing tag. Loading scripts last, after stylesheets and page elements is a proven technique for improving performance. After linking first to jQuery, we link to the `ui.core.js` file that is required by all components (except the effects, which have their own core file). We then link to the component's source file that in this case is `ui.tabs.js`.

After the three required script files from the library, we can turn to our custom `<script>` element in which we add the code that creates the tabs. We simply use the `$(function(){});` shortcut to execute our code when the document is ready. We then call the `tabs()` widget method on the jQuery object, representing our tabs container element (the `<ul>` with an `id` of `myTabs`).

When we run this file in a browser, we should see the tabs as they appeared in the first screenshot of this chapter (without the annotations of course).

Tab CSS framework classes

Using Firebug for Firefox (or another generic DOM explorer) we can see that a variety of class names are added to the different underlying HTML elements that the tabs widget is created from, as shown in the following screenshot:

Let's review these briefly. To the outer container `<div>` the following class names are added:

Class name	Purpose
ui-tabs	Allows tab-specific structural CSS to be applied.
ui-widget	Sets generic font styles that are inherited by nested elements.
ui-widget-content	Provides theme-specific styles.
ui-corner-all	Applies rounded corners to container.

The first element within the container is the `<ul>` element. This element receives the following class names:

Class name	Purpose
ui-tabs-nav	Allows tab-specific structural CSS to be applied.
ui-helper-reset	Neutralizes browser-specific styles applied to `<ul>` elements.
ui-helper-clearfix	Applies the clear-fix as this element has children that are floated.
ui-widget-header	Provides theme-specific styles.
ui-corner-all	Applies rounded corners.

The individual `<li>`elements are given the following class names:

Class name	Purpose
ui-state-default	Applies theme-specific styles.
ui-corner-top	Applies rounded corners to the top edges of the elements.
ui-tabs-selected	This is only applied to the active tab. On page load of the default implementation this will be the first tab. Selecting another tab will remove this class from the currently selected tab and apply it to the new tab.
ui-state-active	Applies theme-specific styles to the currently selected tab. This class name will be added to the tab that is currently selected, just like the previous class name. The reason there are two class names is that `ui-tabs-selected` provides the functional CSS, while `ui-state-active` provides the visual, decorative styles.

The `<a>` elements within each `<li>` are not given any class names, but they still have both structural and theme-specific styles applied to them by the framework.

Finally, the elements that hold each tab's content are given the following class names:

Class name	Purpose
ui-tabs-panel	Applies structural CSS to the content panels.
ui-widget-content	Applies theme-specific styles.
ui-corner-bottom	Applied rounded corners to the bottom edges of the content panels.

All of these classes are added to the underlying elements automatically by the library, we don't need to manually add them when coding the page.

As these tables illustrate, the CSS framework supplies the complete set of both structural CSS styles that control how the tabs function and theme-specific styles that control how the tabs appear, but not how they function. We can easily see which selectors we'll need to override if we wish to tweak the appearance of the widget, which is what we'll do in the following section.

Applying a custom theme to the tabs

In the next example, we can see how to change the tabs' basic appearance. We can override any rules used purely for display purposes with our own style rules for quick and easy customization without changing the rules related to the tab functionality or structure.

In a new file in your text editor, create the following very small stylesheet.

```
#myTabs {
  border:1px solid #636363; width:400px;
  background:#c2c2c2 none; padding:5px;
}
.ui-widget-header {
  border:0; background:#c2c2c2 none; font-family:Georgia;
}
#myTabs .ui-widget-content {
  border:1px solid #aaaaaa; background:#ffffff none;
  font-size:80%;
}
.ui-state-default, .ui-widget-content .ui-state-default {
  background:#a2a2a2 none; border:1px solid #636363;
}
.ui-state-active, .ui-widget-content .ui-state-active {
  background:#ffffff none; border:1px solid #aaaaaa;
}
```

This is all we need. Save the file as `tabsTheme.css` in your `css` folder. If you compare the class names with the tables on the previous pages you'll see that we're overriding the theme-specific styles. Because we're overriding the theme file, we need to meet or exceed the specificity of the selectors in `theme.css`. This is why we target multiple selectors sometimes.

In this example we override some of the rules in `ui.tabs.css`. We need to use the ID selector of our container element along with the selector from `ui.theme.css` (`.ui-widget-content`) in order to beat the double class selector `.ui-tabs .ui-tabs-panel`.

Don't forget to link to the new stylesheet from the `<head>` of the underlying HTML file, and make sure the custom stylesheet we just created appears after the `ui.tabs.css` file:

```
<link rel="stylesheet" type="text/css" href="css/tabsTheme.css">
```

The rules that we are trying to override will be not overridden by our theme file if the stylesheets are not linked to in the correct order. Save the altered file as `tabs2.html` in the `jqueryui` folder and view it in a browser. It should look like the following screenshot:

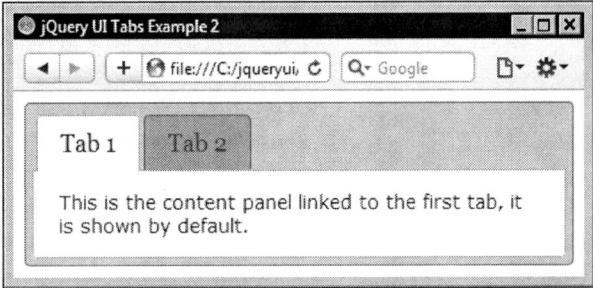

Our new theme isn't dramatically different from the default smoothness. However, we can tweak its appearance to suit our own needs and preferences by adding just a few additional styles.

Configurable options

Each of the different components in the library has a series of different options that control which features of the widget are enabled by default. An object literal can be passed in to the `tabs` widget method to configure these options.

The available options to configure non-default behaviors when using the tabs widget are shown in the following table:

Option	Default value	Usage
ajaxOptions	{}	When using AJAX tabs and importing remote data into the tab panels, additional AJAX options are supplied via this property. We can use any of the options exposed by jQuery's $.ajax method such as data, type, url, and so on.
cache	false	Load remote tab content only once (lazy-load).
collapsible	false	Allows an active tab to be unselected if it is clicked.
cookie	null	Show active tab using cookie data on page load.
disabled	[]	Disable specified tabs on page load. Supply an array of index numbers to disable specific tabs.
event	"click"	The tab event that triggers the display of content.
fx	null	Specify an animation effect when changing tabs. Supply a literal object or an array of animation effects.
idPrefix	"ui-tabs-"	Used to generate a unique ID and fragment identifier when a remote tab's link element has no title attribute.
panelTemplate	"<div></div>"	A string specifying the elements used for the content section of a dynamically created tab widget.
selected	0	The tab selected by default when the widget is rendered (overrides the cookie property).
spinner	"Loading&#B230"	Specify the loading spinner for remote tabs.
tabTemplate	<li><a href="#{ href}"><span>#{ label} </span></a></ li>	A string specifying the elements used when creating new tabs dynamically. Notice that both an <a> and a <span> tag are created when new tabs are added by the widget. The #{href} and #{label} parts of the string are used internally by the widget and are replaced with actual values by the widget.

Selecting a tab

Let's look at how these configurable properties can be used. For example, let's configure the widget so that the second tab is displayed when the page loads. Remove the `<link>` for tabsTheme.css in the `<head>` and change the final `<script>` element so that it appears as follows:

```
<script type="text/javascript">
  $(function(){
    var tabOpts = {
      selected: 1
    };
    $("#myTabs").tabs(tabOpts);
  });
</script>
```

Save this as tabs3.html. The different tabs and their associated content panels are represented by a numerical index starting at zero, much like a standard JavaScript array. Specifying a different tab to open by default is as easy as supplying its index number as the value for the selected property. When the page loads, the second tab should be selected.

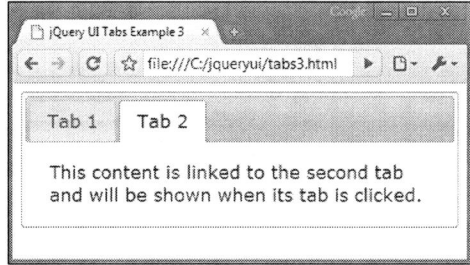

We've switched to the default smoothness theme so that we can focus on how the properties work. Along with changing which tab is selected we can also specify that no tabs should be initially selected by supplying null as the value for this property. This will cause the widget to appear as follows on page load:

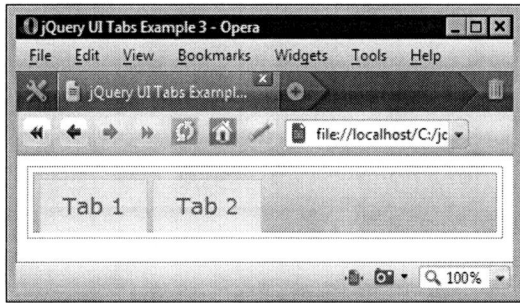

Disabling a tab

You may want a particular tab to be disabled until a certain condition is met. This is easily achieved by manipulating the `disabled` property of the tabs. Change the configuration object in `tabs3.html` to this:

```
var tabOpts = {
  disabled: [1]
};
```

Save this as `tabs4.html` in your `jqueryui` folder. In this example, we remove the `selected` property and add the index of the second tab to the `disabled` array. We could add the indices of other tabs to this array as well, separated by a comma, to disable multiple tabs by default.

When the page is loaded in a browser, the second tab has the class name `ui-widget-disabled` applied to it, and will pick up the disabled styles from `ui.theme.css`. It will not respond to mouse interactions in any way as shown in the following screenshot:

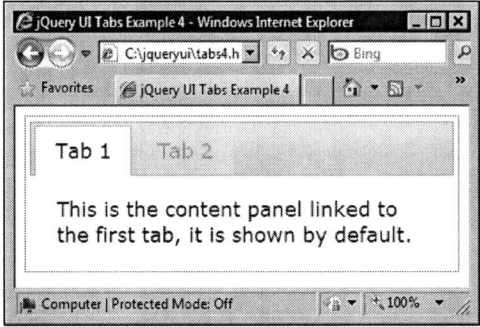

Transition effects

We can easily add attractive transition effects using the `fx` property. These are displayed when tabs are open and close. This property is configured using another object literal (or an array) inside our configuration object, which enables one or more effects. Let's enable fading effects using the following configuration object:

```
var tabOpts = {
  fx: {
    opacity: "toggle",
    duration: "slow"
  }
};
```

Save this file as `tabs5.html` in your `jqueryui` folder. The `fx` object that we created has two properties. The first property is the animation. To use fading, we specify `opacity` as this is what is adjusted. We would specify `height` as the property name instead to use opening animations. Toggling the `opacity` simply reverses its current setting. If it is currently visible, it is made invisible and vice-versa.

The second property, `duration`, specifies the speed at which the animation occurs. The values for this property are `slow`, `normal` (default value), or `fast`. We can also supply an integer representing the number of milliseconds the animation should run for.

When we run the file we can see that the tab content slowly fades out as a tab closes and fades in when a new tab opens. Both animations occur during a single tab interaction. To only show the animation once, when a tab closes for example, we would need to nest the `fx` object within an array. Change the configuration object in `tabs5.html` so that it appears as follows:

```
var tabOpts = {
     fx: [{
        opacity: "toggle",
        duration: "slow"
     },
     null]
};
```

The closing effect of the currently open content panel is contained within an object in the first item of the array, and the opening animation of the new tab is the second. By specifying `null` as the second item in the array we disable the opening animations when a new tab is selected.

We can also specify different animations and speeds for opening and closing animations by adding another object as the second array item instead of `null`. Save this as `tabs6.html` and view the results in a browser.

Collapsible tabs

By default when the currently active tab is clicked, nothing happens. But we can change this so that the currently open content panel closes when its tab heading is selected. Change the configuration object in `tabs6.html` so that it appears as follows:

```
var tabOpts = {
  collapsible: true
};
```

Save this version as `tabs7.html`. This option allows all of the content panels to be closed, much like when we supplied `null` to the `selected` property earlier on. Clicking a deactivated tab will select the tab and show its associated content panel. Clicking the same tab again will close it, shrinking the widget down so that only the header and tabs are displayed).

Tab events

The tab widget defines a series of useful options that allow you to add callback functions to perform different actions when certain events exposed by the widget are detected. The following table lists the configuration options that are able to accept executable functions on an event:

Option	Usage
add	Execute a function when a new tab is added.
disable	Execute a function when a tab is disabled.
enable	Execute a function when a tab is enabled.
load	Execute a function when a tab's remote data has loaded.
remove	Execute a function when a tab is removed.
select	Execute a function when a tab is selected.
show	Execute a function when the content section of a tab is shown.

Each component of the library has callback options (such as those in the previous table), which are tuned to look for key moments in any visitor interaction. Any function we use with these callbacks are usually executed *before* the change happens. Therefore, you can return `false` from your callback and prevent the action from occurring.

In our next example, we will look at how easy it is to react to a particular tab being selected using the standard non-bind technique. Change the final `<script>` element in `tabs7.html` so that it appears as follows:

```
<script type="text/javascript">
  $(function(){

    function handleSelect(event, tab) {
      $("<p>").text("The tab at index " + tab.index +
        " was selected").addClass("status-message ui-corner-all").
        appendTo($(".ui-tabs-nav", "#myTabs")).fadeOut(5000);
    }
```

```
    var tabOpts = {
      select:handleSelect
    };

    $("#myTabs").tabs(tabOpts);
  });
</script>
```

Save this file as `tabs8.html`. We also need a little CSS to complete this example, in the `<head>` of the page we just created add the following `<link>` element:

```
<link rel="stylesheet" type="text/css" href="css/tabSelect.css">
```

Then in a new page in your text editor add the following code:

```
.status-message {
  position:absolute; right:3px; top:4px; margin:0;
  padding:11px 8px 10px; font-size:11px;
  background-color:#ffffff; border:1px solid #aaaaaa;
}
```

Save this file as `tabSelect.css` in the `css` folder.

We made use of the `select` callback in this example, although the principle is the same for any of the other custom events fired by tabs. The name of our callback function is provided as the value of the `select` property in our configuration object.

Two arguments will be passed automatically to the function we define by the widget when it is executed. These are the original event object and a custom object containing useful properties from the tab which is in the function's execution context.

To find out which of the tabs was clicked, we can look at the `index` property of the second object (remember these are zero-based indices). This is added, along with a little explanatory text, to a paragraph element that we create on the fly and append to the widget header.

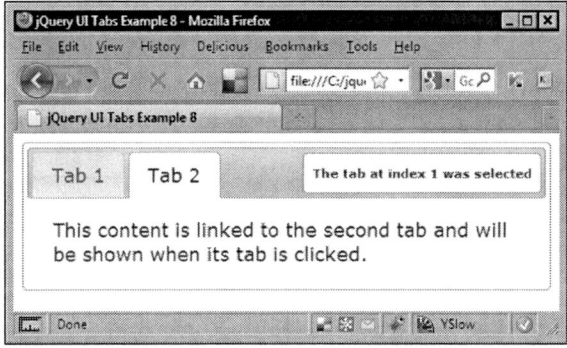

In this example, the callback function was defined outside the configuration object, and was instead referenced by the object. We can also define these callback functions inside our configuration object to make our code more efficient. For example, our function and configuration object from the previous example could have been defined like this:

```
var tabOpts = {
  select: function(event, tab) {
    $("<p>").text("The tab at index " + tab.index +
      " was selected").addClass("status-message ui-corner-all").
      appendTo($(".ui-tabs-nav", "#myTabs")).fadeOut(5000);
  }
}
```

Check `tabs8inline.html` in the code download for further clarification on this way of using event callbacks. Whenever a tab is selected, you should see the paragraph before it fades away. Note that the event is fired before the change occurs.

Binding to events

Using the event callbacks exposed by each component is the standard way of handling interactions. However, in addition to the callbacks listed in the previous table we can also hook into another set of events fired by each component at different times.

We can use the standard jQuery `bind()` method to bind an event handler to a custom event fired by the tabs widget in the same way that we could bind to a standard DOM event, such as a `click`.

The following table lists the tab widget's custom binding events and their triggers:

Event	Trigger
tabsselect	A tab is selected.
tabsload	A remote tab has loaded.
tabsshow	A tab is shown.
tabsadd	A tab has been added to the interface.
tabsremove	A tab has been removed from the interface.
tabsdisable	A tab has been disabled.
tabsenable	A tab has been enabled.

The first three events are fired in succession in the order event in which they appear in the table. If no tabs are remote then `tabsselect` and `tabsshow` are fired in that order. These events are sometimes fired before and sometimes after the action has occurred, depending on which event is used.

Let's see this type of event usage in action, change the final `<script>` element in `tabs8.html` to the following:

```
<script type="text/javascript">
  $(function() {
    $("#myTabs").tabs();
    $("#myTabs").bind("tabsselect", function(e, tab) {
      alert("The tab at index " + tab.index + " was selected");
    });
  });
</script>
```

Save this change as `tabs9.html`. Binding to the `tabsselect` in this way produces the same result as the previous example using the `select` callback function. Like last time, the alert should appear before the new tab is activated.

All the events exposed by all the widgets can be used with the `bind()` method, by simply prefixing the name of the widget to the name of the event.

Using tab methods

The tabs widget contains many different methods, which means it has a rich set of behaviors. It also supports the implementation of advanced functionality that allows us to work with it programmatically. Let's take a look at the methods which are listed in the following table:

Method	Usage
abort	Stops any animations or AJAX requests that are currently in progress.
add	Add a new tab programmatically, specifying the URL of the tab's content, a label, and optionally its index number as arguments.
destroy	Completely remove the tabs widget.
disable	Disable a tab based on index number.
enable	Enable a disabled tab based on index number.
length	Return the number of tabs in the widget.
load	Reload an AJAX tab's content, specifying the index number of the tab.
option	Get or set any property after the widget has been initialized.
remove	Remove a tab programmatically, specifying the index of the tab to remove.
rotate	Automatically changes the active tab after a specified number of milliseconds have passed, either once or repeatedly.
select	Select a tab programmatically, which has the same effect as when a visitor clicks a tab, based on index number.
url	Change the URL of content given to an AJAX tab. The method expects the index number of the tab and the new URL. See also `load` (above).

Enabling and disabling tabs

We can make use of the `enable` or `disable` methods to programmatically enable or disable specific tabs. This will effectively switch on any tabs that were initially disabled or disable those that are currently active. Let's use the `enable` method to switch on a tab, which we disabled by default in an earlier example. Add the following new `<button>` directly after the markup for the tabs widget in `tabs4.html`:

```
<button id="enable">Enable!<
    /button><button id="disable">Disable!</button>
```

Next change the final <script> element so that it appears as follows:

```
<script type="text/javascript">
  $(function(){

    var tabOpts = {
      disabled:[1]
    };
    $("#myTabs").tabs(tabOpts);

    $("#enable").click(function() {

      $("#myTabs").tabs("enable", 1);
    });

    $("#disable").click(function() {

      $("#myTabs").tabs("disable", 1);
    });
  });
</script>
```

Save the changed file as `tabs10.html`. On the page we've added two new `<button>` elements — one will be used to enable the disabled tab and the other used to disable it again.

In the JavaScript, we use the `click` event of the **Enable!** button to call the `tabs` constructor. This passes the string `"enable"`, which specifies the `enable` method and the index number of the tab we want to enable. The `disable` method is used in the same way. Note that a tab cannot be disabled while it is active.

All methods exposed by each component are used in this same easy way which you'll see more of as we progress through the book.

I mentioned in *Chapter 1* that each widget has a set of common methods consisting of `enable`, `disable`, and `destroy`. These methods are used in the same way across each of the different components, so we won't be looking at these methods again.

Adding and removing tabs

Along with enabling and disabling tabs programmatically, we can also remove them or add completely new tabs dynamically. In `tabs10.html` add the following new code directly after the underlying HTML of the widget:

```
<label>Enter a tab to remove:</label>
  <input id="indexNum"><button id="remove">Remove!</button><br>
<button id="add">Add a new tab!</button>
<div id="newTab" class="ui-helper-hidden"> This content was added
  after the widget was initialized!</div>
```

Then change the final `<script>` element to this:

```
<script type="text/javascript">
  $(function(){
    $("#myTabs").tabs();
    $("#remove").click(function() {
      var indexNumber = $("#indexNum").val();
      $("#myTabs").tabs("remove", indexNumber);
    });
    $("#add").click(function() {
      var newLabel = "A New Tab!"
      $("#myTabs").tabs("add", "#newTab", newLabel);
    });
  });
```

Save this as `tabs11.html`. On the page we've changed the `<button>` from the last example and have added a new `<label>`, an `<input>`, and another `<button>`. These new elements are used to add a new tab.

We have also added some new content on the page, which will be used as the basis for each new tab that is added. We make use of the `ui-helper-hidden` framework class to hide this content, so that it isn't available when the page loads,. Even though this class name will remain on the element once it has been added to the tab widget, it will still be visible when its tab is clicked. This is because the class name will be overridden by classes within `ui.tabs.css`.

In the `<script>`, the first of our new functions handles removing a tab using the `remove` method. This method requires one additional argument—the index number of the tab to be removed. In this example, we get the value entered into the text box and pass it to the method as the argument. If no index is passed to the method, the first tab will be removed.

The `add` method that adds a new tab to the widget, can be made to work in several different ways. In this example, we've specified that content already existing on the page (the `<div>` with an `id` of `newTab`) should be added to the tabs widget. In addition to passing the string `"add"` and specifying a reference to the element we wish to add to the tabs, we also specify a label for the new tab.

Optionally, we can also specify the index number where the new tab should be inserted. If the index is not supplied, the new tab will be added as the last tab. We can continue adding new tabs and each one will reuse the `<div>` for its content because our content `<div>` will retain its `id` attribute after it has been added to the widget. After adding and perhaps removing tabs, the page should appear something like this:

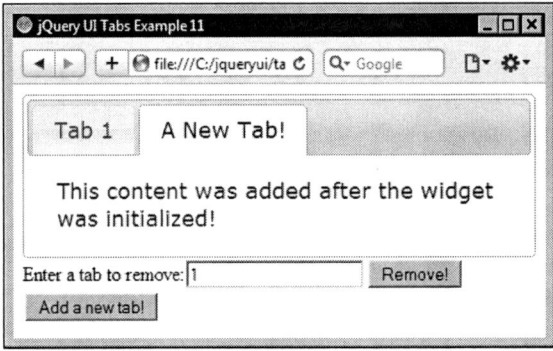

Simulating clicks

There may be times when you want to programmatically select a particular tab and show its content. This could happen as the result of some other interaction by the visitor. We can use the `select` method to do this, which is completely analogous with the action of clicking a tab. Alter the final `<script>` block in `tabs11.html` so that it appears as follows:

```
<script type="text/javascript">
  $(function(){

    $("#myTabs").tabs();

    $("#remove").click(function() {

      var indexNumber = $("#indexNum").val() - 1;

      $("#myTabs").tabs("remove", indexNumber);

    });

    $("#add").click(function() {
      var newLabel = "A New Tab!"
```

```
$("#myTabs").tabs("add", "#newTab", newLabel);

var newIndex = $("#myTabs").tabs("length") - 1;

$("#myTabs").tabs("select", newIndex);

    });
  });
</script>
```

Save this as `tabs12.html` in your `jqueryui` folder. Now when a new tab is added, it is automatically selected. The `select` method requires just one additional parameter, which is the index number of the tab to select.

As any tab we add will be the last tab in the interface (in this example) and as the tab indices are zero based, all we have to do is use the `length` method to return the number of tabs and then subtract 1 from this figure to get the index. The result is passed to the `select` method.

Creating a tab carousel

One method that creates quite an exciting result is the `rotate` method. The `rotate` method will make all of the tabs (and their associated content panels) display one after the other automatically.

It's a great visual effect and is useful for ensuring that all, or a lot, of the individual tab's content panels get seen by the visitor. For an example of this kind of effect in action, see the homepage of `http://www.cnet.com`. There is a tabs widget (not a jQuery UI one) that shows blogs, podcasts, and videos.

Like the other methods we've seen, the `rotate` method is easy to use. Change the final `<script>` element in `tabs9.html` to this:

```
<script type="text/javascript">
  $(function(){

    $("#myTabs").tabs().tabs("rotate", 1000, true);
  });
</script>
```

Save this file as `tabs13.html`. We've reverted back to a simplified page with no additional elements other than the underlying structure of the widget. Although we can't call the `rotate` method directly using the initial `tabs` method, we can chain it to the end like we would with methods from the standard jQuery library.

Chaining UI Methods

Chaining widget methods is possible because like the methods found in the underlying jQuery library, they always return the jQuery ($) object.

The `rotate` method is used with two additional parameters. The first parameter is an integer, that specifies the number of milliseconds each tab should be displayed before the next tab is shown. The second parameter is a Boolean that indicates whether the cycle through the tabs should occur once or continuously.

The tab widget also contains a `destroy` method. This is a method common to all the widgets found in jQuery UI. Let's see how it works. In `tabs13.html`, after the widget add a new `<button>` as follows:

```
<button id="destroy">Destroy the tabs!</button>
```

Next change the final `<script>` element to this:

```
<script type="text/javascript">
  $(function(){
    $("#myTabs").tabs();
    $("#destroy").click(function() {
      $("#myTabs").tabs("destroy");
    });
  });
</script>
```

Save this file as `tabs14.html`. The `destroy` method that we invoke with a click on the button, completely removes the tab widget, returning the underlying HTML to its original state. After the button has been clicked, you should see a standard HTML list element and the text from each tab, just like in the following screenshot:

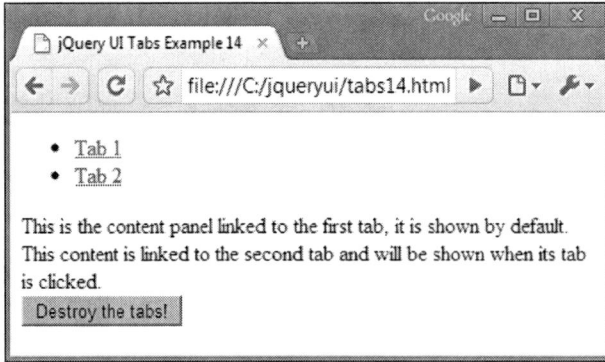

Once the tabs have been reduced to this state it would be common practice to remove them using jQuery's `remove()` method. As I mentioned with the `enable` and `disable` methods earlier, the `destroy` method is used in exactly the same way for all widgets and therefore will not be discussed again.

Getting and setting options

Like the `destroy` method the `option` method is exposed by all the different components found in the library. This method is used to work with the configurable options and functions in both getter and setter modes. Let's look at a basic example, add the following `<button>` after the tabs widget in `tabs9.html`:

```
<button id="show">Show Selected!</button>
```

Then change the final `<script>` element so that it is as follows:

```
<script type="text/javascript">
  $(function(){

  $("#myTabs").tabs();

    $("#show").click(function() {
      $("<p>").text("The tab at index " + $("#myTabs").
        tabs("option", "selected") + " is active").addClass(
        "status-message ui-corner-all").appendTo($(".ui-tabs-nav",
        "#myTabs")).fadeOut(5000);
    });
  });
</script>
```

Save this file as `tabs15.html`. The `<button>` on the page has been changed so that it shows the currently active tab. All we do is add the index of the selected tab to a status bar message as we did in the earlier example. We get the `selected` option by passing the string `selected` as the second argument. Any option can be accessed in this way.

To trigger setter mode instead, we can supply a third argument containing the new value of the option that we'd like to set. Therefore, to change the value of the `selected` option, we could use the following HTML to specify the tab to select:

```
<label>Enter a tab index to activate</label><input id="newIndex"
  type="text"><button id="set">Change Selected!</button>
```

And the following click-handler:

```
<script type="text/javascript">
  $(function(){
$("#set").click(function() {
  $("#myTabs").tabs("option", "selected", parseInt($("#newIndex").
    val()));
});
```

Save this as `tabs16.html`. The new page contains a `<label>` and an `<input>`, as well as a `<button>` that is used to harvest the index number that the `selected` option should be set to. When the button is clicked, our code will retrieve the value of the `<input>` and use it to change the `selected` index. By supplying the new value we put the method in setter mode.

When we run this page in our browser, we should see that we can switch to the second tab by entering its index number and clicking the **Changed Selected** button.

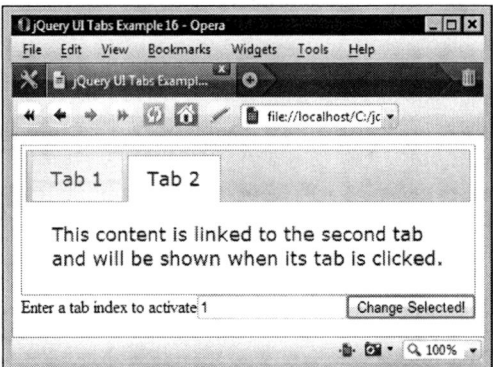

AJAX tabs

We've looked at adding new tabs from already existing content on the page. In addition to this we can also create AJAX tabs that load content from remote files or URLs. Let's extend our previous example of adding tabs so that the new tab content is loaded from an external file. In `tabs16.html` remove the `<label>` and the `<input>` from the page and change the `<button>` so that it appears as follows:

```
<button id="add">Add a new tab!</button>
```

Then change the click-handler so that it appears as follows:

```
$("#add").click(function() {
  $("#myTabs").tabs("add", "tabContent.html", "A Remote Tab!");
});
```

Save this as `tabs17.html`. This time, instead of specifying an element selector as the second argument of the `add` method, we supply a relative file path. Instead of generating the new tab from inline content, the tab becomes an AJAX tab and loads the contents of the remote file.

The file used as the remote content in this example is basic and consists of just the following code:

```
<div>This is some remote content!</div>
```

Save this as `tabContent.html` in the `jqueryui` folder. After the `<button>` has been clicked, the page should appear like this:

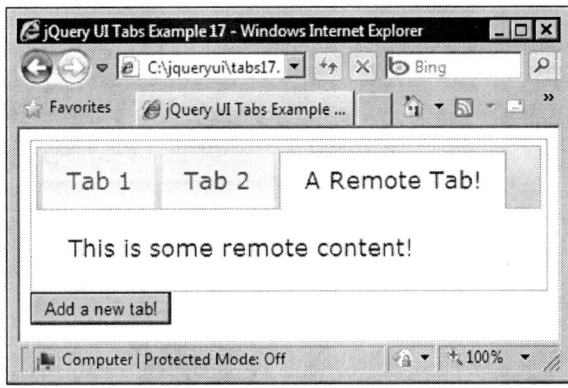

Instead of using JavaScript to add the new tab, we can use plain HTML to specify an AJAX tab as well. In this example, we want the tab that will display the remote content to be available all the time, not just after clicking the button. Add the following new `<a>` element to the underlying HTML for the widget in `tabs17.html`:

```
<li><a href="tabContent.html">AJAX Tab</a></li>
```

The final `<script>` element can be used to just call the `tabs` method:

```
$("#myTabs").tabs();
```

Save this as `tabs18.html`. All we're doing is specifying the path to the remote file (the same one we created in the previous example) using the `href` attribute of an `<a>` element in the underlying markup from which the tabs are created.

Unlike static tabs, we don't need a corresponding `<div>` element with an `id` that matches the `href` of the link. The additional elements required for the tab content will be generated automatically by the widget.

If you use a DOM explorer, you can see that the file path we added to link to the remote tab has been removed. Instead, a new fragment identifier has been generated and set as the `href`. The new fragment is also added as the `id` of the new tab (minus the # symbol of course).

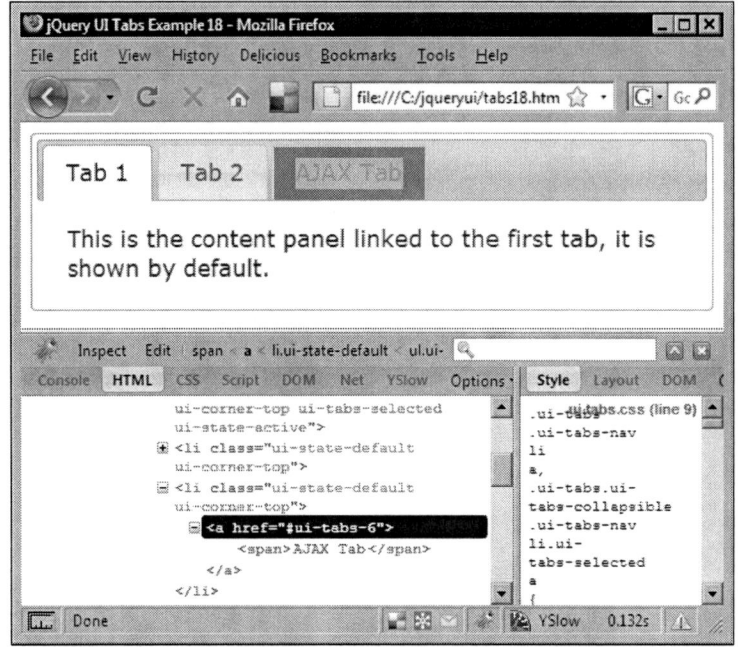

There is no inherent cross-domain support built into the AJAX functionality of tabs widget. Therefore, unless additional PHP or some other server-scripting language is employed as a proxy, or you wish to make use of JSON structured data and jQuery's JSONP functionality, files and URLs should be under the same domain as the page running the widget.

Along with loading data from external files, it can also be loaded from URLs. This is great when retrieving content from a database using query strings or a web service. Methods related to AJAX tabs include the `load` and `url` methods. The `load` method is used to load and reload the contents of an AJAX tab, which could come in handy for refreshing content that changes very frequently.

The `url` method is used to change the URL that the AJAX tab retrieves its content from. Let's look at a brief example of these two methods in action. There are also a number of properties related to AJAX functionality. Add the following new `<select>` element in `tabs18.html`:

```
<select id="fileChooser">
  <option>tabContent.html</option>
  <option>tabContent2.html</option>
</select>
```

Then change the final `<script>` element to this:

```
<script type="text/javascript">
  $(function(){
    $("#myTabs").tabs();
    $("#fileChooser").change(function() {
      this.selectedIndex == 0 ? loadFile1() : loadFile2();
      function loadFile1() {
        $("#myTabs").tabs("url", 2, "tabContent.html").tabs(
          "load", 2);
      }
      function loadFile2() {
        $("#myTabs").tabs("url", 2, "tabContent2.html").tabs(
          "load", 2);
      }
    });
  });
</script>
```

Save the new file as `tabs19.html`. We've added a simple `<select>` element to the page that lets you choose the content to display in the AJAX tab. In the JavaScript, we set a `change` handler for the `<select>` and specified an anonymous function to be executed each time the event is detected.

This function checks the `selectedIndex` of the `<select>` element and calls either the `loadFile1` or `loadFile2` function. The `<select>` element is in the execution scope of the function, so we can refer to it using the `this` keyword.

These functions are where things get interesting. We first call the `url` method, specifying two additional arguments, which are the index of the tab whose URL we want to change followed by the new URL. We then call the `load` method that is chained to the `url` method, specifying the index of the tab whose content we want to load.

We'll need a second local content file, change the text on the page of `tabContent1.html` and resave it as `tabContent2.html`.

Run the new file in a browser and select a tab. Then use the dropdown `<select>` to choose the second file and watch as the content of the tab is changed. You'll also see that the tab content will be reloaded even if the AJAX tab isn't active when you use the `<select>` element.

The slight flicker in the tab heading is the string value of the `spinner` option that by default is set to `Loading...`. Although, we don't get a chance to see it in full as the tab content is changed quickly when running it locally. Here's how the page should look after selecting the remote page in the dropdown select and the third tab:

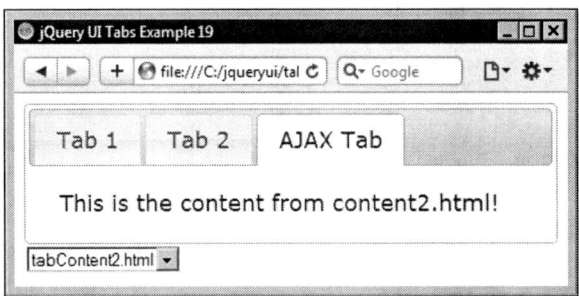

Displaying data obtained via JSONP

Let's pull in some external content for our final tabs example. If we use the tabs widget, in conjunction with the standard jQuery library `getJSON` method, we can bypass the cross-domain exclusion policy and pull in a feed from another domain to display in a tab. In a new file in your text editor, create the following new page:

```
<!DOCTYPE HTML PUBLIC "-//W3C//DTD HTML 4.01//EN"
"http://www.w3.org/TR/html4/strict.dtd">
<html lang="en">
  <head>
    <link rel="stylesheet" type="text/css"
      href="development-bundle/themes/smoothness/ui.all.css">
    <link rel="stylesheet" type="text/css"
      href="css/flickrTabTheme.css">
    <meta http-equiv="Content-Type"
      content="text/html; charset=utf-8">
    <title>jQuery UI AJAX Tabs Example</title>
  </head>
  <body>
    <div id="myTabs">
      <ul>
        <li><a href="#a"><span>Nebula Information</span></a></li>
        <li><a href="#flickr"><span>Images</span></a></li>
      </ul>
      <div id="a">
```

```
    <p>A nebulae is an interstellar cloud of dust, hydrogen gas,
and plasma. It is the first stage of a star's cycle. In these regions
the formations of gas, dust, and other materials clump together to
form larger masses, which attract further matter, and eventually will
become big enough to form stars. The remaining materials are then
believed to form planets and other planetary system objects. Many
nebulae form from the gravitational collapse of diffused gas in the
interstellar medium or ISM. As the material collapses under its own
weight, massive stars may form in the center, and their ultraviolet
radiation ionizes the surrounding gas, making it visible at optical
wavelengths.</p>
      </div>
      <div id="flickr"></div>
    </div>
    <script type="text/javascript"
      src="development-bundle/jquery-1.3.2.js"></script>
    <script type="text/javascript"
      src="development-bundle/ui/ui.core.js"></script>
    <script type="text/javascript"
      src="development-bundle/ui/ui.tabs.js"></script>
  </body>
</html>
```

The HTML seen here is nothing new. It's basically the same as the previous examples
so I won't describe it in any detail. The only point worthy noting is that unlike the
previous AJAX tab examples, we have specified an empty `<div>` element that will be
used for the AJAX tab's content. Now, just before the `</body>` tag, add the following
script block:

```
<script type="text/javascript">
  $(function(){

    var tabOpts = {
      select: function(event, ui) {
        ui.tab.toString().indexOf("flickr") != -1 ? getData() : null ;
        function getData() {
          $("#flickr").empty();
    $.getJSON("http://api.flickr.com/services/feeds/photos_public.gne?
      tags=nebula&format=json&jsoncallback=?", function(data) {
            $.each(data.items, function(i,item){
              $("<img/>").attr("src",
              item.media.m).appendTo("#flickr").height(100).width(100);
               return (i == 5) ? false : null;
            });
          });
        }
      }
```

```
        }
      $("#myTabs").tabs(tabOpts);
    });
</script>
```

Save the file as `flickrTab.html` in your `jqueryui` folder. Every time a tab is selected, our `select` callback will check to see if it was the tab with an `id` of `flickr` that was clicked. If it is, then the `getData()` function is invoked that uses the standard jQuery `getJSON` method to retrieve an image feed from `http://www.flickr.com`.

Once the data is returned, the anonymous callback function iterates over each object within the feed and creates a new image. We also remove any preexisting images from the content panel to prevent a buildup of images following multiple tab selections.

Each new image has its `src` attribute set using the information from the current feed object and is then added to the empty Flickr tab. Once iteration over six of the objects in the feed has occurred, we exit jQuery's `each` method. It's that simple.

We also require a bit of CSS to make the example look right. In a new file in your text editor add the following selectors and rules:

```
#myTabs { width:335px; }
#myTabs .ui-tabs-panel { padding:10px 0 0 7px; }
#myTabs p { margin:0 0 10px; font-size:75%; }
#myTabs img { border:1px solid #aaaaaa; margin:0 5px 5px 0; }
```

Save this as `flickrTabTheme.css` in your `css` folder. When you view the page and select the **Images** tab, after a short delay you should see six new images, as seen in the following screenshot:

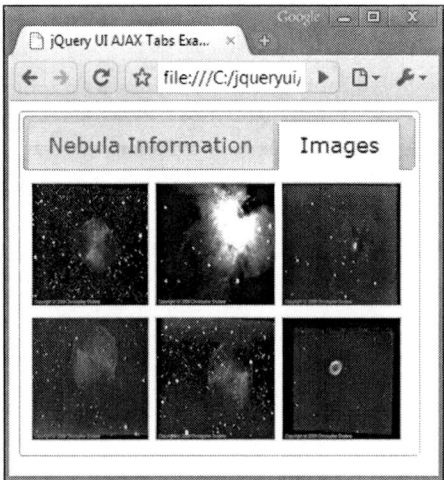

Summary

The tabs widget is an excellent way of saving space on your page by organizing related (or even completely unrelated) sections of content that can be shown or hidden, with simple click-input from your visitors. It also lends an air of interactivity to your site that can help improve the overall functionality and appeal of the page on which it is used.

Let's review what was covered in this chapter. We first looked at how, with just a little underlying HTML and a single line of jQuery-flavored JavaScript code, we can implement the default tabs widget.

We then saw how easy it is to add our own basic styling for the tabs widget so that its appearance, but not its behavior, is altered. We already know that in addition to this we can use a predesigned theme or create a completely new theme using ThemeRoller.

We then moved on to look at the set of configurable options exposed by the tabs API. With these, we can enable or disable different options that the widget supports, such as whether tabs are selected by clicks or another event, whether certain tabs are disabled when the widget is rendered, and so on.

We took some time to look at how we can use a range of predefined callback options that allow us to execute arbitrary code when different events are detected. We also saw that the jQuery `bind()` method can listen for the same events if it becomes necessary.

Following the configurable options, we covered the range of methods that we can use to programmatically make the tabs perform different actions, such as simulating a click on a tab, enabling or disabling a tab, and adding or removing tabs.

We briefly looked at some of the more advanced functionality supported by the tabs widget such as AJAX tabs and the tab carousel. Both these techniques are easy to use and can add value to any implementation.

4
The Accordion Widget

The accordion widget is another UI widget that allows you to group content into separate panels which can be opened or closed by visitor interaction. Therefore, most of its content is initially hidden from view, much like tabs widget that we looked at in the previous chapter.

Each container has a heading element associated with it that is used to open the container and display the content. When you click on a heading its content will slide into view below it. The currently visible content is hidden while the new content is shown when you click on another heading.

The **accordion widget** is a robust and highly configurable widget that allows you to save space on your web pages by displaying only a single panel of content at any time. This is like a tabbed interface but positioned vertically instead of horizontally. The following screenshot shows an example of an accordion widget:

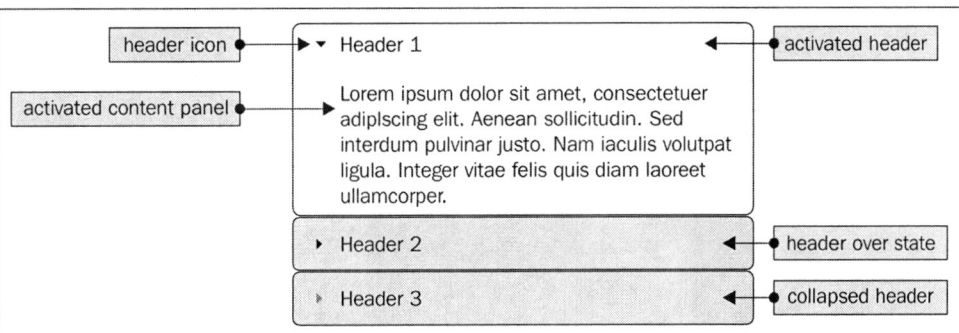

It's easy to use for your visitors and easy to implement for us. It has a range of configurable options that can be used to customize its appearance and behavior. It also has a series of methods that allow you to control it programmatically.

The height of the accordion's container element will be set automatically so that there is room to show the tallest content panel in addition to the headers. Also, the size of the widget will remain fixed so that it won't push other elements out of the way when content panels open or close.

In this chapter, we are going to cover the following topics:

- The structure of an accordion widget
- The default implementation of an accordion
- Adding custom styling
- Using the configurable options to set different behaviors
- Working with methods for controlling the accordion
- The built-in types of animation
- Custom accordion events

Accordion's structure

Let's take a moment to familiarize ourselves with the underlying markup that an accordion is made of. Within the outer container is a series of links. These links are the headings within the accordion and each heading will have a corresponding content panel that opens when the header is clicked.

It's worth remembering that only one content panel can be open at any one time when using the accordion widget. Let's implement a basic accordion now. In a blank page in your text editor, create the following page:

```
<!DOCTYPE HTML PUBLIC "-//W3C//DTD HTML 4.01//EN"
  "http://www.w3.org/TR/html4/strict.dtd">
<html lang="en">
  <head>
    <link rel="stylesheet" type="text/css"
      href="development-bundle/themes/smoothness/ui.all.css">
    <meta http-equiv="Content-Type"
      content="text/html; charset=utf-8">
    <title>jQuery UI Accordion Widget Example 1</title>
  </head>
  <body>
    <div id="myAccordion">
      <h2><a href="#">Header 1</a></h2>
      <div>Lorem ipsum dolor sit amet, consectetuer adipiscing elit.
        Aenean sollicitudin. Sed interdum pulvinar justo. Nam iaculis
        volutpat ligula. Integer vitae felis quis diam laoreet
        ullamcorper.</div>
      <h2><a href="#">Header 2</a></h2>
      <div>Etiam tincidunt est vitae est. Ut posuere, mauris at
```

```
        sodales rutrum, turpis tellus fermentum metus,
        ut bibendum velit enim eu lectus. Suspendisse potenti.</div>
      <h2><a href="#">Header 3</a></h2>
      <div>Donec at dolor ac metus pharetra aliquam. Suspendisse
        purus. Fusce tempor ultrices libero. Sed quis nunc.
        Pellentesque tincidunt viverra felis. Integer elit mauris,
        egestas ultricies, gravida vitae, feugiat a, tellus.</div>
    </div>
    <script type="text/javascript"
      src="development-bundle/jquery-1.3.2.js"></script>
    <script type="text/javascript"
      src="development-bundle/ui/ui.core.js"></script>
    <script type="text/javascript"
      src="development-bundle/ui/ui.accordion.js"></script>
    <script type="text/javascript">
      $(function() {
        $("#myAccordion").accordion();
      });
    </script>
  </body>
</html>
```

Save the file as `accordion1.html` in your `jqueryui` folder and try it out in a browser. The widget should appear as it did in the screenshot at the start of the chapter, fully skinned and ready for action.

Less coding is required for a basic working version of the accordion widget. The following list shows the required dependencies of the widget:

- `ui.all.css`
- `jquery-1.3.2.js`
- `ui.core.js`
- `ui.accordion.js`

Each widget also has its own source file, and may depend on other components as well. For example, we could include some effects files to use non-standard animations on the opening accordion panels.

The order in which these files appear is important. The jQuery library must always appear first, followed by the `ui.core.js` file. After these files, any other files that the widget depends upon should appear before the widget's own script file. The library components will not function as expected if files are not loaded in the correct order.

The underlying markup required for the accordion is flexible and the widget can be constructed from a variety of different structures. In this example, the accordion headings are formed from links wrapped in `<h2>` elements and the content panels are simple `<div>` elements.

For the accordion to function correctly, each content panel should appear directly after its corresponding header. All of the elements for the widget are enclosed within a container `<div>` that is targeted with the `accordion()` widget method.

After the required script dependencies from the library we use a custom `<script>` block to transform the underlying markup into the accordion. We can use the jQuery object shortcut `$` to specify an anonymous function that will be executed as soon as the document is ready.

Following this, we use the simple `id` selector `$("#myAccordion")` to specify the element that contains the markup for the widget and then chain the `accordion()` method after the selector to create the accordion.

In this example, we used an empty fragment (#) as the value of the `href` attribute in our tab heading elements, such as:

```
<h2><a href="#">Header 1</a></h2>
```

You should note that any URLs supplied for accordion headers will not be followed when the header is clicked in the default implementation.

Similar to the tabs widget that we looked at in the last chapter, the underlying markup that is transformed into the accordion has a series of class names added to it when the widget is initialized. The following screenshot shows the widget in Firebug:

As you can see from the previous screenshot, a number of different elements that make up the widget are given `role` and `aria-` attributes. **ARIA** that stands for **Accessible Rich Internet Applications,** is a W3C recommendation for ensuring that rich Internet applications remain accessible to assisted technologies.

The accordion panels that are initially hidden from view are given the attribute `aria-expanded="false"` to ensure that screen readers don't discard or cannot access content that is hidden using `display:none`. This makes the accordion widget highly accessible.

Styling the accordion

ThemeRoller is the recommended tool for choosing or creating the theme of the accordion widget, but there may be times when we want to considerably change the look and style of the widget beyond what is possible with ThemeRoller. In that case we can just style our own accordion.

In a new page in your text editor add the following code:

```
#myAccordion {
    width:400px; border:1px solid #636363; padding-bottom:1px;
}
.ui-accordion-header {
    font-family:Georgia; background:#e2e2e2 none;
    border:1px solid #ffffff;
}
.ui-widget-content { font-size:70%; border:none; }
.ui-corner-bottom {
    -moz-border-radius-bottomleft:0;
    -moz-border-radius-bottomright:0;
    -webkit-border-bottom-left-radius:0;
    -webkit-border-bottom-right-radius:0;
}
.ui-corner-all {
    -moz-border-radius-topleft:0; -moz-border-radius-topright:0;
    -moz-border-radius-bottomleft:0;
    -moz-border-radius-bottomright:0;
    -webkit-border-top-left-radius:0;
    -webkit-border-top-right-radius:0;
    -webkit-border-bottom-left-radius:0;
    -webkit-border-bottom-right-radius:0;
}
.ui-accordion .ui-accordion-header { margin:0 0 -1px; }
```

```
#myAccordion .ui-state-active, #myAccordion .ui-widget-content .ui-
state-active { background:#ffffff; }
.ui-state-hover, .ui-widget-content .ui-state-hover {
  background:#d2d2d2;
}
```

Save this file as `accordionTheme.css` in the `css` folder and link to it after the jQuery UI stylesheet in the head of `accordion1.html`.

```
<link rel="stylesheet" type="text/css"
  href=" css/accordionTheme.css">
```

Save the new file as `accordion2.html` in the `jqueryui` folder and view it in a browser. It should appear something like this:

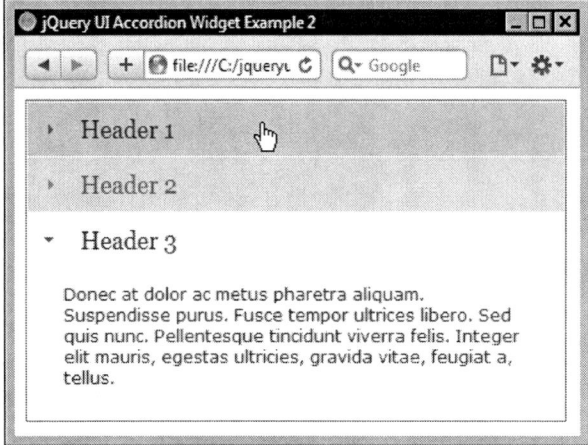

As you can see from the previous screenshot, we've disabled the built-in rounded corners that are added by the `ui.theme.css` file and have set alternative fonts, background colors, and border colors.

We haven't changed the widget much, but we haven't used many style rules. It would be easy to continue overriding rules in this way to build a much more complex custom theme.

Configuring an accordion

The accordion has a range of configurable options that allow us to change the default behavior of the widget. The following table lists the available options, their default value, and gives a brief description of their usage:

Option	Default value	Usage
`active`	first child	Sets the active heading on page load.
`animated`	`"slide"`	Animate the opening of content panels.
`autoHeight`	`true`	Automatically set height according to the biggest drawer.
`clearStyle`	`false`	Clear height and overflow styles after a panel opens.
`collapsible`	`false`	Allows all of the content panels to be closed.
`event`	`"click"`	The event on headers that trigger drawers to open.
`fillSpace`	`false`	Allows the accordion to fill the height of its container instead of sizing itself according to the content within it.
`header`	`"> li >:first-child,> :not(li):even"`	The selector for header elements. Although it looks complex, this is a standard jQuery selector that simply targets the first-child within every odd `<li>` element.
`icons`	`'header': 'ui-icon-triangle-1-e', 'headerSelected': 'ui-icon-triangle-1-s'`	Sets the icons for the header element and selected state.
`navigation`	`false`	Enables navigation for accordion.
`navigationFilter`	`location.href`	Changes the function used to obtain the ID of the content panel that should be open when the widget is initialized.

Changing the trigger event

Most of the options are self-explanatory, and the values they accept are usually Booleans, strings, or element references. Let's put some of them to use so that we can explore their functionality. Change the final `<script>` element in `accordion2.html` so that it appears as follows:

```
<script type="text/javascript">
  $(function() {

    var accOpts = {
    event:"mouseover"
    }
    $("#myAccordion").accordion(accOpts);

  });
</script>
```

First, we create a new object literal called `accOpts` that contains one property key and a value. We pass this object to the `accordion()` method as an argument and it overrides the default options of the widget.

The string we specified for the value of the `event` option becomes the event that triggers the selection of a header and the opening of its content panel, making this a useful option. Save these changes as `accordion3.html`.

You should note that you can also set options using an inline object within the widget's constructor method without creating a separate object (see `accordion3Inline.html`). Using the following code would be equally as effective, and would often be the preferred way of coding:

```
<script type="text/javascript">
  $(function() {
    $("#myAccordion").accordion({
      event:"mouseover"
    });
  });
</script>
```

Changing the default active header

By default the first header of the accordion will be selected when the widget is rendered, with its content panel open. We can change which header is selected on page load using the `active` option. Change the configuration object in `accordion3.html` so that it appears as follows:

```
var accOpts = {
  active: 2
};
```

We set the `active` option to the integer `2` to open the last content panel by default and like the tab headers that we saw in the last chapter accordion's headers use a zero-based index. Along with an integer this option also accepts a jQuery selector, a raw HTML element, or a Boolean value.

We can use the Boolean value of `false` to configure the accordion so that none of the content panels are open by default. Change the configuration object once again to the following:

```
var accOpts = {
   active: false
};
```

Save this as `accordion5.html`. Now when the page loads all of the content panels are hidden from view.

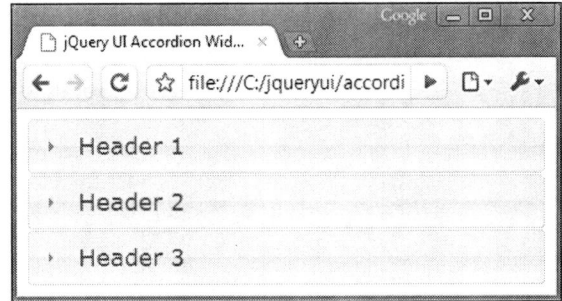

The widget will only remain closed until one of the headers is selected and then one panel will remain open at all times. This behavior can be changed by employing the `collapsible` option in the configuration object:

```
var accOpts = {
   active: false,
   collapsible: true
};
```

Save this as `accordion6.html`. Now, not only is the accordion closed when the page loads, but clicking an active header will close its associated content panel as well. As expected, when a closed header is clicked, it will show its content panel in the usual way. For usability, it is best to avoid configuring both this and the `mouseover event` option together in the same implementation.

Filling the height of its container

If the `fillSpace` option is set, then it will override `autoHeight` and force the accordion to take the full height of its container. In our examples so far, the container of the accordion has been the body of the page, and the height of the body will only be the height of its largest element. We'll need to use a new container element with a fixed height to see this option in action.

In the `<head>` of `accordion6.html` add the following `<style>` element:

```
<style type="text/css">
  #container { height:600px; width:400px; }
</style>
```

Then wrap all of the underlying markup for the accordion in a new container element:

```
<div id="container">
  <div id="myAccordion">
    <h2><a href="#">Header 1</a></h2><div>Lorem ipsum dolor sit
      amet, consectetuer adipiscing elit. Aenean sollicitudin.
      Sed interdum pulvinar justo. Nam iaculis volutpat ligula.
      Integer vitae felis quis diam laoreet ullamcorper.</div>
    <h2><a href="#">Header 2</a></h2><div>Etiam tincidunt est
      vitae est. Ut posuere, mauris at sodales rutrum, turpis
      tellus fermentum metus, ut bibendum velit enim eu lectus.
      Suspendisse potenti.</div>
    <h2><a href="#">Header 3</a></h2><div>Donec at dolor ac metus
      pharetra aliquam. Suspendisse purus. Fusce tempor ultrices
      libero. Sed quis nunc. Pellentesque tincidunt viverra
      felis. Integer elit mauris, egestas ultricies, gravida
      vitae, feugiat a, tellus.</div>
  </div>
</div>
```

Finally, change the configuration object to use the `fillSpace` option.

```
var accOpts = {
  fillSpace: true
};
```

Save the changes as `accordion7.html`. The new container is given a fixed height and width using the CSS specified in the `<head>` of the page. Please note, this is not the right way to style elements! But when we only have a single selector and two rules, it seems excessive to create a new stylesheet.

The `fillSpace` option forces the accordion to take the entire height of its container, and restricting the width of the container naturally reduces the width of the widget too. This page should appear as follows:

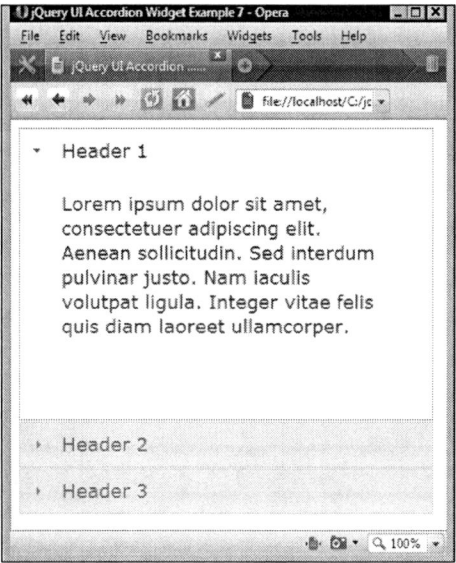

Accordion animation

The accordion widget comes with the built-in `slide` animation that is enabled by default and has been present in all of our examples so far. Disabling this animation is as easy as supplying `false` as the value of the `animated` option. Remove the `<style>` tag from the `<head>` of the page and remove the additional container `<div>`, then change the configuration object in `accordion7.html` so that it appears as follows:

```
var accOpts = {
   animated: false
};
```

Save this as `accordion8.html`. This will cause each content panel to open immediately instead of sliding open nicely whenever a header is clicked. An alternative animation has also been built into the widget—the `bounceslide` animation. However, to use this alternative animation we need to link to the `effects.core.js` file. Directly after the link to `ui.accordion.js` at the bottom of the `<body>` add the following line of code:

```
<script type="text/javascript"
   src="development-bundle/ui/effects.core.js"></script>
```

Now change the configuration object in our custom `<script>` element so that it appears like this:

```
var accOpts = {
    animated: "bounceslide"
};
```

Save these changes as `accordion9.html`. Although the accordion panels close in exactly the same way as they did in previous examples when we run this variant in a browser, when they open they bounce a few times at the end of the animation. It's a great effect and as we saw in this example, easy to use.

In addition to these two animations, we can also use any of the different easing effects defined within the `effects.core.js` file, including the following:

- `easeInQuad`
- `easeInCubic`
- `easeInQuart`
- `easeInQuint`
- `easeInSine`
- `easeInExpo`
- `easeInCirc`
- `easeInElastic`
- `easeInBack`
- `easeInBounce`

Each of these easing methods is complimented by `easeOut` and `easeInOut` counterparts. For the complete list see the `effects.core.js` file, or refer to the easing table in *Chapter 13*.

The easing effects don't change the underlying animation, which will still be based on the slide animation. But they do change how the animation progresses. For example, we can make the content panels bounce both on opening and closing animations by using the `easeOutBounce` easing effect in our configuration object:

```
var accOpts = {
    animated: "easeOutBounce"
};
```

Save this file as `accordion10.html` and view it in a browser. Most of the easing effects have opposites, so instead of making the content panels bounce at the end of the animation, we can make them bounce at the start of the animation. This can be done using the `easeInBounce` effect.

Another option that has an effect on animations is the `clearStyle` property that resets `height` and `overflow` styles after each animation. Remember that animations are enabled by default, but this option isn't. Change the configuration object in `accordion10.html` to the following:

```
var accOpts = {
  clearStyle: true,
  animated: "easeOutBounce"
};
```

Save this as `accordion11.html`. Now when the page is run the accordion will not keep to a fixed size; it will grow or shrink depending on how much content is in each panel. It doesn't make much of a difference in this example, but the property really comes into its own when using dynamic content, when we may not always know how much content will be within each panel.

Accordion events

The accordion exposes two custom events. The `change` event is triggered every time the active header (and its associated content panel) is changed. It fires at the end of the content panel's opening animation, or if animations are disabled it is fired immediately. The other event is `changestart` that is fired as soon as the new header is selected, that is before the opening animation.

Let's see how we can use these events in our accordion implementations. In `accordion11.html` change the configuration object so that it appears as follows:

```
var accOpts = {
  change: function(e, ui) {
    $("<div>").addClass("
      notify ui-corner-all").text(ui.newHeader.find("a").text() +
      " was activated, " + ui.oldHeader.find("a").text() +
      " was closed").appendTo("body").fadeOut(5000,
      function(){ $(this).remove(); }); }
  };
  $("#myAccordion").accordion(accOpts);
});
```

Save this as `accordion12.html`. In this example, we use the `change` configuration property to specify an anonymous callback function that is executed every time the event is triggered. This function will automatically receive two objects as arguments. The first object is the `event` object that contains information about the event.

The second object contains useful information about the accordion widget, such as the header element that was activated (`ui.newHeader`) and the header that was deactivated (`ui.oldHeader`).

These objects are jQuery objects, so we can call jQuery methods on them. In this example we navigate down to the `<a>` element within the header and display its text content in our alert. For reference, the `ui` object also provides information on the content panels in the form of `ui.newContent` and `ui.oldContent` properties. However, I find working with the header objects much more reliable.

Once a header has been activated and its content panel shown, the notification will be generated.

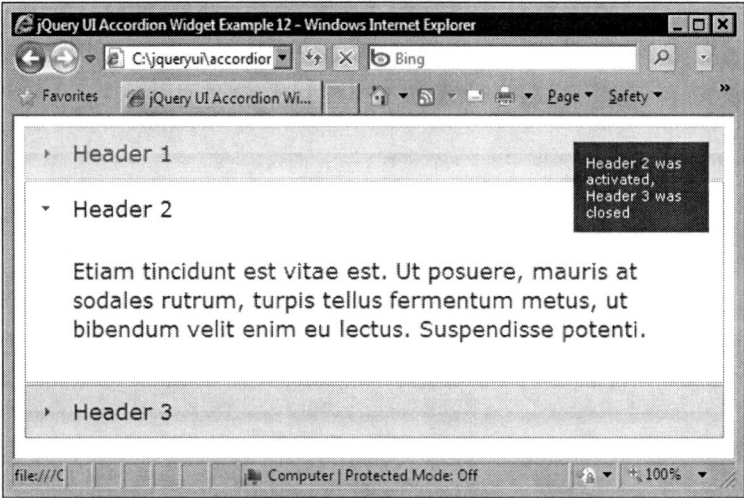

The changestart event

The `changestart` event can be used in exactly the same way and any callback function we specify using this event also receives the `e` and `ui` objects to use. Change the configuration object from the last example to as follows:

```
var accOpts = {
  changestart: function(e, ui) {
    $("<div>").addClass("
      notify ui-corner-all").text(ui.newHeader.find("a").text() +
      " was activated, " + ui.oldHeader.find("a").text() +
      " was closed").appendTo("body").fadeOut(5000,
      function(){ $(this).remove(); });
  }
};
```

Save this as `accordion13.html`. All that's changed is the property that we're targeting with our configuration object. When we run the page we should find that everything is exactly as it was before, except that our notification is produced before the content panel animation instead of after it.

There are also events such as `accordionchange` and `accordionchangestart` for use with the standard jQuery `bind()` method, so that we can specify a callback function to execute outside of the accordion configuration.

Accordion navigation

Along with a standard content accordion, the widget can also be put to good use as a navigation menu through the simple addition of some proper `href` attributes and the `navigation` option. We'll need to create two new pages to fully appreciate the effect of this option, in `accordion13.html` change the underlying markup for the accordion to the following:

```
<div id="container" class="ui-helper-clearfix">
  <div id="navCol">
    <a class="header" href="#me" title="About Me">About Me</a>
    <div>
      <a href="accordion14.html#me" title="Bio">My Bio</a>
      <a href="accordion14.html#me" title="Contact Me">Contact
        Me</a>
      <a href="accordion14.html#me" title="Resume">My Resume</a>
    </div>
    <a class="header" href="#js"
      title="JavaScript">JavaScript</a>
      <div>
        <a href="accordion14a.html#js" title="JavaScript
          Tutorials">JavaScript Tutorials</a>
        <a href="accordion14a.html#js" title="AJAX">AJAX</a>
        <a href="accordion14a.html#js" title="JavaScript
          Apps">JavaScript Apps</a>
      </div>
    </div>
  <div id="contentCol">
    <h1>Page 1</h1>
  </div>
</div>
```

Then change the configuration object so that it appears as follows:

```
var accOpts = {
  fillSpace: true,
  header: ".header",
  navigation: true
};
```

Save this file as `accordion14.html`, then save it again as `accordion14a.html` to give us the two pages we need for this example. In the `<body>` of the page we've added a new outer container to hold all the page content and have added two inner containers within this — one for the accordion widget that will appear as a navigation menu, and the other for content. In this example, the two pages just have `<h1>` elements denoting which page is open.

The underlying markup that the accordion is built from has also changed. We've removed the `<h2>` elements wrapping the `<a>` elements that form the accordion headings and have added class names and document fragment `href` attributes. Both of these additions are critical to the functioning of the navigation accordion.

In the final `<script>` element we use the `fillSpace` property to give the navigation accordion a consistent height and set both the header and navigation properties. In a standard accordion, the `<h2>` elements were used automatically as the header elements for the widget, but now that these have been removed (which is required for navigation accordions) we need to tell the widget to use the `<a>` elements with the class name `header` for the accordion headers instead.

The `navigation` option changes how the widget appears when the page is initially loaded. Instead of activating the first header when the accordion is initialized, it instead looks at the `location.href` property of the window. If the contents of the `location.href` property matches the `href` attribute of one of the accordion headers, that header will be activated.

When we run `accordion14.html` in a browser and select one of the links in the second content panel, the page will navigate to `accordion14a.html` and the second header will automatically be activated. The navigation property gives us a great way of maintaining state between pages for the widget.

We also need some additional styles in order to make sure the accordion and the page appear correctly. In a new page in your text editor create the following file:

```
#container { width:800px; margin:auto; }
#navCol { width:250px; height:400px; float:left; }
#contentCol { width:550px; height:400px; float:left; }
#contentCol h1 { text-indent:20px; font-family:Georgia; }
#navCol .ui-accordion-header {
  display:block; padding-left:40px;
}
.ui-accordion-content a {
  font-size:70%; text-decoration:none; display:block;
}
.ui-accordion-content a:hover { text-decoration:underline; }
```

Save this in the `css` folder as `accordionTheme2.css`. We don't need many styles for this example, we just need to arrange the containers and set some basic aesthetics for the accordion and the links within it.

The following screenshot shows how the second page will appear on load when navigating to it from the second content panel on the first page:

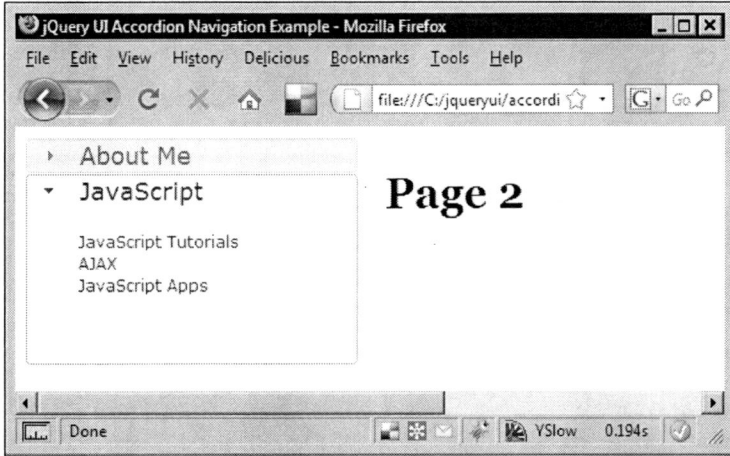

When going back to the first page from the second page, the first header should once again be activated.

Accordion methods

The accordion includes a selection of methods that allow you to control and manipulate the behavior of the widget programmatically. Some of the methods are common to each component of the library, such as the `destroy` method that is used by every widget. The following table lists the single unique method for the accordion widget:

Method	Use
`activate`	Programmatically activate a header. This is analogous to the header being selected by the visitor.

Remember, in addition to the accordion-specific `activate` method, the `destroy`, `enable`, `disable`, and `option` methods are also available. We looked at the `enable` and `disable` methods in the last chapter, so we won't go over those again.

Destruction

The destroy method is one of the common methods exposed by all library components. This method removes the widget class names and returns the underlying markup to its original state. We'll use the default options associated with accordion instead of the ones we configured for the last example. In accordion13.html add the following <button> to the page after the widget:

```
<button id="destroy">Destroy</button>
```

Then change the final <script> element so that it appears as follows:

```
<script type="text/javascript">
  $(function() {
    $("#myAccordion").accordion();
    $("#destroy").click(function() {
      $("#myAccordion").accordion("destroy");
    });
  });
</script>
```

Save this file as accordion15.html. The <body> of the page contains our new <button> element that can be used to destroy the accordion. The final <script> block contains the new click handler and anonymous function.

We use the standard jQuery library's click() method to execute some code when the targeted <button> element is clicked. We use the same accordian() method to destroy it as we did to create it. But this time, we supply the string "destroy" as an argument.

This causes the class names added by the library to be removed, the opening and closing behavior of the headers to no longer be effective, and all of the previously hidden content to be made visible. This is how the page will appear once the button has been clicked:

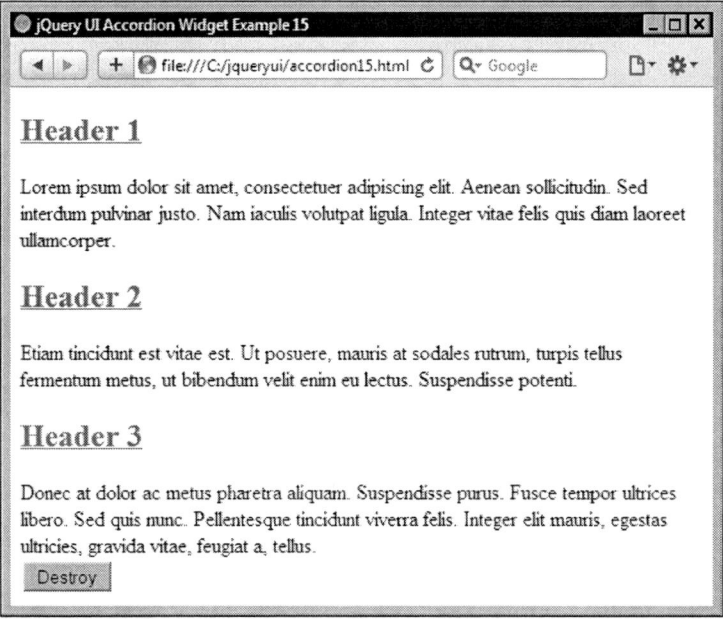

Header activation

The single unique method exposed by accordion is the `activate` method. This can be used to programmatically show or hide different drawers. We can easily test this method using a text box and a new button. In `accordion15.html` add the following new markup in place of the `<button>` elements from the last example:

```
<label>Enter a header index to activate</label>
<input id="activateChoice" type="text">
<button id="activate">Activate</button>
```

Now change the final `<script>` element so that it appears as follows:

```
<script type="text/javascript">
  $(function() {
    $("#myAccordion").accordion();
      $("#activate").click(function() {
        $("#myAccordion").accordion("activate",
        parseInt($("#activateChoice").val()));
    });
  });
</script>
```

Save the new file as `accordion16.html`. The `activate` method takes an additional argument. It expects to receive the index (zero-based) number of the header element to activate. In this example, we obtain the header to activate by returning the value of the text input. We convert it to an integer using the `parseInt()` function of JavaScript because the `val()` jQuery method returns a string.

If an index number that doesn't exist is specified then all of the content panels will close (regardless of whether the collapsible property is set to `true` or `false`). The first header will be activated if no index is specified,.

Accordion interoperability

Does the accordion widget play nicely with other widgets in the library? Let's take a look and see whether the accordion can be combined with the widget from the last chapter, the tabs widget. Create the following new page in your text editor:

```
<!DOCTYPE HTML PUBLIC "-//W3C//DTD HTML 4.01//EN" "http://www.w3.org/
TR/html4/strict.dtd">
<html lang="en">
  <head>
    <link rel="stylesheet" type="text/css"
      href="development-bundle/themes/smoothness/ui.all.css">
    <meta http-equiv="Content-Type"
      content="text/html; charset=utf-8">
    <title>jQuery UI Accordion Widget Example 17</title>
  </head>
  <body>
    <div id="myAccordion">
      <h2><a href="#">Header 1</a></h2><div>Lorem ipsum dolor sit
        amet, consectetuer adipiscing elit. Aenean sollicitudin. Sed
        interdum pulvinar justo. Nam iaculis volutpat ligula. Integer
        vitae felis quis diam laoreet ullamcorper.</div>
      <h2><a href="#">Header 2</a></h2><div>Etiam tincidunt est vitae
        est. Ut posuere, mauris at sodales rutrum, turpis tellus
        fermentum metus, ut bibendum velit enim eu lectus.
        Suspendisse potenti.</div>
      <h2><a href="#">Header 3</a></h2>
      <div>
        <div id="myTabs">
          <ul>
            <li><a href="#0"><span>Tab 1</span></a></li>
            <li><a href="#1"><span>Tab 2</span></a></li>
          </ul>
          <div id="0">This is the content panel linked to the first
            tab, it is shown by default.</div>
          <div id="1">This content is linked to the second tab and
            will be shown when its tab is clicked.</div>
```

```
        </div>
      </div>
    </div>
    <script type="text/javascript"
      src="development-bundle/jquery-1.3.2.js"></script>
    <script type="text/javascript"
      src="development-bundle/ui/ui.core.js"></script>
    <script type="text/javascript"
      src="development-bundle/ui/ui.accordion.js"></script>
    <script type="text/javascript"
      src="development-bundle/ui/ui.tabs.js"></script>
    <script type="text/javascript">
      $(function() {
        $("#myAccordion").accordion();
        $("#myTabs").tabs();
      });
    </script>
  </body>
</html>
```

Save this file as `accordion17.html`. All we've done with this file is to add a simple tab structure to one of the accordion's content panels. In the `<script>` at the end of the page we just call the accordion and tab's widget methods. No additional or special configuration is required.

The page should appear like this when the third accordion heading is activated:

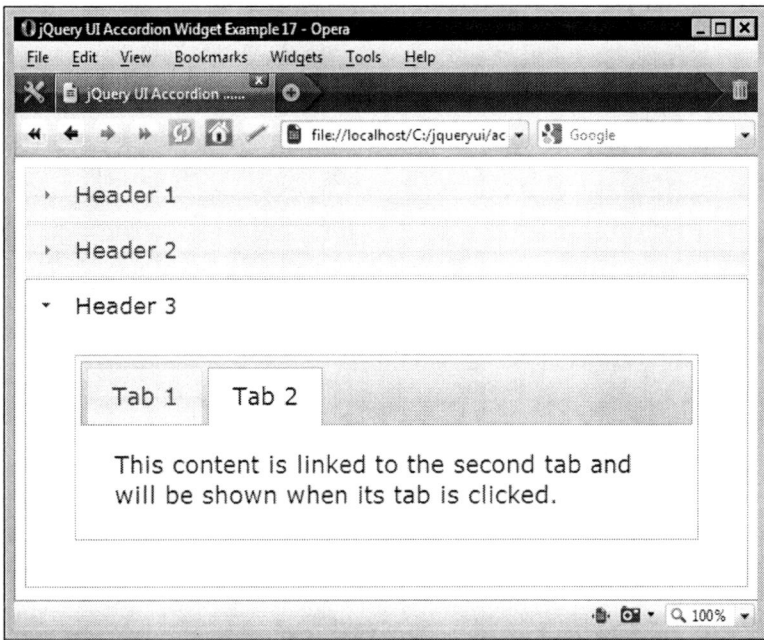

The widgets are compatible the other way round, that is we can have an accordion within one of the tab's content panels.

A del.icio.us accordion

Let's put a sample page together that will make the most of the accordion widget and uses some of the options and methods that we've looked at so far in this chapter.

One thing we haven't looked at yet is dynamic content within an accordion's content panel. Although no native methods or options are exposed by the accordion API which relate directly to enabling this functionality, we can add this feature manually ourselves.

The following screenshot shows the finished widget:

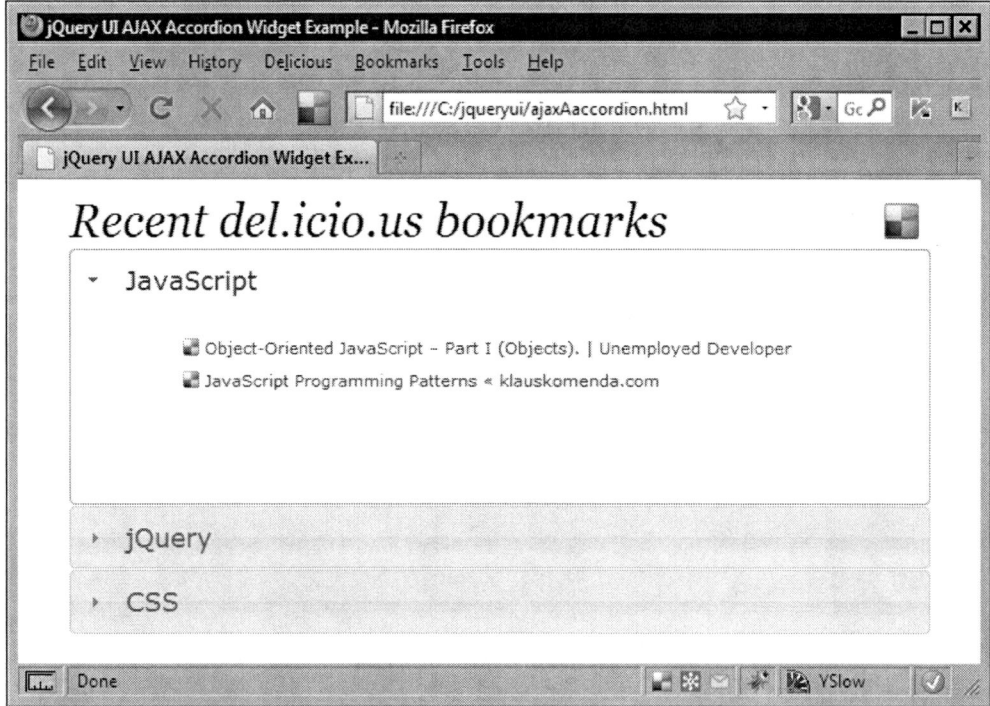

In a new page in your text editor, create the following HTML file:

```
<!DOCTYPE HTML PUBLIC "-//W3C//DTD HTML 4.01//EN" "http://www.w3.org/
TR/html4/strict.dtd">
<html lang="en">
  <head>
```

```html
        <link rel="stylesheet" type="text/css"
          href="development-bundle/themes/smoothness/ui.all.css">
        <link rel="stylesheet" type="text/css"
          href="css/ajaxAccordion.css">
        <meta http-equiv="Content-Type"
          content="text/html; charset=utf-8">
        <title>jQuery UI AJAX Accordion Widget Example</title>
    </head>
    <body>
        <div id="myAccordion">
          <h2><a href="#">Recent del.icio.us bookmarks</a>
            <span id="deliciousLogo"></span></h2><div>Use the headers
              below to look at some of my del.icio.us bookmarks</div>
          <h2><a href="#">JavaScript</a></h2><div id="js">
            <p class="empty-message">No recent JavaScript
              bookmarks</p></div>
          <h2><a href="#">jQuery</a></h2><div id="jquery">
            <p class="empty-message">No recent jQuery bookmarks</p></div>
          <h2><a href="#">CSS</a></h2><div id="css">
            <p class="empty-message">No recent CSS bookmarks</p></div>
        </div>
        <script type="text/javascript"
          src="development-bundle/jquery-1.3.2.js"></script>
        <script type="text/javascript"
          src="development-bundle/ui/ui.core.js"></script>
        <script type="text/javascript"
          src="development-bundle/ui/ui.accordion.js"></script>
        <script type="text/javascript">
          $(function() {
      $.getJSON("http://feeds.delicious.com/v1/json/
        danwellman?callback=?", function(data){

            $.each(data, function(i) {
              ($(".empty-message", $("#" + data[i].t[0])).length > 0) ?
                $(".empty-message", $("#" + data[i].t[0])).
                  remove() : null ;
                  var list = $("<ul>"),
                  li = $("<li>").appendTo(list);
                $("<a>").text(data[i].d).attr("href",
                  data[i].u).appendTo(li);
                list.appendTo("#" + data[i].t[0]);
              });
            });
            $("#myAccordion").accordion({ clearStyle: true });
          });
        </script>
    </body>
</html>
```

Save this file as `ajaxAccordion.html`. In this example, the `<body>` of the page is light as we'll be creating a lot of the elements we need dynamically, so most of our accordion content sections are empty.

The main `<script>` revolves around getting a set of recent bookmarks from Delicious' JSON feed (I've used my username for this example, feel free to use your own). The object returned to us by Delicious contains an array, and each item in the array is an object containing information about a single bookmark. This could include the title, URL, and any tags associated with it, so we use jQuery's `each()` method to iterate over each item in this array.

First we check whether the element with the class `empty-message` exists and remove it if it does. We can use jQuery's selector context facility to target the accordion panel that contains a `<div>` with an `id` matching the Delicious tag name property from the current item in `data` array. Next, we create a new `<ul>` element and a new `<li>` element along with appending the `<li>` immediately to the `<ul>`. We then create a new `<a>` element—the inner text of the new link and its `href` attribute are both set using properties from the Delicious `data` array.

Once the `<a>` has been created we can then append the list of links to the appropriate accordion content panel. We again use the tag name property of the current `data` item to append the new list to the content panel with a matching `id`. For example, all bookmarks tagged with **javascript** will be appended to the `#javascript` content panel.

Our final task is to call the accordion's widget method. Notice that we've set the `clearStyle` option to `true`. Some of the content in our dynamic panels may be hidden if we don't do this.

This is all the JavaScript we'll need, but in addition to this we'll also need a small stylesheet. In another new file in your text editor add the following style rules:

```
h2.title {
   width:600px; margin:auto; position:relative; font-family:Georgia;
font-weight:normal;
   font-size:32px; font-style:italic;
}
#myAccordion { width:600px; margin:auto; }
#deliciousLogo {
   width:24px; height:24px; position:absolute; right:8px; top:8px;
   background:url(../img/accordion/delicious.png) no-repeat;
}
```

```
#myAccordion .ui-accordion-content ul { margin:0; pading:0; }
#myAccordion .ui-accordion-content ul li {
   font-size:11px; list-style-type:none; padding-left:16px; margin-
bottom:8px;
   background:url(../img/accordion/delicious_small.png) no-repeat 0
1px;
}
#myAccordion .ui-accordion-content ul li a
{ text-decoration:none; padding:4px 16px 0 0; }
#myAccordion .ui-accordion-content ul li a:hover {
   background:url(../img/accordion/external.png) no-repeat 100% 4px;
}
```

Save this in the `css` folder as `ajaxAccordion.css`. We basically set the size of the widget and added a few icons. This code (along with the images from the code download) should give us a fully working AJAX accordion listing some of our recent bookmarks:

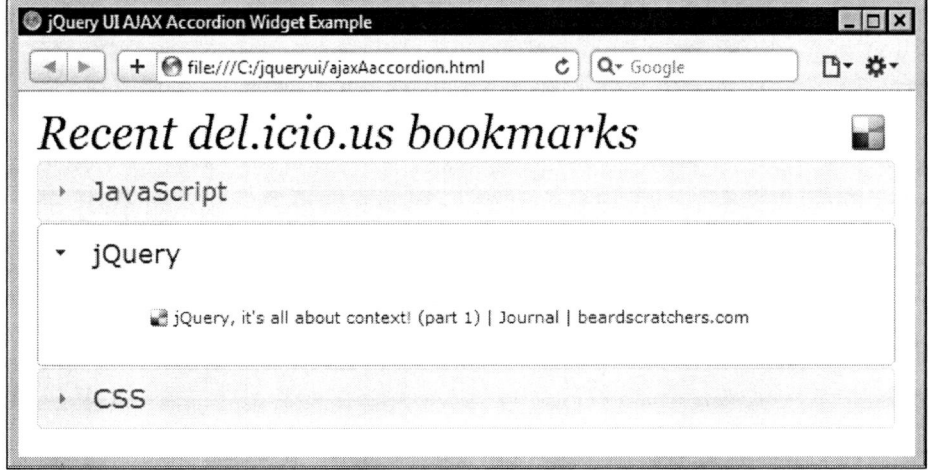

Summary

The accordion widget allows us to implement an object on the page that will show and hide different blocks of content. This is a popular and much sought-after effect, which is implemented by big players on the Web today, such as Apple.

We then moved on to look at the configurable options that can be used with accordion. We saw that we can use these options to change the behavior of the widget, such as specifying an alternative heading to be open by default, whether the widget should expand to fill the height of its container, or the event that triggers the opening of a content drawer.

Along with configurable options, we saw that the accordion exposes several custom events. Using them we can specify to callback functions during configuration, or bind to after configuration to execute additional functionality in reaction to different things happening to the widget.

We then looked at the accordion's default animation and how we can add simple transition effects to the opening of content panels in the form of easing effects. We saw that to make use of non-standard animations or easing effects, the `effects.core.js` file needs to be included.

In addition to looking at these options, we also saw that there are a range of methods which can be called on the accordion to make it do things programmatically. For example, we can specify a header to `activate`, `enable`, and `disable` the widget, or even completely `destroy` the widget and return the markup to its original state.

Like the tabs widget that we looked at in the previous chapter, the accordion is a flexible and robust widget that provides essential functionality and interaction in an aesthetically pleasing format.

5
The Dialog

Traditionally, the way to display a brief message or ask a visitor a question would've been to use one of JavaScript's native dialog boxes (such as `alert` or `confirm`) or to open a new web page with a predefined size, styled to look like a dialog box.

Unfortunately, as I'm sure you're aware, neither of these methods is particularly flexible to us as developers, or particularly engaging for our visitors. For each problem they solve, several new problems are usually introduced.

The dialog widget lets us display a message, supplemental content (such as images or text), or even interactive content (like forms). It's also easy to add buttons, such as simple **ok** and **cancel** buttons to the dialog and define callback functions for them in order to react to their being clicked.

The following screenshot shows a dialog widget and the different elements that it is made of:

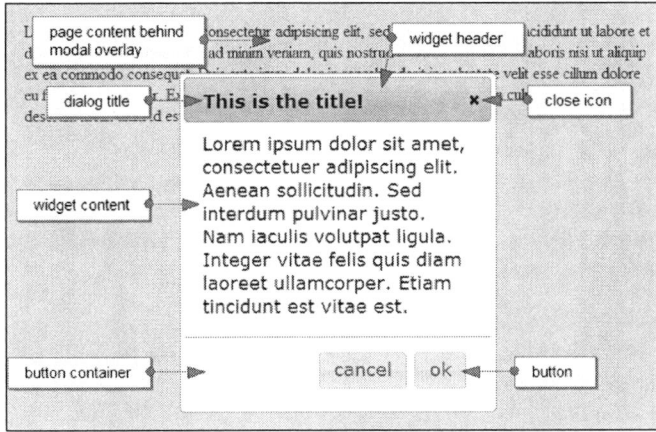

In this chapter, we will cover the following topics:

- Creating a basic dialog
- Work with dialog options
- Modality
- Enabling the built-in animations
- Adding buttons to the dialog
- IE6 and the selectbox z-index bug
- Working with dialog callbacks
- Controlling the dialog programmatically

A basic dialog

A dialog has a lot of default behavior built-in, but few methods are needed to control it programmatically, making this an easy to use widget that is also highly configurable and powerful.

Generating the widget is simple and requires a minimal underlying markup structure. The following page contains the minimum markup that's required to implement the dialog widget:

```
<!DOCTYPE HTML PUBLIC "-//W3C//DTD HTML 4.01//EN" "http://www.w3.org/
TR/html4/strict.dtd">
<html lang="en">
  <head>
    <link rel="stylesheet" type="text/css"
      href="development-bundle/themes/smoothness/ui.all.css">
    <meta http-equiv="Content-Type"
      content="text/html; charset=utf-8">
    <title>jQuery UI Dialog Example 1</title>
  </head>
  <body>
    <div id="myDialog" title="This is the title!">
      Lorem ipsum dolor sit amet, consectetuer adipiscing elit.
      Aenean sollicitudin. Sed interdum pulvinar justo. Nam iaculis
      volutpat ligula. Integer vitae felis quis diam laoreet
      ullamcorper. Etiam tincidunt est vitae est.
    </div>
    <script type="text/javascript"
      src="development-bundle/jquery-1.3.2.js"></script>
    <script type="text/javascript"
      src="development-bundle/ui/ui.core.js"></script>
    <script type="text/javascript"
      src="development-bundle/ui/ui.dialog.js"></script>
    <script type="text/javascript">
```

```
      $(function(){
        $("#myDialog").dialog();
      });
    </script>
  </body>
</html>
```

Save this file as `dialog1.html` in the `jqueryui` project folder. To use the dialog, the following dependencies are required:

- `ui.all.css`
- `jquery-1.3.2.js`
- `ui.core.js`
- `ui.dialog.js`

The dialog widget is initialized in the same way as the other widgets we have already looked at—by calling the widget's plugin method. When you run this page in your browser, you should see the default dialog widget as shown in the screenshot at the start of this chapter.

As with the previous widgets we've covered, a variety of class names from the CSS framework are added to different elements within the widget to give them the appropriate styling for their respective elements, and any additional elements that are required are created on the fly. The following screenshot show these classes and the structure of the widget as interpreted by Firebug:

The dialog in the first example is fixed both in size and position, and will remain in the center of the viewport until it is closed. We can make the widget draggable, or resizable, or both easily. All we need to do is include the draggable and resizable component's source files with the other `<script>` resources at the end of the `<body>`.

It's not important that the draggable and resizable files are included in the page before the dialog's source file, they can come before or after and the widget will still inherit these behaviors. Any styling that is required, such as the resize indicator that appears in the bottom-left of the dialog, will be picked up automatically from the master CSS file.

Add the following two `<script>` elements directly before the closing `</body>` tag in `dialog1.html`:

```
<script type="text/javascript"
    src="development-bundle/ui/ui.draggable.js"></script>
<script type="text/javascript"
    src="development-bundle/ui/ui.resizable.js"></script>
```

Save this as `dialog2.html` and view it in a browser. The dialog should now be draggable and can be moved to any part of the viewport, but will not cause it to scroll if the widget is moved to an edge.

The dialog should also be resizable—by clicking and holding the resize indicator the widget can be made bigger or smaller. If the dialog is made bigger than the viewport then it will cause the window to scroll.

Dialog options

An options object can be used in a dialog's widget method to configure various dialog options. Let's look at the available options:

Options	Default value	Usage
autoOpen	true	Shows the dialog as soon as the `dialog()` method is called when set to `true`.
bgiframe	false	Creates an `<iframe>` shim to prevent `<select>` elements showing through the dialog in IE6 (at present the `bgiframe` plugin is required). We'll look at this option in more detail shortly. This plugin is due to be retired in version 1.8 of the library and will be replaced by the new `stackfix` component.

Options	Default value	Usage
buttons	{}	Supplies an object containing buttons to be used with the dialog. Each property name becomes the text on the <button> element, and the value of each property is a callback function, which is executed when the button is clicked.
closeOnEscape	true	If set to true, the dialog will close when the *Esc* key is pressed.
dialogClass	""	Sets additional class names on the dialog for theming purposes.
draggable	true	Makes the dialog draggable (use ui.draggable.js).
height	"auto"	Sets the starting height of the dialog.
hide	null	Sets an effect to be used when the dialog is closed.
maxHeight	false	Sets a maximum height for the dialog.
maxWidth	false	Sets a maximum width for the dialog.
minHeight	150	Sets a minimum height for the dialog.
minWidth	150	Sets a minimum width for the dialog.
modal	false	Enables modality while the dialog is open.
position	"center"	Sets the starting position of the dialog in the viewport. Can accept a string, or an array of strings, or an array containing exact coordinates of the dialog offset from the top and left of the viewport.
resizable	true	Makes the dialog resizable (also requires ui.resizable.js).
show	null	Sets an effect to be used when the dialog is opened.
stack	true	Causes the focused dialog to move to the front when several dialogs are open.
title	false	Alternative to specifying the title attribute on the widget's underlying container element.
width	300	Sets the starting width of the dialog.
zIndex	1000	Sets the starting CSS z-index of the widget. When using multiple dialogs and the stack option is set to true the z-index will change as each dialog is moved to the front of the stack.

As you can see, we have a wide range of configurable options to work with when implementing the dialog. Many of these options are Boolean, or numerical, or string-based, making them easy to set and work with.

Showing the dialog

In our examples so far, the dialog has opened as soon as the page has loaded, or when the `dialog` widget method is called, which is as soon as the page is ready in this case.

We can change this so that the dialog is opened when something else occurs, like a button being clicked, by setting the `autoOpen` option to `false`. Change the final `<script>` element at the bottom of `dialog2.html` to the following:

```
<script type="text/javascript">
  $(function(){
    var dialogOpts = {
      autoOpen: false
    };
    $("#myDialog").dialog(dialogOpts);
  });
</script>
```

Save this as `dialog3.html`. The widget is still created; the underlying markup is removed from the page, transformed into the widget, and then reappended to the end of the `<body>`. It will remain hidden until the `open` method is called on it. We'll come back to this option when we look at the `open` method a little later on.

Positioning the dialog

The `position` option controls where the dialog is rendered in the viewport when it is opened and accepts either a string or an array value. The strings may be one of the following values:

- `bottom`
- `center`
- `left`
- `right`
- `top`

We can also supply different sensible combinations of these strings in an array, there's no point supplying an array containing the strings `top` and `bottom`. However, we can supply `right` and `top` for the widget to be positioned in the top-right of the viewport.

An array can also be used when you want to specify the exact coordinates, relative to the top-left corner of the viewport where the dialog should appear. Change the configuration object used in `dialog3.html` so that it appears as follows:

```
var dialogOpts = {
  position: ["left", "bottom"]
};
```

Save this as `dialog4.html`. When using a string-based array we need to supply the values in a specific order—the value of the widget's position on the horizontal axis should be specified first, followed by its position on the vertical axis.

The following screenshot shows where the dialog can be positioned on the page using either a string or a string-based array:

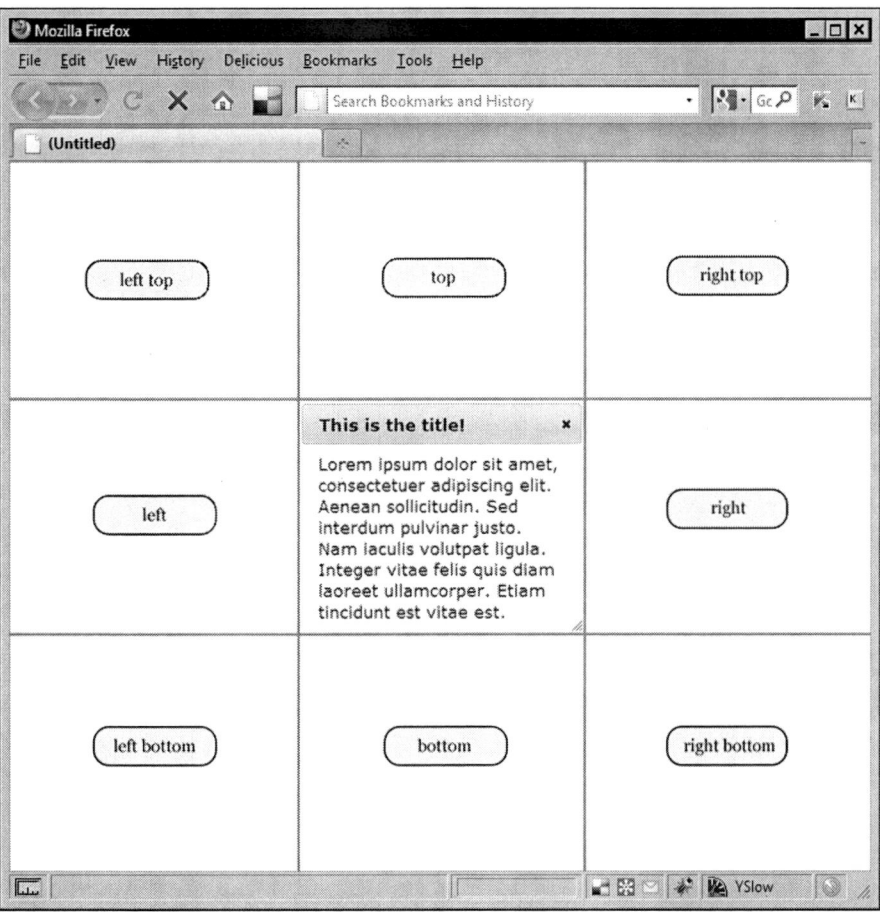

When using integers in the `position` array we can specify any location on the page in which to position the dialog. Change the configuration object in `dialog4.html` to the following:

```
var dialogOpts = {
   position: [100, 100]
};
```

Save this version as `dialog5.html`. This time, the dialog should appear exactly 100 pixels from the top and 100 pixels from the left edges of the viewport. Note that the axis order is the same as when using string values—horizontal followed by vertical. If the dialog is outside the maximum `width` or `height` of the viewport then the page will be scrolled.

The title of the dialog

The options table shows a `title` option. Although the title of the dialog (the actual text in the header of the widget) can be set using the `title` attribute of the underlying HTML container element, using the `title` configuration option gives us more control over how the title (the text) is displayed on the widget.

By default, the title text (in the header) of the dialog will not be selectable and will also not be displayed in the OSs default tooltip style. When using the `title` attribute on the underlying element, the text will appear within a `<span>` element, which is inside a `<div>` with the class name `ui-dialog-titlebar`. These elements will appear in the header of the widget.

If we want to inject additional elements into the DOM structure of the dialog (for additional styling perhaps or different behavior), we could do it using the `title` option. Change the configuration object in `dialog5.html` to the following:

```
var dialogOpts = {
   title: '<a href="#">A link title!</a>'
};
```

Save this file as `dialog6.html`. The change in the widget should be apparent immediately, the span element in the widget header will now contain our new link element. The following screenshot shows our new title:

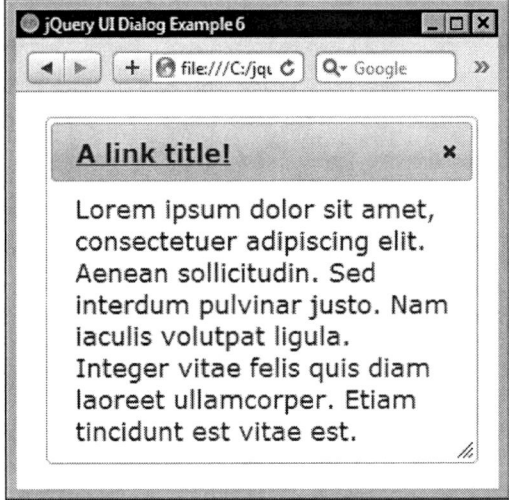

 As a cautionary note, I should advise that the system will display the default OS tooltip if a `title` attribute is specified on any new elements we add to the widget in this way.

Modality

One of the dialog's greatest assets is modality. This feature creates an overlay when the widget that sits above the page content but below the dialog is opened. The overlay is removed as soon as the dialog is closed. None of the underlying page content can be interacted with in any way while the dialog is open.

The benefit of this feature is that it ensures the dialog is closed before the underlying page becomes interactive again, and gives a clear visual indicator to the visitor that the dialog must be interacted with before they can proceed.

Change the configuration object in `dialog6.html` to this:

```
var dialogOpts = {
  modal: true
};
```

This file can be saved as `dialog7.html`. Only a single property is required when adding modality and that is the `modal` option. When you view the page in a browser, you'll see the modal effect immediately.

The repeated background image that is used to create the overlay is styled completely by the CSS framework and is therefore fully themeable via ThemeRoller. We can also use our own image if we need to. The class name `ui-widget-overlay` is added to the overlay, so this is the selector to override if customization is required.

The following screenshot shows the modal effect (I've added some fake content to the page so that the effect of the modal can be fully appreciated):

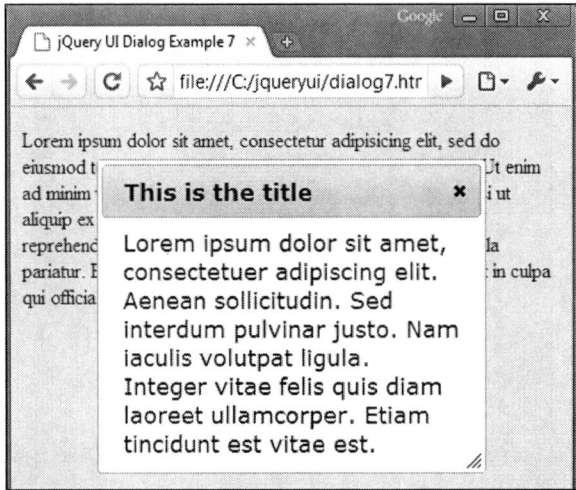

Adding buttons

The `button` option accepts an object literal that is used to specify the different `<button>` elements that should be present on the dialog. Each `property:value` pair represents a single button. Let's add a couple of `<button>` elements to our dialog. Alter the final `<script>` element in `dialog7.html` so that it appears as follows:

```
<script type="text/javascript">
  $(function(){

    var execute = function() {
    }
    var cancel = function() {
    }
    var dialogOpts = {
      buttons: {
        "Ok": execute,
        "Cancel": cancel
```

```
        }
      };
      $("#myDialog").dialog(dialogOpts);
   });
</script>
```

Save the file as `dialog8.html`. The key for each property in the `buttons` object is the text that will form the `<button>` label, and the value is the name of the callback function to execute when the button is clicked.

Each callback function is defined before the configuration object. If this is not done an error will be thrown by the widget when the button is clicked. In this example the functions don't do anything, we'll come back to this example shortly and populate these functions.

The widget will add our new buttons to their own container at the foot of the dialog, and if the dialog is resized then this container will retain its original dimensions. The `<button>` elements are fully themeable and will be styled according to the theme in use. The following screenshot shows how our new `<button>` elements would appear:

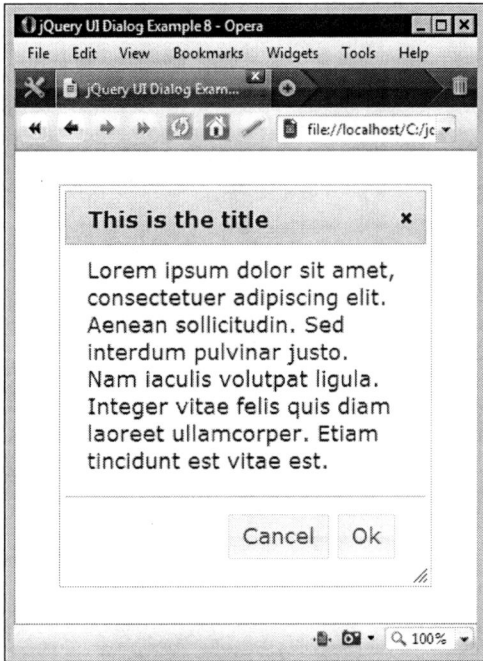

Enabling dialog animations

The dialog provides us with a built-in effect that can be applied to the opening or closing (or both) phases of the widget. There is only a single effect that we can use, which is an implementation of the scale effect (we'll look at this in more detail in *Chapter 13*). Change the final `<script>` element in `dialog8.html` to this:

```
<script type="text/javascript">
  $(function(){

    var dialogOpts = {
      show: true,
      hide: true

    };
    $("#myDialog").dialog(dialogOpts);
  });
</script>
```

Save this as `dialog9.html`. We set both the `hide` and `show` options to the Boolean value `true`; this enables the built-in effect, which gradually reduces the dialog's size and opacity until it gracefully disappears. The following screenshot shows an effect in motion:

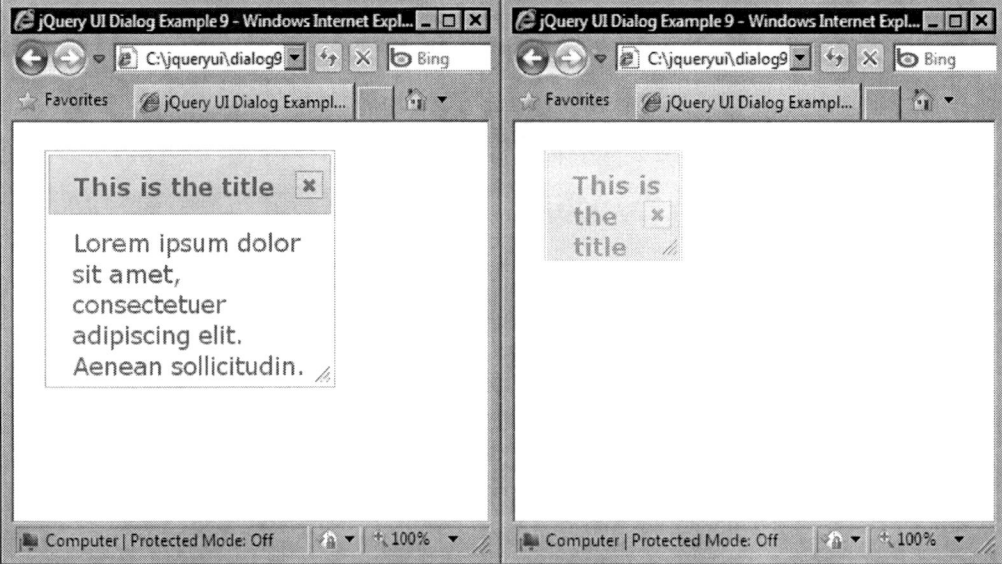

Fixing IE6

I need not say much more than IE6 is anathema to web developers, and at the time of writing is unfortunately still with us. A major problem with this browser (sometimes referred to as the select box z-index bug), is the fact that `<select>` elements appear above any other content on the page. This can cause issues with widgets like the dialog that are supposed to float above any other page content. The following screenshot shows this bug in action:

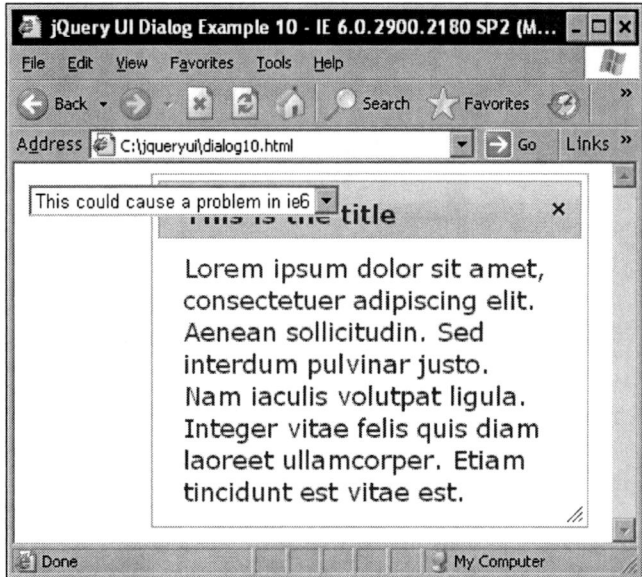

 Fortunately, the jQuery UI dialog comes with built-in protection in the form of the `bgiframe` option that fixes the selectbox issue by inserting an `<iframe>` element into the dialog, which blocks out any underlying `<select>` elements. In `dialog9.html` add a new `<select>` element to the page, and then change the configuration object so that it is like this:

```
var dialogOpts = {
   bgiframe: true
};
```

Don't forget to link to the `bgiframe` plugin that can be found in the `external` directory, with the other `<script>` resources at the end of the `<body>`:

```
<script type="text/javascript"
   src="development-bundle/external/bgiframe/jquery.bgiframe.js">
</script>
```

Save the changed file as `dialog10.html`. Now in IE6, the widget will float above the select box as it should:

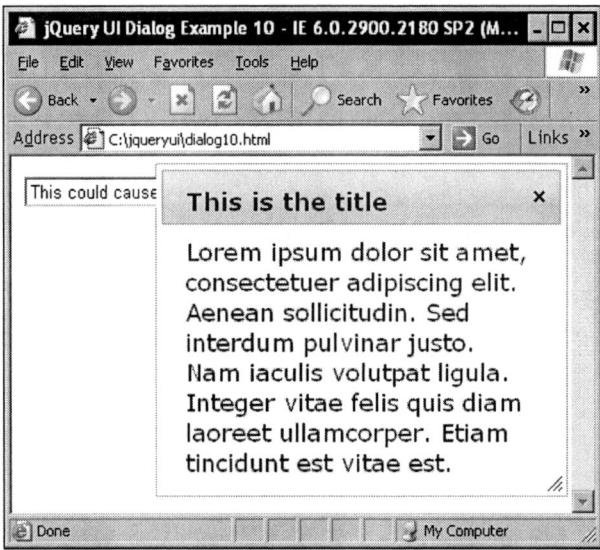

The `<iframe>` element will only be added in IE6, no other browsers will need it. It will receive all the attributes that it requires automatically, no further configuration or styling is required.

Configuring the dialog's dimensions

There are several options related to the dialog's size, and the minimum and maximum size that it can be resized to. We can add all of these options to the next example as they're all related, to save looking at them individually. Remove the `<select>` box and the link to the `bgiframe` plugin, and change the configuration object in `dialog10.html` to the following:

```
var dialogOpts = {
    width: 300,
    height: 300,
    minWidth: 150,
    minHeight: 150,
    maxWidth: 450,
    maxHeight: 450
};
```

Save this file as `dialog11.html`. The effect these options have on the widget is simple; the `width` and `height` options define how big the dialog is when it is first opened while the `min-` and `max-` options define how small or large the dialog can be resized to respectively. Care should be taken that the minimum `width` and `height` of the dialog do not cause the title to overflow or it may end up looking something like this:

As an additional note, assistive technologies and keyboard users may find the content difficult to navigate if the dialog is made too small. There is a usability tenant that insists dialog boxes should always be non-resizable, whereas windows should always be resizable.

While I don't think this a black-and-white rule, it may be wise to keep small, informational, text-based dialogs at a fixed size, while allowing dialogs richer in content, composed of both images and text to be resizable.

Stacking

The dialog is made so that it appears above any of the existing page content, and even provides the `zIndex` option in case we need to raise it slightly to cover our existing content. But what if we have two dialogs on the page? Do we need to separately define the `zIndex` for each dialog? How is focus taken into consideration?

Let's see if we can answer these questions by looking at another example, change the
`<body>` of `dialog11.html` so that it has two dialog boxes on it:

```
<div id="dialog1" title="Dialog 1">
    Lorem ipsum dolor sit amet, consectetuer adipiscing elit.
        Aenean sollicitudin. Sed interdum pulvinar justo. Nam iaculis
        volutpat ligula. Integer vitae felis quis diam laoreet
        ullamcorper. Etiam tincidunt est vitae est.
    </div>
<div id="dialog2" title="Dialog 2">
    Lorem ipsum dolor sit amet, consectetuer adipiscing elit. Aenean
        sollicitudin. Sed interdum pulvinar justo. Nam iaculis volutpat
        ligula. Integer vitae felis quis diam laoreet ullamcorper.
        Etiam tincidunt est vitae est.
    </div>
```

Now change the final `<script>` element so that it appears like this:

```
<script type="text/javascript">
    $(function(){

        $("#dialog1").dialog();

        $("#dialog2").dialog();

    });
</script>
```

Save this file as `dialog12.html`. We've added another dialog to the page, which is
basically just a clone of the original with a different `id` attribute. In the `<script>`
we simply call the widget method of both our underlying elements, we don't need a
configuration object.

Because the widget method is called on the second dialog last, this dialog will
automatically have a higher `zIndex`, so we don't need to worry about configuring
this separately. It doesn't matter the order in which the dialogs appear in the
underlying markup, it's the order of the widget methods that dictate each
dialog's `zIndex`.

Because neither dialog has its position explicitly set, only the second dialog will be
visible when our example page loads. However, both are draggable and we can align
them so that they overlap slightly by dragging the second dialog away. If we click on
the first dialog box its `zIndex` will automatically be increased to one higher than the
second dialog box.

The `stack` option is set to `true` by default, so all of this behavior is automatically available with no additional configuration from us. If for some reason this behavior is not desired then we can disable it by supplying `false` as the value of the `stack` option.

Dialog's event model

The dialog widget gives us a wide range of callback options that we can use to execute arbitrary code at different points in any dialog interaction. The following table lists the option available to us:

Option	Fired when
beforeclose	The dialog is about to be closed.
close	The dialog is closed.
drag	The dialog is being dragged.
dragStart	The dialog starts being dragged.
dragStop	The dialog stops being dragged.
focus	The dialog receives focus.
open	The dialog is opened.
resize	The dialog is being resized.
resizeStart	The dialog starts to be resized.
resizeStop	The dialog stops being resized.

Some of these callbacks are only available in certain situations, such as the `drag` and `resize` callbacks, which will only be available when the draggable and resizable components are included. We won't be looking at these callback options in this chapter as they'll be covered in detail later in the book.

Other callbacks such as the `beforeClose`, `open`, `close`, and `focus` callbacks will be available in any implementation. Let's look at an example in which we make use of some of these callback options. In a new page in your text editor, add the following code:

```
<!DOCTYPE HTML PUBLIC "-//W3C//DTD HTML 4.01//EN"
  "http://www.w3.org/TR/html4/strict.dtd">
<html lang="en">
  <head>
    <link rel="stylesheet" type="text/css"
      href="development-bundle/themes/smoothness/ui.all.css">
    <link rel="stylesheet" type="text/css" href="css/dialogTheme.css">
    <meta http-equiv="Content-Type" content="text/html; charset=utf-8">
```

```
    <title>jQuery UI Dialog Example 13</title>
  </head>
  <body>
    <div id="status" class="ui-widget">
      <div class="ui-widget-header">Dialog Status</div>
      <div class="ui-widget-content"></div>
    </div>
    <div id="myDialog" title="This is the title">Lorem ipsum dolor sit
      amet, consectetuer adipiscing elit. Aenean sollicitudin. Sed
      interdum pulvinar justo. Nam iaculis volutpat ligula. Integer
      vitae felis quis diam laoreet ullamcorper. Etiam tincidunt est
      vitae est.</div>
    <script type="text/javascript"
      src="development-bundle/jquery-1.3.2.js"></script>
    <script type="text/javascript"
      src="development-bundle/ui/ui.core.js"></script>
    <script type="text/javascript"
      src="development-bundle/ui/ui.dialog.js"></script>
    <script type="text/javascript"
      src="development-bundle/ui/ui.draggable.js"></script>
    <script type="text/javascript"
      src="development-bundle/ui/ui.resizable.js"></script>
    <script type="text/javascript">
      $(function(){

        var dialogOpts = {
          open: function() {

            $("#status").find(".ui-widget-content").text("The dialog
              is open");
          },
          close: function() {
            $("#status").find(".ui-widget-content").text("The dialog
              is closed");
          },
          beforeclose: function() {

            if (parseInt($(".ui-dialog").css("width")) == 300 ||
              parseInt($(".ui-dialog").css("height")) == 300) {
              return false
            }
          }
        };
        $("#myDialog").dialog(dialogOpts);
      });
    </script>
  </body>
</html>
```

Save this as `dialog13.html`. The page contains a new status box which will be used to report whether the dialog is open or closed. We've given the elements that make up the status box several CSS framework classes to make it fit with the theme in use and to cut down on the amount of styling we need to worry about.

Our configuration object uses the `open`, `close`, and `beforeclose` options to specify simple callback functions. The `open` and `close` callbacks simply set the text of the status box accordingly. The `beforeclose` callback that is fired after the close button on the dialog has been clicked but before it is actually closed, is used to determine whether or not to close the dialog.

We use a simple `if` statement to check the `width` and `height` of the dialog; if the dialog has not been resized we return `false` from the callback and the dialog remains open. This kind of behavior is of course a big no in terms of usability, but it does serve to highlight how we can use the `beforeclose` callback to prevent the dialog being closed.

We also use a custom stylesheet for this example. It's simple and contains the following rules:

```
#status { width:200px; }
#status .ui-widget-header {
  font-family:Georgia; padding:5px;
}
#status .ui-widget-content { font-size:12px; padding:5px; }
```

Save this as `dialogTheme.css` in the `css` folder. When the page loads and the dialog is opened (as it is by default), the `open` callback will be executed and the status box should display a message as shown in the following screenshot:

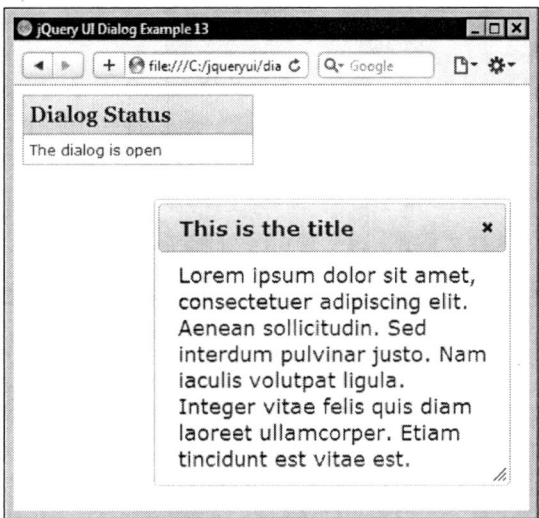

One thing I should make clear is that the dialog widget only passes a single object (the original event object) to the callback functions. It does not pass the second `ui` object in version 1.7 (the current version at the time of writing). The second object will be introduced in version 1.8 of the library.

Controlling a dialog programmatically

The dialog requires few methods in order to function. The full list of the methods we can call on a dialog is as follows:

Method	Used to
close	Close or hide the dialog.
destroy	Permanently disable the dialog. The destroy method for a dialog works in a slightly different way than it does for the other widgets we've seen so far. Instead of just returning the underlying HTML to its original state, the dialog's destroy method also hides it.
disable	Temporarily disable the dialog.
enable	Enable the dialog if it has been disabled.
isOpen	Determine whether a dialog is open or not.
moveToTop	Move the specified dialog to the top of the stack.
open	Open the dialog.
option	Get or set any configurable option after the dialog has been initialized.

Toggling the dialog

We first take a look at opening the widget, which can be achieved with the simple use of the `open` method. Let's revisit `dialog3.html` in which the `autoOpen` option was set to `false`, so the dialog did not open when the page was loaded. Add the following `<button>` to the page:

```
<button id="toggle">Toggle dialog!</button>
```

Then add the following click-handler directly after the dialog's widget method:

```
$("#toggle").click(function() {
  ($("#myDialog").dialog("isOpen") == false) ?
    $("#myDialog").dialog("open") : $("#myDialog").dialog("close") ;
});
```

Save this file as `dialog14.html`. To the page we've added a simple `<button>` that can be used to either open or close the dialog depending on its current state. In the `<script>` element, we've added a click handler for the `<button>` that uses the JavaScript ternary conditional to check the return value of the `isOpen` method. If it returns `false`, the dialog is not open so we call its `open` method else we call the `close` method instead.

The `open` and `close` methods both trigger any applicable events, for example, the `close` method fires first the `beforeclose` and then the `close` events. Calling the `close` method is analogous to clicking the close button on the dialog.

Getting data from the dialog

Because the widget is a part of the underlying page, passing data to and from it is simple. The dialog can be treated as any other standard element on the page. Let's look at a basic example.

We looked at an example earlier in the chapter which added some `<button>` elements to the dialog. The callback functions in that example didn't do anything, but this example gives us the opportunity to use them. Add the following code above the `<script>` tags in `dialog14.html`.

```
<p>Please answer the opinion poll:</p>
<div id="myDialog" title="Best Widget Library">
  <p>Is jQuery UI the greatest JavaScript widget library?</p>
  <label for="yes">Yes!</label><input type="radio" id="yes"
    value="yes" name="question" checked="checked"><br>
  <label for="no">No!</label><input type="radio" id="no"
    value="no" name="question">
</div>
<script type="text/javascript" src="development-bundle/jquery-
1.3.2.js"></script>
```

Now change the final `<script>` element to as follows:

```
<script type="text/javascript">
  $(function(){

  var execute = function(){

    var answer;
      $("input").each(function(){
        (this.checked == true) ? answer = $(this).val() : null;
      });
      $("<p>").text("Thanks for selecting " +
        answer).appendTo($("body"));
          $("#myDialog").dialog("close");
```

```
    }
    var cancel = function() {
      $("#myDialog").dialog("close");
    }
    var dialogOpts = {
      buttons: {
        "Ok": execute,
        "Cancel": cancel
      }
    };
    $("#myDialog").dialog(dialogOpts);
  });
</script>
```

Save this as `dialog15.html`. Our dialog widget now contains a set of radio buttons, `<label>` elements, and some text. The purpose of the example is to get the result of which radio is selected, and then do something with it when the dialog closes.

We start the `<script>` by filling out the `execute` function that will be attached as the value of the `Ok` property in the `buttons` object later in the script. It will therefore be executed each time the **Ok** button is clicked.

In this function we use jQuery's `each()` method to look at both of the radio buttons and determine which one is selected. We set the value of the `answer` variable to the radio button's value and then created a short message along with appending it to the `<body>` of the page. The callback mapped to the **Cancel** button is simple, all we do is close the dialog using the `close` method.

The following screenshot shows how the page should appear once a radio button has been selected and the **Ok** button has been clicked:

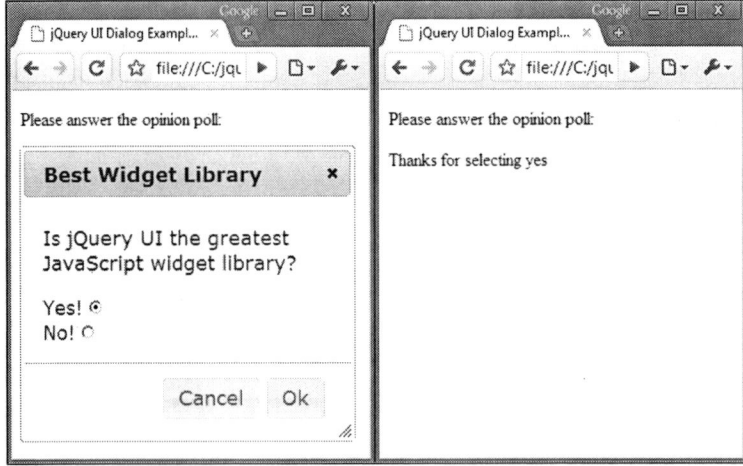

The point of this trivial example was to see that getting data from the dialog is as simple as getting data from any other component on the page.

Dialog interoperability

In previous chapters we've combined several widgets so that we can see how well they work together and this chapter will be no exception. We can easily place other UI widgets into the dialog, such as the accordion widget that we looked at in the last chapter. In a new file in your text editor create the following page:

```
<!DOCTYPE HTML PUBLIC "-//W3C//DTD HTML 4.01//EN" "http://www.w3.org/
TR/html4/strict.dtd">
<html lang="en">
  <head>
    <link rel="stylesheet" type="text/css"
      href="development-bundle/themes/smoothness/ui.all.css">
    <meta http-equiv="Content-Type" content="text/html;
      charset=utf-8">
    <title>jQuery UI Dialog Example 17</title>
  </head>
  <body>
    <div id="myDialog" title="An Accordion Dialog">
      <div id="myAccordion">
        <h2><a href="#">Header 1</a></h2><div>Lorem ipsum dolor sit
          amet, consectetuer adipiscing elit. Aenean
          sollicitudin.</div>
        <h2><a href="#">Header 2</a></h2><div>Etiam tincidunt est
          vitae est. Ut posuere, mauris at sodales rutrum,
          turpis.</div>
        <h2><a href="#">Header 3</a></h2><div>Donec at dolor ac metus
          pharetra aliquam. Suspendisse purus.</div>
      </div>
    </div>
    <script type="text/javascript"
      src="development-bundle/jquery-1.3.2.js"></script>
    <script type="text/javascript"
      src="development-bundle/ui/ui.core.js"></script>
    <script type="text/javascript"
      src="development-bundle/ui/ui.dialog.js"></script>
    <script type="text/javascript"
      src="development-bundle/ui/ui.draggable.js"></script>
    <script type="text/javascript"
      src="development-bundle/ui/ui.resizable.js"></script>
    <script type="text/javascript"
      src="development-bundle/ui/ui.accordion.js"></script>
    <script type="text/javascript">
      $(function(){
```

```
            $("#myDialog").dialog();
            $("#myAccordion").accordion();
        });
    </script>
  </body>
</html>
```

Save this file as `dialog16.html`. The underlying markup for the accordion widget is placed into the dialog's container element, and we just call each component's widget method in the `<script>`. The combined widget should appear like this:

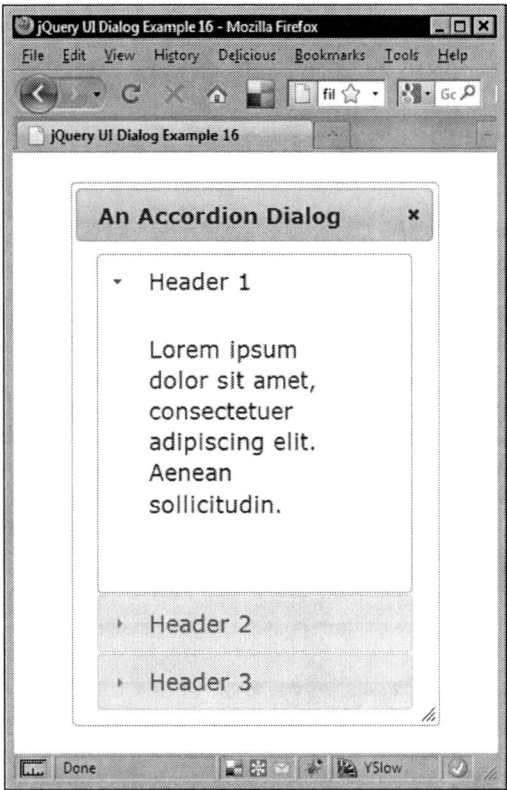

A dynamic image-based dialog

The class behind the dialog widget is compact and caters to a small range of specialized behavior, much of which we have already looked at. We can still have some fun with a dynamic dialog box, which loads different content depending on which element triggers it. The following image shows the kind of page we'll end up with:

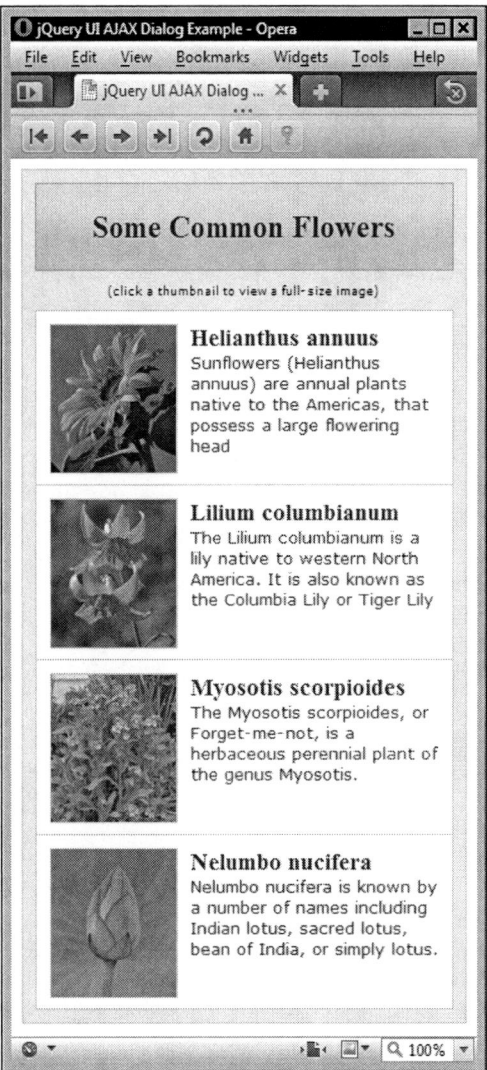

In a new page in your text editor add the following code:

```
<!DOCTYPE HTML PUBLIC "-//W3C//DTD HTML 4.01//EN" "http://www.w3.org/
TR/html4/strict.dtd">
<html lang="en">
  <head>
    <link rel="stylesheet" type="text/css"
      href="development-bundle/themes/smoothness/ui.all.css">
    <link rel="stylesheet" type="text/css" href="css/ajaxDialog.css">
    <meta http-equiv="Content-Type" content="text/html;
```

```
    charset=utf-8">
  <title>jQuery UI AJAX Dialog Example</title>
</head>
<body>
  <div id="thumbs">
    <div class="ui-widget-header">
      <h2>Some Common Flowers</h2>
    </div>
    <p>(click a thumbnail to view a full-size image)</p>
    <div class="thumb ui-helper-clearfix ui-widget-content">
      <a href="img/dialog/flowers/fullsize/helianthus_annuus.jpg"
        title="Helianthus annuus"><img
        src="img/dialog/flowers/thumbs/helianthus_annuus.jpg"
        alt="Helianthus annuus"></a>
      <h3>Helianthus annuus</h3>
      <p>Sunflowers (Helianthus annuus) are annual plants native to
        the Americas, that possess a large flowering head</p>
    </div>
    <div class="thumb ui-helper-clearfix ui-widget-content">
      <a href="img/dialog/flowers/fullsize/lilium_columbianum.jpg"
        title="Lilium columbianum"><img
        src="img/dialog/flowers/thumbs/lilium_columbianum.jpg"
        alt="Lilium columbianum"></a>
      <h3>Lilium columbianum</h3>
      <p>The Lilium columbianum is a lily native to western North
        America. It is also known as the Columbia Lily or Tiger
        Lily</p>
    </div>
    <div class="thumb ui-helper-clearfix ui-widget-content">
      <a
        href="img/dialog/flowers/fullsize/myosotis_scorpioides.jpg"
        title="Myosotis scorpioides"><img
        src="img/dialog/flowers/thumbs/myosotis_scorpioides.jpg"
        alt="Myosotis scorpioides"></a>
      <h3>Myosotis scorpioides</h3>
      <p>The Myosotis scorpioides, or Forget-me-not, is a
        herbaceous perennial plant of the genus Myosotis.</p>
    </div>
    <div class="thumb ui-helper-clearfix ui-widget-content last">
      <a href="img/dialog/flowers/fullsize/nelumbo_nucifera.jpg"
        title="Nelumbo nucifera"><img
        src="img/dialog/flowers/thumbs/nelumbo_nucifera.jpg"
        alt="Nelumbo nucifera"></a>
      <h3>Nelumbo nucifera</h3>
      <p>Nelumbo nucifera is known by a number of names including
        Indian lotus, sacred lotus, bean of India, or simply
```

```
lotus.</p>
      </div>
    </div>
    <div id="ajaxDialog"></div>
    <script type="text/javascript"
      src="development-bundle/jquery-1.3.2.js"></script>
    <script type="text/javascript"
      src="development-bundle/ui/ui.core.js"></script>
    <script type="text/javascript"
      src="development-bundle/ui/ui.dialog.js"></script>
    <script type="text/javascript"
      src="development-bundle/ui/ui.draggable.js"></script>
  </body>
</html>
```

Save this file as `ajaxDialog.html`. The page is relatively straightforward—we've got an outer container which encloses everything and an element which we've given the class name `ui-widget-header`. We've used the latter in order to pick up some of the default styling from the theme in use.

Following this we have some explanatory text followed by a series of containers. Several class names are given to these container, some of which are so that we can style them, and others (such as `ui-helper-clearfix`) in order to pick up framework or theme styles.

Within each of these containers is an image wrapped in an anchor, a subheading, and some descriptive text. After the outer container comes the empty `<div>` element, which will form the basis of our dialog. We don't use the Resizable component in this example as this behavior is not required.

Each of the thumbnail images is wrapped in a link in order for the page to function even with JavaScript disabled. The dialog widget won't work in this situation but the visitor will still be able to see a full-sized version of each image. Progressive enhancement such as this is essential is this kind of application.

Now add the following `<script>` block directly before the closing `</body>` tag:

```
<script type="text/javascript">
  $(function(){
    var filename, titleText;
    var dialogOpts = {
      modal: true,
      width: 388,
      height: 470,
      autoOpen: false,
```

```
      open: function() {
        $("#ajaxDialog").empty();
          $("<img>").attr("src", filename).appendTo("#ajaxDialog");
        $("#ajaxDialog").dialog("option", "title", titleText);
      }
    };
    $("#ajaxDialog").dialog(dialogOpts);
    $("#thumbs").find("a").click(function(e) {
      filename = $(this).attr("href");
      titleText = $(this).attr("title");
      $("#ajaxDialog").dialog("open");
      e.preventDefault();
    });
  });
</script>
```

The first thing we do is define two variables, which we'll use to add the path to the full-sized image of whichever thumbnail was clicked to the dialog's inner content area, and store the image title to use as the text for the widget's title. We then add the configuration object for the dialog. We've seen all of these properties in action already so I won't go over most of them in much detail.

The open callback, called directly before the dialog is opened, is where we add the full-sized image to the dialog. We first create a new <img> element and set its src to the value of the filename variable. The new <img> is then appended to the inner content area of the dialog.

We then use the option method to set the title option to the value of the titleText variable. Once the open callback has been defined we then call the dialog's widget method as normal.

We can use the wrapper <a> elements as the triggers to open the dialog. Within our click-handler, we set the contents of our two variables using the href and title attributes. We then call the dialog's open method to display the dialog.

We'll also need a new stylesheet for this example. In a new page in your text editor, add the following code:

```
#thumbs {
  width:342px; background-color:#eeeeee; border:1px solid
  #cccccc; padding:10px 0 10px 10px;
}
#thumbs p {
  font-family:Verdana; font-size:9px; width:330px;
  text-align:center;
}
.thumb {
```

```
        width:310px; height:114px; border:1px solid #cccccc;
        border-bottom:none; padding:10px;
    }
    .last { border-bottom:1px solid #cccccc; }
    .thumb img {
        float:left; margin-right:10px; cursor:pointer;
        border:1px solid #cccccc;
    }
    .thumb h3 { margin:0; float:left; width:198px; }
    #thumbs .thumb p {
        margin:0; font-family:Verdana; font-size:13px;
        text-align:left; width:310px;
    }
    #thumbs .ui-widget-header { width:330px; text-align:center; }
    .ui-dialog-titlebar { text-transform:capitalize; }
```

Many of these styles have been used in previous examples, but adding some new rules for the other page elements lets us see the dialog in real-world context. Save this as `ajaxDialog.css` in the `css` folder. This should now give us the page that we saw in the previous screenshot and when a thumbnail is clicked, the full size version of the same image will be displayed:

Summary

The dialog widget is specialized and caters to the display of a message or question in a floating panel that sits above the page content. Advanced functionality such as draggability and resizability, are directly built-in, and features such as the excellent modality and overlay are easy to configure.

We started out by looking at the default implementation, which is as simple as it is with the other widgets we have looked at so far. However, there are several optional components that can also be used in conjunction with the dialog, such as the draggables and resizable components.

We also examined the range of configurable options exposed by the dialog's API. We can make use of them to enable or disable built-in behavior such as modality or set the dimensions of the widget. It also gives us a wide range of callbacks that allow us to hook into custom events fired by the widget during an interaction.

We then took a brief look at the built-in opening and closing effects that can be used with the dialog, before moving on to see the basic methods we can invoke in order to make the dialog do things, such as open or close.

6
Slider

The slider component allows us to implement an engaging and easy-to-use widget that our visitors should find attractive and intuitive to use. Its basic function is simple. The slider background represents a series of values that are selected by dragging the thumb along the background.

Before we roll up our sleeves and begin creating a slider, let's look at the different elements that it is made from. The following screenshot shows a typical slider widget:

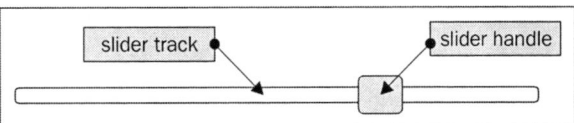

It's a simple widget, as you can see, comprised of just two main elements — the slider handle, also called the thumb, and the slider background, also called the track. In this chapter, we will cover the following topics:

- The default slider implementation
- Custom styling for sliders
- Changing configuration options
- Creating a vertical slider
- Setting minimum, maximum, and default values
- Enabling multiple handles and ranges
- The slider's built-in event callbacks
- Slider methods

Implementing a slider

Creating the default, basic slider takes no more code than any of the other widgets we have looked at so far. The underlying HTML markup required is also minimal. Let's create a basic one now. In a new page in your text editor, add the following code:

```
<!DOCTYPE HTML PUBLIC "-//W3C//DTD HTML 4.01//EN"
  "http://www.w3.org/TR/html4/strict.dtd">
<html lang="en">
  <head>
    <link rel="stylesheet" type="text/css"
      href="development-bundle/themes/smoothness/ui.all.css">
    <meta http-equiv="Content-Type" content="text/html; charset=utf-8">
    <title>jQuery UI Slider Example 1</title>
  </head>
  <body>
    <div id="mySlider"></div>
    <script type="text/javascript"
      src="development-bundle/jquery-1.3.2.js"></script>
    <script type="text/javascript"
      src="development-bundle/ui/ui.core.js"></script>
    <script type="text/javascript"
      src="development-bundle/ui/ui.slider.js"></script>
    <script type="text/javascript">
      $(function(){

        $("#mySlider").slider();
      });
    </script>
  </body>
</html>
```

Save this file as slider1.html and view it in your browser. On the page is a simple container element; this will be transformed by the widget into the slider track. In the <script> at the end of the <body> we select this element and call the slider method on it. The <a> element that is used for the slider handle will be automatically created by the widget.

When we run this page in a browser we should see something similar to the previous screenshot. We've used several library resources for the default implementation, including the following files:

- ui.all.css
- jquery-1.3.2.js
- ui.core.js
- ui.slider.js

The default behavior of a basic slider is simple but effective. The thumb can be moved horizontally along any pixel of the track on the x axis by dragging the thumb with the mouse pointer, or using the *left/down* or *right/up* arrow keys of the keyboard. Clicking anywhere on the track with the left or right mouse button will instantly move the handle to that position.

Custom styling

Because of its simplicity, the slider widget is extremely easy to create a custom theme for. Using ThemeRoller is the recommended method of theming, but to completely change the look and feel of the widget we can easily create our own theme file; in your text editor create the following stylesheet:

```
background-div {
    background:url(../img/slider/slider_outerbg.gif) no-repeat;
    height:50px; width:217px; padding:36px 0 0 24px;
}
#mySlider {
    background:url(../img/slider/slider_bg.gif) no-repeat;
    width:184px; height:23px; position:relative; left:4px;
    top:4px; border:none;
}
.ui-slider-handle {
    background:url(../img/slider/slider_handle.gif) no-repeat;
    width:14px; height:30px; top:-4px;
}
```

Save this file as `sliderTheme.css` in the `css` directory. Link to this file in the usual way, after the link to `ui.all.css` then save the new page as `slider2.html`. With a minimum of CSS and a few images (these can be found in the code download) we can easily but considerably alter the widget's appearance, as shown in the following screenshot:

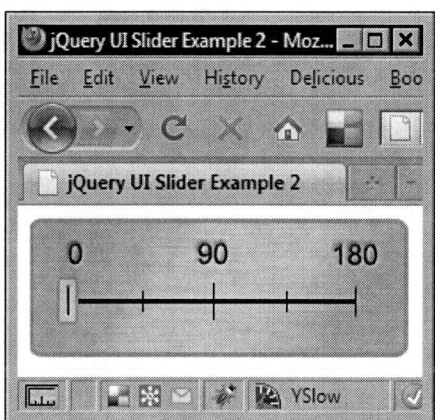

Of course, this example is completely arbitrary and was intended purely to show how to override the default theme.

Configurable options

Additional functionality, such as vertical sliders, multiple handles, and stepping, can also be configured using an object literal passed into the widget method when the slider is initialized. The options that can be used in conjunction with the slider widget are listed in the following table:

Option	Default value	Usage
animate	false	Enables a smooth animation of the slider handle when the track is clicked.
max	100	Sets the maximum value of the slider.
min	0	Sets the minimum value of the slider.
orientation	"auto"	Sets the axis that the slider thumb is moved along. This can accept the strings vertical or horizontal.
range	false	If two handles are in use this option creates a styleable range element between them.
step	1	Sets the distance of the step the handle will take along the track. The max value must be equally divisible by the supplied number.
value	0	The current value of the slider thumb.
values	null	This option accepts an array of values, each supplied integer will become the value of a slider handle.

Creating a vertical slider

To make a vertical slider, all we need to do is set the orientation option to true; the widget will do the rest for us.

In slider2.html change the final <script> element so that it appears like this:

```
<script type="text/javascript">
  $(function(){

    var sliderOpts = {
      orientation: "vertical"
    };
    $("#mySlider").slider(sliderOpts);
  });
</script>
```

Save the new file as `slider3.html`. We just need to set this single option to put the slider into vertical mode. When we launch the page, we see that the slider operates exactly as it did before, except that it now moves along the y axis, as in the following screenshot:

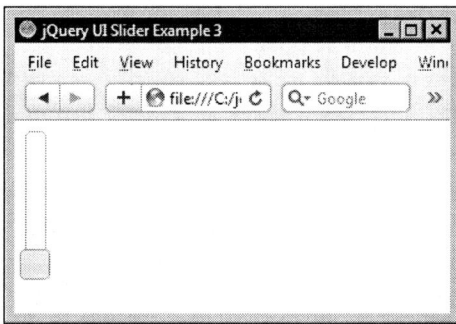

The widget defaults to `100px` in height if we don't provide our own CSS `height` rule for the slider track.

Minimum and maximum values

By default the minimum value of the slider is `0` and the maximum value is `100`, but we can change these values easily using the `min` and `max` options. Change the configuration object in `slider3.html` to this:

```
var sliderOpts = {
   min: -50,
   max: 50
};
```

Save this as `slider4.html`. We simply specify the integers that we'd like set as the starting and end values. Because the `value` option is set to `0` by default when we run this file the slider thumb will start in the middle of the track:

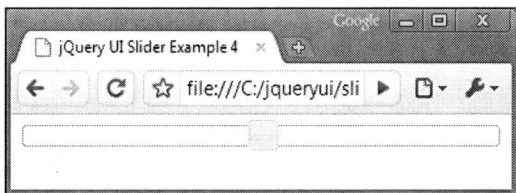

These options affect the state of the slider handle as reported by some of the widget's methods. For example, when the slider handle in this example is at the minimum value, the `value` method (see the methods section) will return `-50` as we would expect.

Slider steps

The `step` option refers to the number and position of steps along the track that the slider's handle jumps when moving from the minimum to the maximum positions on the track. The best way to understand how this option works is to see it in action, so change the configuration object in `slider4.html` to the following:

```
var sliderOpts = {
   step: 25
};
```

Save this as `slider5.html`. We set the step option to 25 in this example; we haven't set the `min` or `max` options, so they will take the default values of 0 and 100 respectively. Hence, by setting `step` to 25 we're saying that each step along the track should be a quarter of the track's length because 100 (the maximum) divided by 25 (the step value) is 4. The thumb will therefore take four steps along the track from beginning to end.

The `max` value of the slider should be equally divisible by whatever value we set as the `step` option, other than that we're free to use whatever value we wish. This is a useful option for confining the value selected by visitors to one of a set of predefined values.

If we were to set the value of `step` option in this example to 27 instead of 25, the slider would still work, but the points along the track that the handle stepped to would not be equal.

Slider animation

The slider widget comes with a built-in animation that moves the slider handle smoothly to a new position whenever the slider track is clicked. This animation is switched off by default but we can easily enable it by setting the `animate` option to `true`. Change the configuration object in `slider5.html` so that it is as follows:

```
var sliderOpts = {
   animate: true
}
```

Save this version as `slider6.html`. The difference this option makes to the overall effect of the widget is extraordinary. Instead of the slider handle just moving instantly to a new position when the track is clicked, it smoothly slides there.

If the `step` option is configured to a value other than one and the `animate` option is enabled the thumb will slide to the nearest step mark on the track. This may mean that the slider thumb moves past the point on the track that was clicked.

Setting the slider's value

The `value` option when set to `true` in a configuration object determines the starting value for the slider thumb. Depending on what we want the slider to represent, the starting value of the handle may not be `0`. If we wanted to start at half way across the track instead of at the beginning, we could use the following configuration object:

```
var sliderOpts = {
   value: 50
}
```

Save this file as `slider7.html`. When the file is loaded in a browser, we see that the handle starts halfway along the track instead of at the beginning, exactly as it did when we set the `min` and `max` options earlier on. We can also set this option after initialization to programmatically select a new value.

Using multiple handles

I mentioned earlier that a slider may have multiple handles; adding additional handles can be done using a single option—the `values` option. It accepts an array where each item in the array is a starting point for a handle. We can specify as many items as we wish up to the `max` value (taking `step` into account).

```
var sliderOpts = {
   values: [25, 75]
};
```

Save this variation as `slider8.html`. This is all we need to do; we don't need to supply any additional underlying markup; the widget has created both new handles for us and, as you'll see, they both function exactly as a standard single handle does. The following screenshot shows our dual-handled slider:

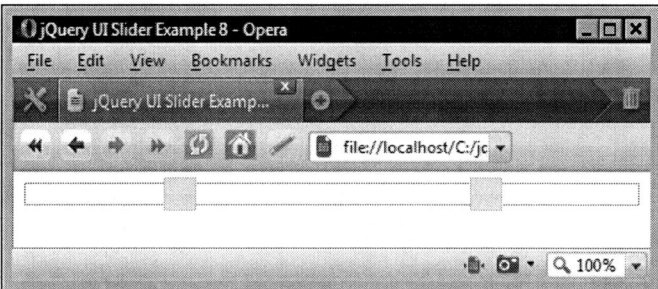

The range element

When working with multiple handles, we can set the `range` option to `true`. This adds a styled range element between two handles. In `slider8.html` supply the following configuration object:

```
var sliderOpts = {
  values: [25, 75],
  range: true
};
```

Save this page as `slider9.html`. When the page loads we should see that a styled `<div>` element now connects our two handles, as in the following screenshot:

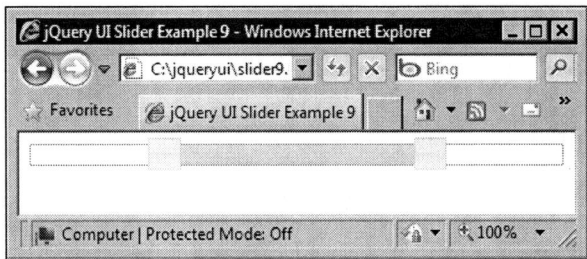

A maximum of two handles can be used in conjunction with the `range` option, but we can also enable it with a single handle as well; change the configuration object in the previous example to this:

```
var sliderOpts = {
  range: "min"
};
```

Save this as `slider10.html`. As well as the Boolean value `true`, we can also supply one of the string values `"min"` or `"max"`, but only when a single handle is in use.

In this example, we set it to `"min"` so when we move the slider handle along the track the range element will stretch from the start of the track to the slider handle. If we set the option to `"max"` the range will stretch from the end of the track to the handle.

Using slider's event API

In addition to the options we saw earlier, there are an additional four options that can be used to define functions which are executed at different times during a slider interaction. Any callback functions we use are automatically passed the standard event object and an object representing the slider. The following table lists the event options we can use with slider:

Function	Usage
change	Called when the slider handle stops and its value has changed.
slide	Called every time the slider handle moves.
start	Called when the slider handle starts moving.
stop	Called when the slider handle stops.

Hooking into these built-in callback functions is extremely easy. Let's put a basic example together to see. Change the configuration object in `slider10.html` so that it appears as follows:

```
var sliderOpts = {
   start: function() {

      $("#tip").fadeOut(function() {
         $(this).remove();
      });
   },
   change: function(e, ui) {

      $("<div>").attr("id", "tip").text(ui.value + "%").css({
         left: e.clientX - 35, top: -40 }).addClass(
         "ui-widget-header ui-corner-all").appendTo("#mySlider");
   }
};
```

Save this as `slider11.html`. We use two of the callback options in this example—`start` and `change`. In the start function we select the tooltip element if it exists and fade it out with jQuery's `fadeOut()` method. Once hidden from view, it is removed from the page.

The `change` function will be executed each time the value of the slider handle changes; when the function is called we create the tooltip and append it to the slider. We position it so that it appears above the center of the slider handle and give it some of the framework class names in order to style it with the theme in use.

In several places we use the second object pass to the callback function, the prepared `ui` object that contains useful information from the slider. In this example we use the `value` option of the object to obtain the new value of the slider handle.

We also need a very small custom stylesheet for this example; in a new page in your text editor add the following code:

```
#mySlider { margin:60px auto 0; }
#tip {
  position:absolute; display:inline; padding:5px 0;
  width:50px; text-align:center; font:bold 11px Verdana;
}
```

Save this file as `sliderTip.css` in the `css` folder and link to it from the `<head>` of `slider11.html`. When displayed, our tooltip should appear like this:

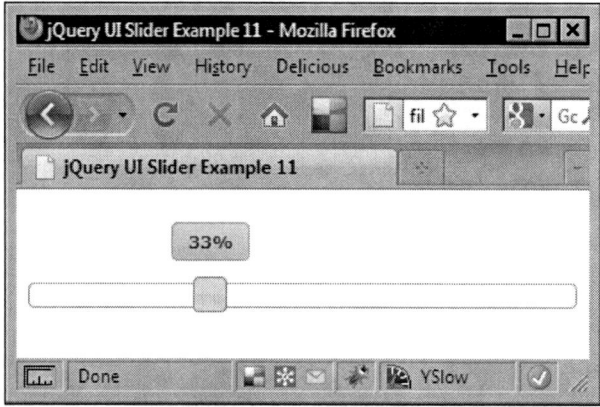

When all of the event options are used the callback will be executed in the following order:

- `start`
- `slide`
- `stop`
- `change`

The `slide` callback can be quite an intensive event as it is fired on every mouse move while the handle is selected, but it can also be used to prevent a slide in certain situations by returning `false` from the callback function. When using the `stop` and `change` callbacks together, the `change` callback may override the `stop` callback.

As with all library components each of these events can also be used with jQuery's `bind()` method by prepending the word `slider` to the event name, for example `sliderstart`.

Slider methods

The slider is intuitive and easy-to-use, and like the other components in the library it comes with a range of methods that are used to programmatically control the widget after it has been initialized. The methods we can use are shown in the following table.

Method	Usage
value	Set a single slider handle to a new value. This will move the handle to the new position on the track automatically. This method accepts a single argument which is an integer representing the new value.
values	Set the specified handle to move to a new value when multiple handles are in use.This method is exactly the same as the value method except that it takes two arguments — the index number of the handle followed by the new value.

The methods destroy, disable, enable, and option are common to all components and work in the same way with slider that we would expect them to.

The value and values methods are exclusive to the slider and are used to get or set the value of single or multiple handles. Of course, we can also do this using the option method so these two methods are merely shortcuts to cater for common implementational requirements. Let's take a look at them in action. First of all let's see how the value method can be used.

In slider11.html remove the <link> to sliderTip.css and add a new <button> element to the page directly after the slider container:

```
<button id="setMax">Set to max value</button>
```

Now change the final <script> element so that it is as follows:

```
<script type="text/javascript">
  $(function(){
    $("#mySlider").slider();
    $("#setMax").click(function() {
      var maxVal = $("#mySlider").slider("option", "max");
      $("#mySlider").slider("value", maxVal);
    });
  });
</script>
```

Save this file as `slider12.html`. We add a click handler for our new `<button>`; whenever it is clicked this method will first determine what the maximum value for the slider is by setting a variable to the result of the `option` method specifying `max` as the option we'd like to get. We don't need a configuration object in this example.

Once we have the maximum value we then call the `value` method, passing in the variable that holds the maximum value as the second argument; our variable will be used as the new value. Whenever the button is clicked, the slider handle will instantly move to the end of the track.

Working with multiple handles is just as easy but involves a slightly different approach; remove the `setMax` button in `slider12.html` and add these two buttons directly after the slider container:

```
<button class="preset" id="low">Preset 1 (low)</button>
<button class="preset" id="high">Preset 2 (high)</button>
```

Now change the final `<script>` element at the end of the `<body>` to this:

```
<script type="text/javascript">
  $(function(){

    var sliderOpts = {
      values: [25, 75]
    };
    $("#mySlider").slider(sliderOpts);

    $(".preset").click(function() {

      if ($(this).attr("id") === "low") {
        $("#mySlider").slider("values", 0, 0);
        $("#mySlider").slider("values", 1, 25);
      } else {
        $("#mySlider").slider("values", 0, 75);
        $("#mySlider").slider("values", 1, 100);
      }
    });
  });
</script>
```

Save this file as `slider13.html`. To trigger multiple handles we specify the values of two handles in our configuration object. When either of the two `<button>` elements on the page are clicked, we work out which button was clicked and then set the handles to either low values or high values depending on which button was clicked.

The values method takes two arguments. The first argument is the index number of the handle we'd like to change and the second argument is the value that we'd like the handle to be set to. Notice that we have to set each handle individually and that we can't chain the two methods together. This is because the method returns the new value and not a jQuery object.

The following screenshot shows how the page should appear after the second button is clicked:

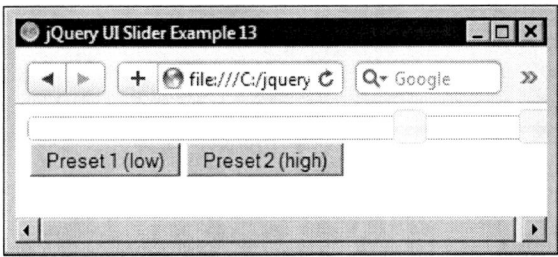

Future uses

The next specification of HTML is looming before us, with newer browsers, such as Firefox 3.5 beginning to implement more and more of the specification. One new element that may lend itself particularly well to implementations of the slider widget is the `<audio>` (and potentially the `<video>`) element. This element will automatically add controls that enable the visitor to play, pause, and adjust the volume of the media being played.

The default controls however, at this point anyway, do not appear to be style-able, so if we wish to change their appearance, we need to create our own controls. The slider widget would of course make an excellent substitution for the default volume control.

This next example should be considered highly experimental, and will, at the time of writing, work only in Firefox 3.5. Create the following new page in your text editor:

```
<!DOCTYPE HTML>
<html lang="en">
  <head>
    <link rel="stylesheet" type="text/css"
      href="development-bundle/themes/smoothness/ui.all.css">
    <meta http-equiv="Content-Type" content="text/html; charset=utf-8">
    <title>jQuery UI Slider Example 14</title>
  </head>
  <body>
```

```
<audio id="audio" src="http://upload.wikimedia.org/wikipedia/
  en/7/77/Jamiroquai_-_Snooze_You_Lose.ogg">
  Your browser does not support the <code>audio</code>
    element.
</audio>
<div id="volume"></div>
<script type="text/javascript"
  src="development-bundle/jquery-1.3.2.js"></script>
<script type="text/javascript"
  src="development-bundle/ui/ui.core.js"></script>
<script type="text/javascript"
  src="development-bundle/ui/ui.slider.js"></script>
<script type="text/javascript">
  $(function(){

    var audio = $("audio")[0];

    audio.volume = 0.5;
    audio.play();

    var sliderOpts = {
      value: 5,
      min: 0,
      max: 10,
      step: 1,
      orientation: "vertical",
      change: function() {
        var vol = $(this).slider("value") / 10;
        audio.volume = vol;
      }
    };
    $("#volume").slider(sliderOpts);
  });
</script>
</body>
</html>
```

Save this as `slider14.html`. On the page we have the `<audio>` tag which has its `src` attribute set to a copyright-free audio clip hosted on Wikipedia. We also have the empty container element for our volume control.

In the script we first select the `<audio>` element using the standard jQuery syntax. Then we set the volume of the audio clip using the `volume` property and begin playing the clip immediately with the `play()` method.

Next we configure our slider; the volume range for the `<audio>` element is from `0.1` to `1` but we can't use these values in the slider so we instead we use the range `1` to `10`. We use the `change` method to alter the volume of the audio. Whenever the value of the slider is changed we get the new value and convert it to the required format for the `volume` option by dividing it by `10`.

When we run this example in a supporting browser, the only thing visible on the page will be the volume slider, but we should also be able to hear the audio clip. Whenever the slider handle is moved, the volume of the clip should increase or decrease.

In a proper real-world implementation of this example we would probably provide a standard flash video solution for cases when browsers that don't support the `<audio>` tag are used.

A color slider

A fun implementation of the slider widget, which could be very useful in certain applications, is the color slider. Let's put what we've learned about this widget into practice to produce a basic color choosing tool. The following screenshot shows the page that we'll be making:

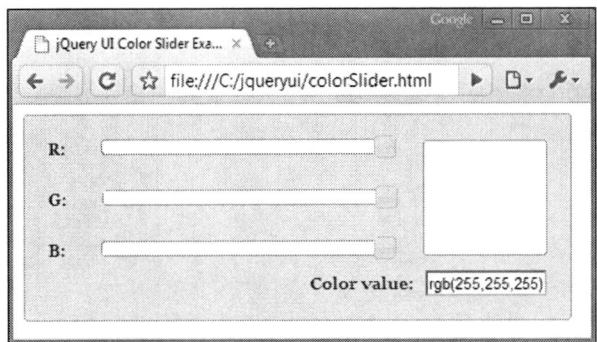

In a new file in your text editor, create the following page:

```
<!DOCTYPE HTML PUBLIC "-//W3C//DTD HTML 4.01//EN" "http://www.w3.org/
TR/html4/strict.dtd">
<html lang="en">
  <head>
    <link rel="stylesheet" type="text/css"
      href="development-bundle/themes/smoothness/ui.all.css">
    <link rel="stylesheet" type="text/css"
      href="css/colorSliderTheme.css">
```

```
    <meta http-equiv="Content-Type" content="text/html;
      charset=utf-8">
    <title>jQuery UI Color Slider Example</title>
  </head>
  <body>
    <div id="container" class="ui-corner-all ui-widget-content
      ui-helper-clearfix">
      <label>R:</label><div id="rSlider"></div><br>
      <label>G:</label><div id="gSlider"></div><br>
      <label>B:</label><div id="bSlider"></div>
      <div id="colorBox" class="ui-corner-all ui-widget-
        content"></div>
      <input id="output" type="text" value="rgb(255,255,255)">
      <label id="outputLabel">Color value:</label>
    </div>
    <script type="text/javascript"
      src="development-bundle/jquery-1.3.2.js"></script>
    <script type="text/javascript"
      src="development-bundle/ui/ui.core.js"></script>
    <script type="text/javascript"
      src="development-bundle/ui/ui.slider.js"></script>
    <script type="text/javascript">
      $(function(){
        var r = 255,
          g = 255,
          b = 255,
          rgbString;
        var sliderOpts = {
          min:0,
          max: 255,
          value: 255,
          slide: function(e, ui) {
            r = $("#rSlider").slider("value");
            g = $("#gSlider").slider("value");
            b = $("#bSlider").slider("value");
            rgbString = "rgb(" + r + "," + g + "," + b + ")";

            $("#colorBox").css({ backgroundColor: rgbString });
            $("#output").val(rgbString);
          }
        };
        $("#rSlider, #gSlider, #bSlider").slider(sliderOpts);
      });
    </script>
  </body>
</html>
```

Save this as `colorSlider.html`. The page itself is simple enough. We've got some elements used primarily for displaying the different components of the color slider, as well as the individual container elements which will be transformed into slider widgets. We use three sliders for our color chooser, one for each RGB channel.

We give various elements, like the container and color box elements, class names from the CSS framework so that we can take advantage of effects like the rounded corners, and so that we can cut down on the amount of CSS we need to write ourselves.

The JavaScript is as simple as the underlying markup. We set some variables equal to the maximum value of each RGB channel and define the `colorString` variable here as well. All of these variables will be updated when the widget is used.

As RGB color values range from 0 to 255, we set the max option to 255 in our configuration object. The color box will have a white background when the page loads so setting the value initially of each slider to 255 makes sense. We also set the `value` option to 255 as well so that the widget handles start in the correct location.

The `slide` callback is where the action happens. Every time a handle is moved we update each of the r, g, and b variables by using the value method in getter mode, and then construct a new RGB string from the values of our variables. This is necessary as we can't pass the variables directly into jQuery's `css()` method. We also update the value in the `<input>` field.

We'll need some CSS as well to complete the overall appearance of our widget. In a new page in your text editor, create the following stylesheet:

```css
#container {
  width:426px; height:150px; position:relative;
  font:bold 13px Georgia; padding:20px 20px 0;
  background:#eeeeee;
}
#container label {
  float:left; text-align:right; margin:0 30px 26px 0;
  clear:left;
}
.ui-slider { width:240px; float:left; }
.ui-slider-handle { width:15px; height:27px; }
#colorBox {
  width:104px; height:94px; float:right; margin:-83px 0 0 0;
  background:#ffffff;
}
#container #outputLabel {
  float:right; margin:-14px 10px 0 0;
```

```
}
#output {
  width:100px; text-align:center; float:right; clear:both;
  margin-top:-17px;
}
```

Save this as `colorSliderTheme.css` in the `css` folder. When we run the example, we should find that everything works as expected; as soon as we start moving any of the slider handles the color box begins to change color and the `<input>` updates:

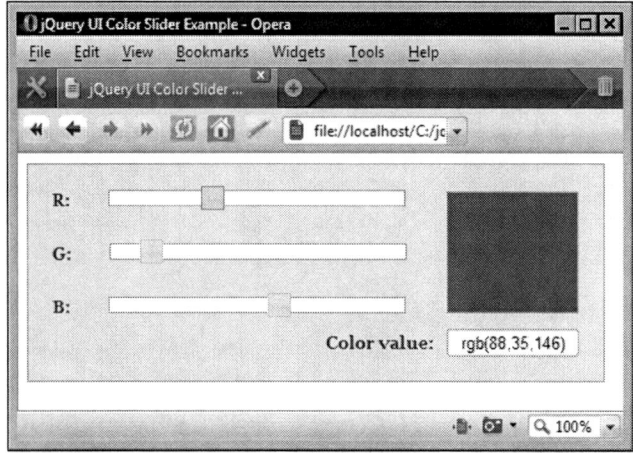

Summary

In this chapter, we looked at the slider widget and saw how quickly and easily it can be put on the page. It requires minimal underlying markup and just a single line of code to initialize.

We looked at the different options that we can set in order to control how the slider behaves and how it is configured once it's initialized. It can be fine-tuned to suit a range of implementations.

We also saw the rich event model that can easily be hooked into, and reacted to, with up to four separate callback functions. This allows us to execute code at important times during an interaction.

Finally, we looked at the range of methods that can be used to programmatically interact with the slider, including methods for setting the value of the handle(s), or getting and setting configuration options after initialization.

These options and methods turn the widget into a useful and highly functional interface tool that adds an excellent level of interactivity to any page.

7
Datepicker

The jQuery UI datepicker widget is probably the most refined and documented widget found in the library. It has the biggest API and probably provides the most functionality out of all the widgets. It works completely out of the box but is also highly configurable and robust.

Quite simply, the datepicker widget provides an interface that allows visitors to your site or application to select dates. Wherever a form field is required that asks for a date to be entered, the datepicker widget can be added. This means your visitors get to use an attractive, engaging widget and you get dates in the format in which you expect them. It's easy for everyone, and that's the attraction.

Additional functionality built into the datepicker includes automatic opening and closing animations along with the ability to navigate the interface of the widget using the keyboard. While holding down the *Ctrl* key (or Command key on the Mac), the arrows on the keyboard can be used to choose a new day cell, which can then be selected using the *Return* key.

While easy to create and configure, the datepicker is a complex widget made up of a wide range of underlying elements, as the following screenshot shows:

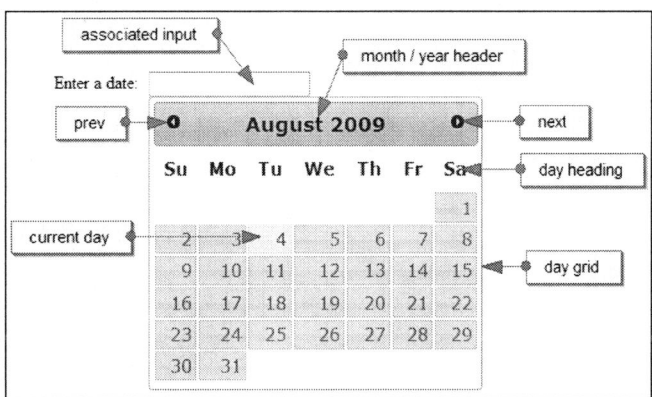

Despite this complexity, we can implement the default datepicker with just a single line of code, much like the other widgets in the library that we have covered so far. In this section, we will look at the following topics:

- The default datepicker implementation
- Exploring the configurable options
- Implementing a trigger button
- Configuring alternative animations
- The `dateFormat` option
- Easy internationalization
- Multiple month datepickers
- Date range selection
- Datepicker's methods
- Using AJAX with the datepicker

The default datepicker

To create the default datepicker add the following code to a new page in your text editor:

```
<!DOCTYPE HTML PUBLIC "-//W3C//DTD HTML 4.01//EN"
  "http://www.w3.org/TR/html4/strict.dtd">
<html lang="en">
  <head>
    <link rel="stylesheet" type="text/css"
      href="development-bundle/themes/smoothness/ui.all.css">
    <meta http-equiv="Content-Type"
      content="text/html; charset=utf-8">
    <title>jQuery UI Datepicker Example 1</title>
  </head>
  <body>
    <label>Enter a date: </label><input id="date">
    <script type="text/javascript"
      src="development-bundle/jquery-1.3.2.js"></script>
    <script type="text/javascript"
      src="development-bundle/ui/ui.core.js"></script>
    <script type="text/javascript"
      src="development-bundle/ui/ui.datepicker.js"></script>
    <script type="text/javascript">
      $(function(){
        $("#date").datepicker();
      });
    </script>
  </body>
</html>
```

Save this as `datePicker1.html` in the `jqueryui` project folder. All we have on the page is a `<label>` and a standard text `<input>` element. We don't need to specify any empty container elements for the datepicker widget to be rendered into. All of the markup required to produce the widget is automatically added by the library.

The JavaScript required is equally simple. We use the `$(function(){});` jQuery construct to execute some code when the page loads. The code that we execute is the `datepicker` method, which is called on a jQuery object representing the `<input>` field.

When you run the page in your browser and focus on the `<input>` element, the default datepicker should appear below the input and will look like the screenshot at the start of the chapter. Along with an `<input>`, the datepicker can also be attached to a `<div>` element.

Apart from great looks, the default datepicker also comes with a lot of built-in functionality. When the calendar opens, it is smoothly animated from zero to full size, it will automatically be set to the present date, and selecting a date will automatically add the date to the `<input>` and close the calendar (again with a nice animation).

With no additional configuration, and a single line of code, we now have a perfectly usable and attractive widget that makes date selection easy. If all you want is to let people pick a date then this is all you need. The source files required for the default datepicker implementation are:

- `jquery-1.3.2.js`
- `ui.core.js`
- `ui.datepicker.js`

Configurable options of the picker

The datepicker has a large range of configurable options (currently thirty-nine to be exact). The following table lists the basic options, their default values, and gives a brief description of their usage.

Option	Default value	Usage
altField	" "	Specify a CSS selector for an alternative <input> field to which the selected date is also added.
altFormat	" "	Specify an alternative format for the date added to the alternative <input>. See the dateFormat option below for clarification on the value this option takes.
appendText	" "	Add text after the datepicker <input> to show the format of the selected date.
buttonImage	" "	Specify a path to the image to use for the trigger <button>.
buttonImageOnly	false	Set to true to use an image instead of a trigger button.
buttonText	"..."	Text to display on a trigger <button> (if present).
changeMonth	false	Show the month change drop-down.
changeYear	false	Show the year change drop-down.
constrainInput	true	Constrains the <input> to the format of the date specified by the widget.
dateFormat	"mm/dd/yy"	The format selected dates should appear in the <input>.
defaultDate	null	Set the date that will be highlighted when the datepicker opens and the <input> is empty.
duration	"normal"	Set the speed at which the datepicker opens.
gotoCurrent	false	Set the current day link to move the datepicker to the currently selected date instead of today.
hideIfNoPrevNext	false	Hide the prev/next links when not needed instead of disabling them.
maxDate	null	Set the maximum date that can be selected. Accepts a date object, a relative number. Example: +7, or a string such as "+6m".

Option	Default value	Usage
minDate	null	Set the minimum date that can be selected. Accepts a number, date object, or string.
navigationAsDateFormat	false	Allows us to specify month names as the Prev, Next, and Current links.
numberOfMonths	1	Set the number of months shown on a single datepicker.
shortYearCutoff	"+10"	This is used to determine the current century when using the y year representation; numbers less than this are deemed to be in the current century.
showAnim	"show"	Set the animation used when the datepicker is displayed.
showButtonPanel	false	Shows a panel of buttons for the datepicker consisting of Close and Current links.
showCurrentAtPos	0	Set the position of the current month in multiple-month datepickers.
showOn	"focus"	Set the event that triggers displaying the datepicker.
showOptions	{}	An object literal containing options to control the configured animation.
showOtherMonths	false	Show the last and first days of the previous and next months.
stepMonths	1	Set how many months are navigated with the previous and next links.
yearRange	"-10:+10"	Specify the range of years in the year drop-down.

Basic Options

Change the final `<script>` element in `datepicker1.html` to this:

```
<script type="text/javascript">
  $(function(){

    var pickerOpts = {
      appendText: "mm/dd/yy",
      defaultDate: "+5",
      showOtherMonths: true
    };

    $("#date").datepicker(pickerOpts);
  });
</script>
```

Save this as `datePicker2.html`. The following image shows how the widget will look after configuring these options:

We've used a number of options in this example because there are simply so many options available — the appearance of the initial page, before the datepicker is even shown, can be changed using the `appendText` option. This adds the specified text string directly after the `<input>` field which is associated with the picker. This helps visitors to clarify the format that will be used for the date.

For styling purposes, we can target this new string using the `.ui-datepicker-append` selector in a stylesheet if necessary, as this is the class name that is given automatically to the `<span>` element containing the specified text.

The `defaultDate` option sets which date is highlighted in the datepicker when it opens initially and the `<input>` is empty. We've used the relative `+5` string in this example so when the datepicker opens initially, the date five days from the current date is selected. Pressing the *Enter* key on the keyboard will select the highlighted date. Along with a relative string, we can also supply `null` as the value of `defaultDate` to set it to the current date (today subjectively), or a standard JavaScript date object.

As we can see in the previous screenshot, the styling of the datepicker date for the current date is different from the styling used to show the default date. This will vary between themes but for reference, the current date is shown in a light yellow color, while the default date has a darker border than normal dates with the default theme.

Once a date has been selected, subsequent openings of the datepicker will show the selected date as the default date, which again has different styling (a preselected date with the Smoothness theme will be white).

By setting the `showOtherMonths` option to `true`, we've added grayed-out (non-selectable) dates from the previous and next months to the empty squares that sit at the beginning and end of the date grid before and after the current month. These are visible in the previous screenshot and are rendered a much lighter color than selectable dates.

Minimum and maximum dates

By default, the datepicker will go forward or backward infinitely, there is no upper or lower boundaries. If we want to restrict the selectable dates to a particular range however we can do this easily using the `minDate` and `maxDate` options. Change the configuration object in `datePicker2.html` to the following:

```
var pickerOpts = {
  minDate: new Date(),
  maxDate: "+10"
};
```

Save this as `datePicker3.html`. In this example we supply a standard, unmodified JavaScript date object to the `minDate` option, which will default to the current date. This will make any dates in the past unselectable.

For the `maxDate` option we use a relative text string of `+10` that will make only the current date and the next ten dates selectable. You can see how these options affect the appearance of the widget in the following screenshot:

Changing the datepicker UI

The datepicker API exposes a number of options directly related to adding or removing additional UI elements within the datepicker. To show `<select>` elements that allow the visitor to choose the month and year we can use the `changeMonth` and `changeYear` configuration options.

```
var pickerOpts = {
   changeMonth: true,
   changeYear: true
};
```

Save this as `datePicker4.html`. Using the month and year `<select>` elements gives the user a much quicker way to navigate to dates that may be far in the past or future. The following screenshot shows how the widget will appear with these two options enabled:

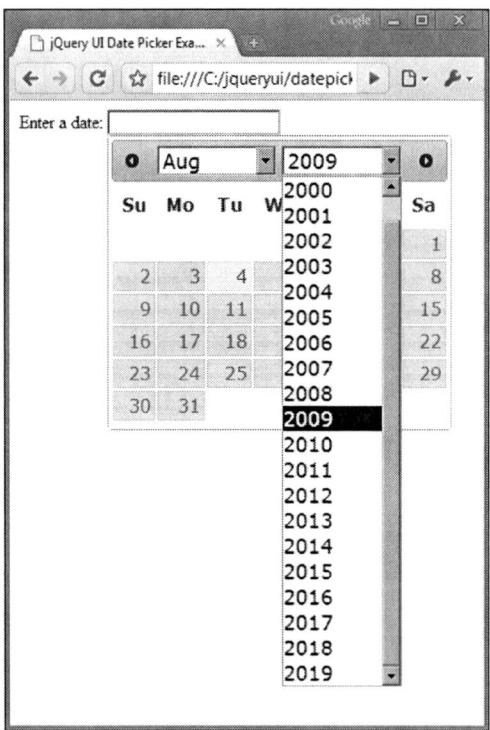

By default the year selectbox will include the previous and next ten years, covering a total range of 20 years. We can navigate further than this using the prev/next arrow links, but if we know beforehand that visitors may be choosing dates very far in the past or future we can change the range of years using the `yearRange` option.

```
var pickerOpts = {
  changeMonth: true,
  changeYear: true,
  yearRange: "-25:+25"
};
```

Save this as `datePicker5.html`. This time when we run the page we should find that the year range now covers 50 years in total.

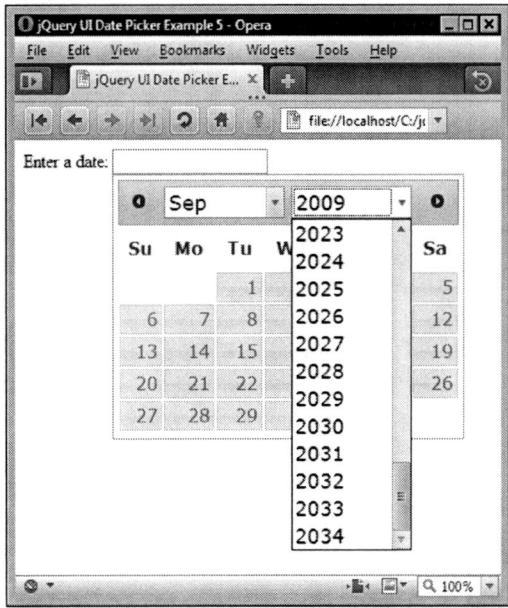

Another change we can make to the UI of the datepicker is to enable the button panel, which adds two buttons to the footer of the widget. Let's see it in action. Change the configuration object in `datepicker5.html` so that it appears as follows:

```
var pickerOpts = {
  showButtonPanel: true
};
```

Save this as `datePicker6.html`. The buttons added to the foot of the widget appear exactly as the buttons in a dialog widget, as you can see in the following screenshot:

The **Today** button will instantly navigate the datepicker back to the month showing the current date, while the **Done** button will close the widget without selecting a date. We can change the **Today** button so that it goes to the selected date instead of the current date using the `gotoCurrent` option.

Adding a trigger button

By default, the datepicker is opened when the `<input>` element it is associated with receives focus. However, we can change this very easily so the datepicker opens when a button is clicked instead. The most basic type of `<button>` can be enabled with just the `showOn` option. Change the configuration object in `datePicker6.html` so that it is as follows:

```
var pickerOpts = {
   showOn: "button"
};
```

Save this as `datePicker7.html`. Setting the `showOn` option to `true` in our configuration object will automatically add a simple `<button>` element directly after the associated `<input>` element. The datepicker will now open only when the `<button>` is clicked, rather than when the `<input>` is focused. This option also accepts the string value `both`, which opens the widget when the `<input>` is focused and when the `<button>` is clicked. The new `<button>` is shown in the following screenshot:

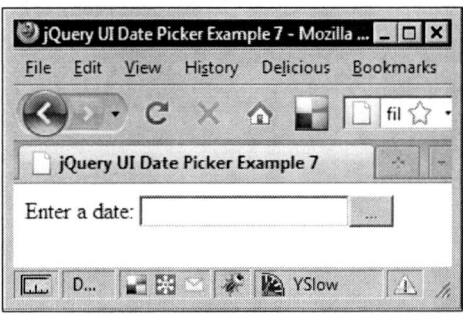

The default text shown on the `<button>` (an ellipsis) can easily be changed by providing a new string as the value of the `buttonText` option; change the previous configuration object to this:

```
var pickerOpts = {
  showOn: "button",
  buttonText: "Open datepicker"
};
```

Save this as `datePicker8.html`. Now the text on the `<button>` should match the value we set as the `buttonText` option.

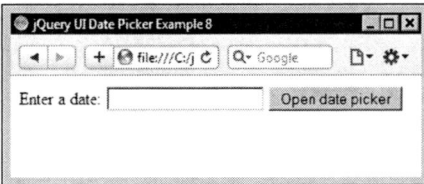

Instead of using text as the label of the `<button>` element, we can use an image instead. This is configured using the `buttonImage` option.

```
var pickerOpts = {
  showOn: "button",
  buttonImage: "img/date-picker/cal.png",
  buttonText: "Open datepicker"
};
```

Save this as `datePicker9.html`. The value of the `buttonImage` option is a string consisting of the path to the image that we'd like to use on the button. Notice that we also set the `buttonText` option in this example too, the reason for this is that the value of the `buttonText` option is automatically used as the `title` and `alt` attributes of the `<img>` element that is added to the `<button>`. Our trigger button should now look as shown in the following screenshot:

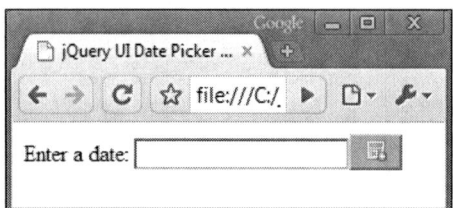

We don't need to use a button at all if we don't want to, we can replace the `<button>` element with an `<img>` element instead. Change the configuration object in `datePicker9.html` so that it appears as follows:

```
var pickerOpts = {
  showOn: "button",
  buttonImage: "img/date-picker/cal.png",
  buttonText: "Open datepicker",
  buttonImageOnly: true
};
```

Save this as `datePicker10.html`. This should give you a nice image-only button as illustrated in the following screenshot:

Configuring alternative animations

The datepicker widget comes with an attractive built-in opening animation that makes the widget appear to grow from nothing to full size. Its flexible API also exposes several options related to animations. These are the `duration`, `showAnim`, and `showOptions` configuration options.

The simplest animation configuration we can set is the speed at which the widget opens and closes. To do this, all we have to do is change the value of the `duration` option. This option requires a simple string that can take a string value of either `slow`, `normal` (default), or `fast`.

Change the configuration object in `datePicker10.html` to the following:

```
var pickerOpts = {
  duration: "fast"
};
```

Save this variation as `datePicker11.html`. When we run this page in a browser we should find that the opening animation is visibly faster.

Along with changing the speed of the animation, we can also change the animation itself using the `showAnim` option. The default animation used is a simple show animation, but we can change this so that it uses any of the other show/hide effects included with the library (refer Chapter 13). Change the configuration object from the last example to this:

```
var pickerOpts = {
  showAnim: "drop",
  showOptions: { direction: "up" }
};
```

Save this as `datePicker12.html`. We also need to use two new `<script>` resources to use alternative effects. These are the `effects.core.js` and the source file of the effect we wish to use in this example, `effects.drop.js`. We'll look at both of these effects in more detail in the last chapter, but they are essential for this example to work. Make sure you add these to the file directly after the source file for the datepicker.

```
<script type="text/javascript"
  src="development-bundle/ui/ui.datepicker.js"></script>
<script type="text/javascript"
  src="development-bundle/ui/effects.core.js"></script>
<script type="text/javascript"
  src="development-bundle/ui/effects.drop.js"></script>
```

Our simple configuration object configures the animation to `drop` using the `showAnim` option, and sets the `direction` option of the effect using `showOptions`. When you now run this example the datepicker should drop down into position instead of opening. Other effects can be implemented in the same way.

Multiple months

So far all of our examples have looked at single-page datepickers, where at a time only one month was shown. However, we can easily adjust this to show a different number of months if we wish using a couple of configuration options. Remove the effect source files before the configuration object in `datePicker12.html` and change the configuration object so that it appears as follows:

```
var pickerOpts = {
  numberOfMonths: 3
};
```

Save this as `datePicker13.html`. The `numberOfMonths` option takes an integer representing the number of months we would like displayed in the widget at any point. Our datepicker should now appear like this:

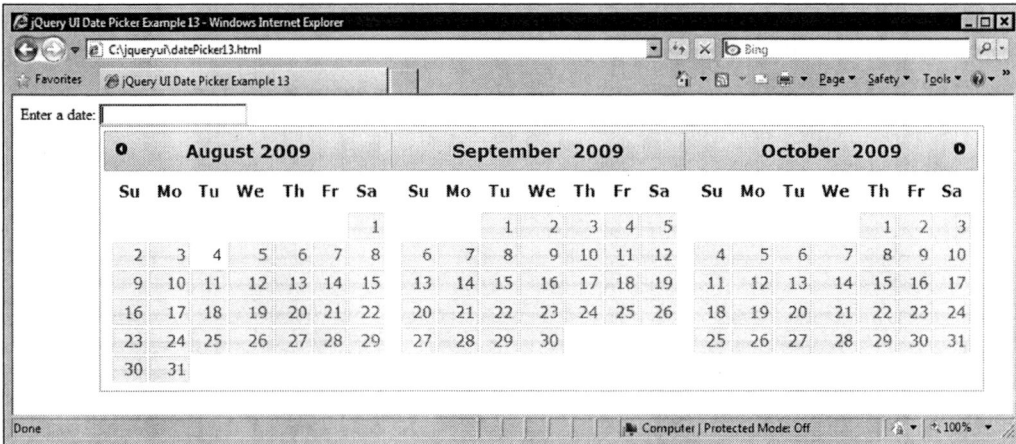

There is no upper limit to the number of months that will be displayed, however, the performance of the widget decreases with each additional month shown. There is also a noticeable lag between focusing the `<input>` and the widget being displayed. Note that in this format the widget doesn't become a calendar, its sole purpose is still to provide an effective UI for selecting a date.

Also, the individual month panels are floated side by side and due to their size will soon overflow the viewport causing a horizontal scrollbar to appear. However, as soon as the scrollbar is used the datepicker will close, making any months that go beyond the boundary of the screen unusable. For these reasons it's best to keep the number of months displayed to a minimum.

There are several other configuration options related to multiple-month datepickers. The stepMonths option controls how many months are changed when the previous or next links are used.

The default value of stepMonths is 1, so in our previous example the widget starts with the current month displayed first and the next two months after it. Each time the previous or next icons are clicked the panels move one space left or right. If we set stepMonths to 3, the same as the number of months shown, each month will move three spaces left or right when the previous or next links are clicked.

The showCurrentAtPos option specifies where the current month is shown when the datepicker is displayed. In our previous example, the current month is shown as the first month panel. Each month panel has a zero-based index number, so if we want the current month to be in the middle of the widget, we would set this option to 1 instead.

Changing the date format

The dateFormat option is one of the localization options at our disposal for advanced datepicker locale configuration. Setting this option allows you to quickly and easily set the format of selected dates (as displayed in the <input>) using a variety of short-hand references. The format of dates can be a combination of any of the following characters (they are case-sensitive):

- d – day of month (single digit where applicable)
- dd – day of month (two digits)
- m – month of year (single digit where applicable)
- mm – month of year (two digits)
- y – year (two digits)
- yy – year (four digits)
- D – short day name
- DD – full day name
- M – short month name
- MM – long month name
- '...' – any literal text string
- @ - UNIX timestamp (milliseconds since 01/01/1970)

We can use these shorthand codes to quickly configure our preferred date format, as in the following example. Change the configuration object in datePicker13.html to the following:

```
var pickerOpts = {
   dateFormat:"d MM yy"
};
```

Save the new file as datePicker14.html. We use the dateFormat option to specify a string containing the short-hand date code for our preferred date format. The format we set is the day of the month (using a single digit if possible) with d, the full name of the month with MM, and the full four-digit year with yy.

When dates are selected and added to the associated <input>, they will be in the format specified in the configuration object, as in the following screenshot:

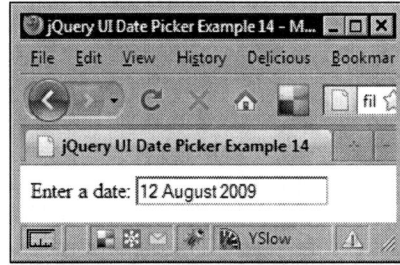

Note that dates returned programmatically via the getDate method (see *Datepicking methods* section) are in the default GMT date and time standard. In order to change the format of the date returned by the API, the $.datepicker.formatDate() utility method should be used.

When using a string as the value of this option to configure dates we can also specify whole strings of text. However, if we do and any letters in the string are those used as short-hand, they will need to be escaped using single quotes.

For example, to add the string Selected: to the start of the date, you would need to use the string Selecte'd': to avoid having the lowercase d picked up as the short day of month format:

```
var pickerOpts = {
   dateFormat:"Selecte'd': d MM yy"
};
```

Save this change as datePicker15.html. Notice how we escape the lowercase d in the string Selected by wrapping it in single quotes. Now when a date is selected, our text string is prepended to the formatted date.

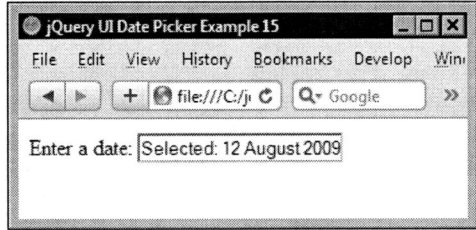

There are also a number of built-in preconfigured date formats that correspond to common standards or RFC notes. These formats are added to the components as constants and can be accessed via the `$.datepicker` object. As an example, let's format the date according to the ATOM standard:

```
var pickerOpts = {
   dateFormat: $.datepicker.ATOM
};
```

Save this as `datePicker16.html`. When a date is selected in this example, the value entered into the `<input>` should be in the format shown in the following screenshot:

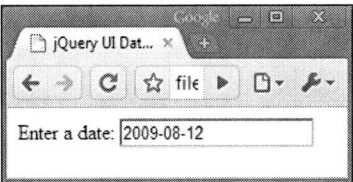

The complete set of predefined date formats is listed below.

Option value	Date format
`$.datepicker.ATOM`	`"yy-mm-dd"`
`$.datepicker.COOKIE`	`"D, dd M y"`
`$.datepicker.ISO_8601`	`"yy-mm-dd"`
`$.datepicker.RFC_822`	`"D,  d M y"`
`$.datepicker.RFC_850`	`"DD, dd-M-y"`
`$.datepicker.RFC_1036`	`"D, d M y"`
`$.datepicker.RFC_1123`	`"D, d M yy"`
`$.datepicker.RFC_2822`	`"D, d M yy"`
`$.datepicker.RSS`	`"D, d M y"`
`$.datepicker.TIMESTAMP`	`@ (UNIX timestamp)`
`$.datepicker.W3C`	`"yy-mm-dd"`

Updating an additional input element

There may be times when we want to update two <input> elements with the selected date, perhaps to show a different date format. The altField and altFormat options can be used to cater for this requirement. Add a second <input> element to the page in date-Picker16.html with an id attribute of alt, and then change the configuration object to this:

```
var pickerOpts = {
    altField: "#alt",
    altFormat: $.datepicker.TIMESTAMP
};
```

Save this as datePicker17.html. The altField option accepts a standard jQuery selector as its value and allows us to select the additional <input> element that is updated when the main <input> is updated. The altFormat option can accept the same formats as the dateFormat option. The next screenshot shows how the page should appear once a date has been selected using the datepicker:

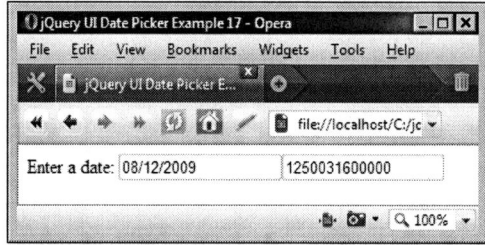

Localization

In addition to the options already listed, there is also a range of regionalization options. They can be used easily to provide custom locale support in order to easily display a datepicker with all the text shown in an alternative language.

Those options that are used specifically for the localization are listed below:

Option	Default	Usage
closeText	"Close"	Text to display on the Close button.
currentText	"Current"	Text to display on the Current link.
dayNames	["Sunday", "Monday", "Tuesday", "Wednesday", "Thursday", "Friday", "Saturday"]	An array of names of days in a week.
dayNamesMin	["Su", "Mo", "Tu", "We", "Th", "Fr", "Sa"]	An array of 2-letter names of days in a week.
dayNamesShort	"Sun", "Mon", "Tue", "Wed", "Thu", "Fri", "Sat"]	An array of abbreviated names of days in a week.
firstDay	0	Specify the first column of days in the datepicker.
isRTL	false	Set the calendar to right-to-left format.
monthNames	["January", "Febru-ary", "March", "April", "May", "June", "July, "August", "September", "October", "November", "December"]	An array of month names.
monthNamesShort	["Jan", "Feb", "Mar", "Apr", "May", "Jun", "Jul", "Aug", "Sep", "Oct", "Nov", "Dec"]	An array of abbreviated month names.
nextText	"Next"	Text to display on the Next link.
prevText	"Prev	Text to display on the Prev link.
showMonthAfterYear	false	Shows the month after the year in the header of the widget.

A wide range of different translations have already been provided and reside within the `i18n` folder in the `development-bundle/ui` directory. Each language translation has its own source file and to change the default language all we have to do is include the source file of the alternative language.

In `datePicker1.html`, add the following new `<script>` element directly after the link to `ui.datepicker.js`:

```
<script type="text/javascript"
    src="development-bundle/ui/i18n/ui.datepicker-fr.js"></script>
```

Save this as `datePicker18.html` and view the results in a browser.

With just a single link to one new resource we've changed all of the visible text in the datepicker to an alternative language, and we don't even need to set any configuration options. If we wanted to truly internationalize the datepicker, there is even a roll-up file containing all of the alternative languages, which we can link to.

Custom localization is also very easy to implement. This can be done using a standard configuration object containing the configured values for the options from the previous table. In this way, any alternative language not included in the roll-up file can be implemented.

For example, to implement a Lolcat datepicker, change the configuration object of `datePicker6.html` to the following:

```
var pickerOpts = {
  closeText: "Kthxbai",
  currentText: "Todai",
  nextText: "Fwd",
  prevText: "Bak",
  monthNames: ["January", "February", "March", "April", "Mai", "Jun",
    "July", "August", "Septembr", "Octobr", "Novembr", "Decembr"],
  monthNamesShort: ["Jan", "Feb", "Mar", "Apr", "Mai", "Jun", "Jul",
    "Aug", "Sep", "Oct", "Nov", "Dec"],
  dayNames: ["Sundai", "Mondai", "Tuesdai", "Wednesdai", "Thursdai",
    "Fridai", "Katurdai"],
  dayNamesShort: ["Sun", "Mon", "Tue", "Wed", "Thu", "Fri", "Kat"],
  dayNamesMin: ["Su", "Mo", "Tu", "We", "Th", "Fr", "Ka"],
  dateFormat: 'dd/mm/yy',
  firstDay: 1,
  isRTL: false,
  showButtonPanel: true
};
```

Save this change as `datePicker19.html`. Most of the options are used to provide simple string substitutions. However, the `monthNames`, `monthNamesShort`, `dayNames`, `dayNamesShort`, and `dayNamesMin` options require arrays.

Note that the `dayNamesMin` and other day-related arrays should begin with Sunday (or the localized equivalent). We've set Monday to appear first in this example using the `firstDay` option. Our datepicker should now appear like this:

Callback properties

The final set of configuration options are related to the event model exposed by the widget. It consists of a series of callback functions we can use to specify code to be executed at different points during an interaction with the datepicker. These are listed below:

Option	Usage
beforeShow	Execute a function just before the datepicker is displayed each time. Called once each time the datepicker is opened.
beforeShowDay	Similar to beforeShow except that this callback is triggered for each day in the current month each time the widget is displayed.
onChangeMonthYear	Set a callback function to be executed when the current month or year changes.
onClose	Set a callback function for the close event.
onSelect	Set a callback function for the select event.

To highlight how useful these callback properties are, we can extend the previous internationalization example to create a page that allows visitors to choose any available language found in the i18n roll-up file.

When using the roll-up file, the language displayed by the datepicker will be whichever language happens to appear last in the source file, which at the time of writing is Taiwanese. We can change this by setting the regional option of the datepicker. In datePicker19.html, add a new <select> box to the page with the following <option> elements:

```
<select id="language">
   <option id="en">English</option>
   <option id="ar">Arabic</option>
   <option id="bg">Bulgarian</option>
   <option id="ca">Catalan</option>
   <option id="cs">Czech</option>
   <option id="da">Danish</option>
   <option id="de">German</option>
   <option id="el">Greek</option>
   <option id="eo">Esperanto</option>
   <option id="es">Spanish</option>
   <option id="fa">Farsi</option>
   <option id="fi">Finnish</option>
   <option id="fr">French</option>
   <option id="he">Hebrew</option>
   <option id="hr">Croatian</option>
```

```
    <option id="hu">Hungarian</option>
    <option id="hy">Armenian</option>
    <option id="id">Indonesian</option>
    <option id="is">Icelandic</option>
    <option id="it">Italian</option>
    <option id="ja">Japanese</option>
    <option id="ko">Korean</option>
    <option id="lt">Lithuanian</option>
    <option id="lv">Latvian</option>
    <option id="ms">Malaysian</option>
    <option id="nl">Dutch</option>
    <option id="no">Norwegian</option>
    <option id="pl">Polish</option>
    <option id="pt-BR">Brazillian</option>
    <option id="ro">Romanian</option>
    <option id="ru">Russian</option>
    <option id="sk">Slovakian</option>
    <option id="sl">Slovenian</option>
    <option id="sq">Albanian</option>
    <option id="sr-SR">Serbian</option>
    <option id="sv">Swedish</option>
    <option id="th">Thai</option>
    <option id="tr">Turkish</option>
    <option id="uk">Ukrainian</option>
    <option id="bg">Bulgarian</option>
    <option id="zh-CN">Chinese</option>
    <option id="zh-TW">Taiwanese</option>
</select>
```

Next link to the `i18n.js` roll-up file as follows:

```
<script type="text/javascript"
  src="development-bundle/ui/i18n/jquery-ui-i18n.js"></script>
```

Now change the final `<script>` element so that it appears as follows:

```
<script type="text/javascript">
  $(function(){
    var pickerOpts = {
      beforeShow: function() {
        var lang = $(":selected", $("#language")).attr("id");
        $.datepicker.setDefaults($.datepicker.regional[lang]);
      }
    };
    $("#date").datepicker(pickerOpts);
    $.datepicker.setDefaults($.datepicker.regional['']);
  });
</script>
```

Save this file as `datePicker20.html`. We use the `beforeShow` callback to specify a function that is executed each time the datepicker is displayed on the screen. Within this function we obtain the `id` attribute of the selected `<option>` element and then pass this to the `$.datepicker.regional` option. This option is set using the `$.datepicker.setDefaults()` utility method.

When the page first loads the `<select>` element won't have a selected `<option>` child, and because of the order of the `i18n` roll-up file, the datepicker will be set to Taiwanese. In order to set it to default English, we can set the `regional` option to an empty string after the datepicker has been initialized.

The following screenshot shows the datepicker after an alternative language has been selected in the `<select>` element:

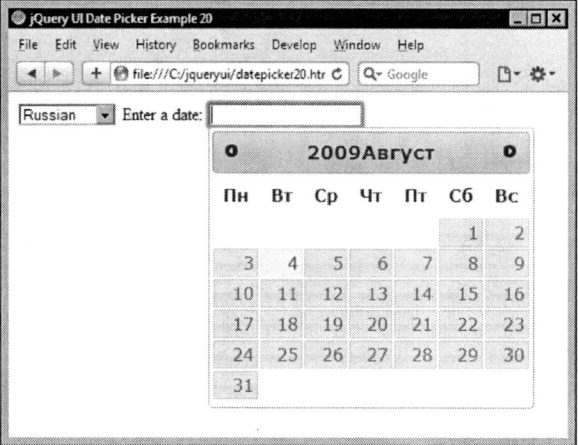

Utility methods

We used one of the utility methods available in a datepicker in the previous example — `setDefaults` is used to set configuration options on all datepicker instances. In addition to this there are several other utility methods that we can use, these are shown in the following table.

Utility	Usage

`formatDate`	This method transforms a date object into a string in a specified format. When using the `dateFormat` option dates are returned in this specified format using the `formatDate` method. This method accepts three arguments — the format to convert the date to (see `dateFormat` in Configurable options of the picker), the date object to convert, and an optional configuration object containing additional settings. The following options can be provided:
	
	`dayNamesShort`
	
	`dayNames`
	
	`monthNamesShort`
	
	`monthNames`

`iso8601Week`	This method returns the week number that a specified date falls on according to the ISO 8601 date and time standard. This method accepts a single argument — the date to show the week number.

`parseDate`	This method does the opposite of `formatDate`, converting a formatted date string into a date object. It also accepts three arguments — the expected format of the date to parse, the date string to parse, and an optional settings object containing the following options:
	
	`shortYearCutoff`
	
	`dayNamesShort`
	
	`dayNames`
	
	`monthNamesShort`
	
	`monthNames`

`setDefaults`	Set configuration options on all datepickers. This method accepts an object literal containing the new configuration options.

All of these methods are called on the singleton instance of the `$.datepicker` manager object which is created automatically by the widget on initialization and used to interact with instances of the datepicker.

Date picking methods

Along with the wide range of configuration options at our disposal, there are also a number of useful methods defined that make working with the datepicker a breeze. The datepicker API exposes the following methods.

Method	Usage
dialog	Open the datepicker in a dialog widget.
getDate	Get the currently selected date.
hide	Programmatically close a datepicker.
isDisabled	Determine whether a datepicker is disabled.
setDate	Programmatically select a date.
show	Programmatically show a datepicker.

Along with the common methods shared by all library components the datepicker also provides a range of unique methods for working with the widget programmatically including show, hide, getDate, setDate, isDisabled, and dialog.

Selecting a date programmatically

There may be times when we want to be able to set a particular date from within our program logic without the visitor using the datepicker widget in the usual way. Let's look at a basic example. Remove the <option> tags in datePicker20.html and directly after the <input> element add the following <button>:

```
<button id="select">Select +7 Days</button>
```

Now change the final <script> element so that it appears like this:

```
<script type="text/javascript">
  $(function(){
  $("#date").datepicker();

    $("#select").click(function() {

      $("#date").datepicker("setDate", "+7");
    });

  });
</script>
```

Save this as `datePicker21.html`. The `setDate` function accepts a single argument, which is the date to set. Like with the `defaultDate` configuration option, we can supply a relative string (as we do in this example), or a date object.

Showing the datepicker in a dialog

The `dialog` method produces the same highly usable and effective datepicker widget, but it displays it in a floating dialog box. The method is easy to use, but makes some aspects of using the widget non-autonomous, as we shall see. Remove the `<button>` from the page and change the final `<script>` element in `datePicker21.html` to this:

```
<script type="text/javascript">
  $(function(){
  function updateDate(date) {
    $("#date").val(date);
    }
    var pickerOpts = {
      beforeShow: function() {
        $("#ui-datepicker-div").css("zIndex",
          1000).next().css("zIndex", 950);
      }
    };
    $("#date").focus(function() {
      $(this).datepicker("dialog", null, updateDate, pickerOpts);
    });
  });
</script>
```

Save this as `datePicker22.html`. First we define a function called `updateDate`. This function will be called whenever a date is selected in the datepicker. All we do within this function is assign the date that is selected, which will be passed to the function automatically to our `<input>` element on the page.

We use a configuration object in this example and due to a minor bug we also use the `beforeShow` callback option once again. This time, our callback function needs to set the z-index of the datepicker and an `<input>` that is automatically generated by the component.

The `dialog` method that is wrapped in a focus-handler callback function, takes three arguments. The first can accept a string that is used to set the initial date of the datepicker. In this example, we've supplied `null`, so the datepicker defaults to the current date.

The second argument is a callback function to execute when a date is selected, which is mapped to our `updateDate` function. The third argument is the configuration object for the datepicker.

We can also supply a fourth argument, if we choose to, which controls the position of the dialog containing the datepicker. By default it will render the dialog in the centre of the screen.

An AJAX datepicker

For our final datepicker example, we'll work a little AJAX magic into the mix and create a datepicker. This datepicker prior to opening, will communicate with a server to see if there are any dates that cannot be selected. In a new page in your text editor, begin with the following code:

```
<!DOCTYPE HTML PUBLIC "-//W3C//DTD HTML 4.01//EN"
  "http://www.w3.org/TR/html4/strict.dtd">
<html lang="en">
  <head>
    <link rel="stylesheet" type="text/css"
      href="development-bundle/themes/smoothness/ui.all.css">
    <link rel="stylesheet" type="text/css"
      href="css/ajaxDatepicker.css">
    <meta http-equiv="Content-Type"
      content="text/html; charset=utf-8">
    <title>jQuery UI AJAX Datepicker</title>
  </head>
  <body>
    <div id="bookingForm" class="ui-widget ui-corner-all">
      <div class="ui-widget-header ui-corner-top">
        <h2>Booking Form</h2>
      </div>
      <div class="ui-widget-content ui-corner-bottom">
        <label>Appointment date:</label><input id="date">
      </div>
    </div>
    <script type="text/javascript"
      src="development-bundle/jquery-1.3.2.js"></script>
    <script type="text/javascript"
      src="development-bundle/ui/ui.core.js"></script>
    <script type="text/javascript"
      src="development-bundle/ui/ui.datepicker.js"></script>
    </script>
  </body>
</html>
```

Save this as `ajaxDatepicker.html`. Our simple example form is made from a series of container elements and a simple `<input>`. Each of the containers has class names from the CSS framework, which allow us to take advantage of the styling offered by the theme in use, helping the elements and the widget to appear consistent.

Now we can add the script that will configure and control the widget, this should go directly before the `</body>` tag:

```
<script type="text/javascript">
  $(function(){
    var months = [], days = [];
    $.getJSON(
      "http://www.danwellman.co.uk/bookedDates.php?jsoncallback=?",
      function(data) {

        for (x = 0; x < data.dates.length; x++) {
          months.push(data.dates[x].month);
          days.push(data.dates[x].day);
        }
    });
    function addDates(date){
      if (date.getDay() == 0 || date.getDay() == 6) {
        return [false, ""];
      }

      for (x = 0; x < days.length; x++) {
        if (date.getMonth() == months[x] - 1 &&
          date.getDate() == days[x]) {
            return [false, "preBooked_class"];
        }
      }

      return [true, ""];
    }
    var pickerOpts = {
      beforeShowDay: addDates,
      minDate: "+1"
    };
    $("#date").datepicker(pickerOpts);
  });
</script>
```

The first part of our script initially declares two empty arrays, and then performs an AJAX request to obtain the JSON object from a PHP file. The JSON object contains a single option called `dates`. The value of this option is an array where each item is also an object.

Each of these sub-objects contain `month` and `day` properties representing one date that should be made unselectable. The `months` or `days` array are populated with the values from the JSON object for use later in the script.

Next, we define the `addDates` callback function that is invoked on the `beforeShowDay` event. This event occurs once for each of the 35 individual day squares in the datepicker. Even the empty squares.

Our function is passed the current date and must return an array containing two items. The first is a Boolean indicating whether the day is selectable, and optionally a class name to give the date.

Our function first checks to see whether the day portion of the current date is equal to either `0` (for Sunday) or `6` (for Saturday). If it is, we return `false` as the first item in the array to make weekends unselectable.

 There is a built-in function of the manager object, `$.datepicker.noWeekends()` that automatically makes weekends unselectable. This is specified as the value of the `beforeShowDay` option when used, but we cannot use it in this example as we are providing our own callback function.

We then loop through each item in our `months` and `days` arrays to see if any of the dates passed to the callback function match the items in the arrays. If both the `month` and `day` items match a date, the array returns with `false` and a custom class name as its items. If the date does not match, we return an array containing `true` to indicate that the day is selectable. This allows us to specify any number of dates that cannot be selected in the datepicker.

Finally we define a configuration object for the datepicker. The properties of the object are simply the callback function to make the dates specified in the JSON object unselectable, and the `minDate` option will be set to the relative value `+1` as we don't want people to book dates in the past, or on the current day.

In addition to the HTML page, we'll also need a little custom styling. In a new page in your editor, create the following stylesheet:

```css
#bookingForm { width:503px; }
#bookingForm h2 { margin-left:20px; }
#bookingForm .ui-widget-content {
  padding:20px 0; border-top:none;
}
label {
  margin:4px 20px 0; font-family:Verdana; font-size:80%;
  float:left;
```

```
}
#date { width:302px; }
.ui-datepicker .preBooked_class { background:none; }
.ui-datepicker .preBooked_class span {
  color:#ffffff;
  background:url(../img/date-picker/red_horizon.gif) no-repeat;
}
```

Save this as `ajaxDatepicker.css` in the `css` folder. We use PHP to provide the JSON object in response to the AJAX request made by our page. If you don't want to install and configure PHP on your web server, you can use the file that I have placed at the URL specified in the example. For anyone that is interested, the PHP used is as follows:

```
<?php
  header('Content-type: application/json');
  $dates = "({
    'dates':[
      {'month':12,'day':2},
      {'month':12,'day':3},
      etc...
  ]})";
  $response = $_GET["jsoncallback"] . $dates;
  echo $response;
?>
```

This can be saved as `bookedDates.php` in the main `jqueryui` project folder. The pre-booked dates are just hardcoded into the PHP file. Again, in a proper implementation, you'd probably need a more robust way of storing these dates, such as in a database.

When we run the page in a browser and open the datepicker, the dates specified by the PHP file should be styled according to our `preBooked_class` and should also be completely non-responsive, as in the following screenshot:

Summary

We looked at the datepicker widget in this chapter that is supported by one of the biggest APIs in the jQuery UI library. This gives us a huge number of options to work with and methods to receive data from. We first looked at the default implementation and how much behavior is added to the widget automatically.

We looked at the rich API exposed by the datepicker, which includes more configurable options than any other component. We also saw how we can use the utility functions that are unique to the datepicker manager object.

We saw how easy the widget makes implementing internationalization. We also saw that there are thirty-four additional languages the widget has been translated into. Each of these are packed into a module that is easy to use in conjunction with the datepicker for adding support for alternative languages. We also saw how we create our own custom language configuration.

We covered some of the events that are fired during a datepicker interaction, and looked at the range of methods available for working with and controlling the datepicker from our code.

8

Progressbar

The progressbar widget is used to show the percentage complete for any arbitrary process. It's a simple and easy-to-use component with an extremely compact API, which provides excellent visual feedback to visitors.

In the current version of the component, the progressbar is purely determinate so we, or the system, must explicitly tell the widget the current amount of progress. An indeterminate progressbar is planned for a future release.

The widget is made up of just two nested `<div>` elements—an outer container `<div>` and an inner `<div>`, which is used to highlight the current progress. The following screenshot shows a progressbar that is 50% complete:

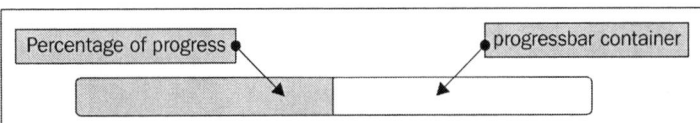

We'll look at the following aspects of the widget during this chapter:

- The default implementation
- The single configurable option
- The event API exposed by the widget
- The unique method exposed by the progressbar
- Some real-world examples

The default progressbar implementation

Let's take a look at the most basic progressbar implementation. In a new file in your text editor create the following file:

```html
<!DOCTYPE HTML PUBLIC "-//W3C//DTD HTML 4.01//EN"
  "http://www.w3.org/TR/html4/strict.dtd">
<html lang="en">
  <head>
    <link rel="stylesheet" type="text/css"
      href="development-bundle/themes/smoothness/ui.all.css">
    <meta http-equiv="Content-Type" content="text/html;
      charset=utf-8">
    <title>jQuery UI Progressbar Widget Example 1</title>
  </head>
  <body>
    <div id="progress"></div>
    <script type="text/javascript"
      src="development-bundle/jquery-1.3.2.js"></script>
    <script type="text/javascript"
      src="development-bundle/ui/ui.core.js"></script>
    <script type="text/javascript"
      src="development-bundle/ui/ui.progressbar.js"></script>
    <script type="text/javascript">
      $(function() {
        $("#progress").progressbar();
      });
    </script>
  </body>
</html>
```

Save this as `progressbar1.html` in the `jqueryui` project folder. With no configuration the progressbar is of course empty. Our example should appear like the first screenshot but without any progress displayed (the container is empty).

The progressbar depends on the following components:

- `ui.all.css`
- `jquery-1.3.2.js`
- `ui.core.js`
- `ui.progressbar.js`

All we need on the page is a simple container element. In this case we've used a `<div>` element, but other block-level elements, like a `<p>` for example, can also be used. The widget will add a nested `<div>` element to the specified container element at initialization which represents the value of the progressbar.

This widget, like some of the other widgets, such as the accordion for example, will naturally fill the width of its container. Both the container and the inner `<div>` are given a series of attributes and class names by the component. The class names pick up styling from the theme file in use and the component is fully ThemeRoller ready. The additional attributes are ARIA-compliant, making the widget fully accessible to visitors using assisted technologies. The following screenshot shows these class names and attributes as they appear in Firebug:

Using progressbar's configuration option

The progressbar has a single configuration option at the time of writing—the `value` option. This option is used to set the `value`, or percentage complete, of the current process. Setting the option at initialization is done using a standard configuration object. Change the final `<script>` element in `progressbar1.html` so that it appears like this:

```
<script type="text/javascript">
  $(function() {
    var progressOpts = {
      value: 50
    };
    $("#progress").progressbar(progressOpts);
  });
</script>
```

Save this as `progressbar2.html`. The `value` option takes an integer and sets the width of the inner `<div>` of the widget to the corresponding percentage. This change will make the widget appear as it did in the first screenshot in this chapter.

Progressbar's event API

The progressbar exposes a single event, the `change` event, which is fired by the widget every time the value of the progressbar is changed. As with the other widgets, we can supply an anonymous callback function as the value of this event in a configuration object and the component will call the function for us automatically each time the event fires.

To see this event in action, add the following `<button>` to the page in `progressbar2.html`:

```
<button id="increase">Increase by 10%</button>
```

Next change the final `<script>` block to this:

```
<script type="text/javascript">
  $(function() {
    var progressOpts = {
      change: function(e, ui) {

        var val = $(this).progressbar("option", "value");
        if(val <= 100) {
          ($("#value").length === 0) ? $("<span>").text(val + "%")
            .attr("id", "value").css({ float: "right", marginTop:
            -28, marginRight:10 }).appendTo("#progress") :
            $("#value").text(val + "%");
        } else {
          $("#increase").attr("disabled", "disabled");
        }
      }
    };
    $("#progress").progressbar(progressOpts);

    $("#increase").click(function() {

      var currentval = $("#progress").progressbar("option", "value"),
        newval = currentval + 10;

      $("#progress").progressbar("option", "value", newval);
    });
  });
</script>
```

Save this file as `progressbar3.html`. Within our callback function, specified as the value of the `change` option, we first obtain the current value of the progressbar which will correspond to the value *after* its last update.

Provided the value is less than or equal to `100` (percent) we check whether the value is already being displayed. If it isn't, we create a new `<span>` element and set its `text` content to the current value. We also give it an `id` attribute and position it so that it appears inside the progressbar. If the element already exists we just update its text to the new value. If the current value is greater than `100` we simply disable the button to prevent further clicks.

We also add a click-handler for the button we added to the page. Whenever the button is clicked we first get the current value of the progressbar by using the `option` method in `getter` mode to get the current value. We then add `10` to the value before using the `option` method in `setter` mode to increase the value of the inner `<div>` by `10` percent.

After clicking the button the page should appear like this:

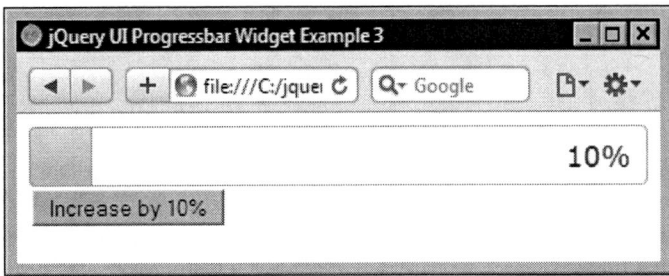

In this example, we set the value of the progressbar manually whenever the button is clicked; we use the standard `option` method, common to all UI library components to retrieve information about the current state of the progressbar.

Don't forget that like the other library components, this event can be used with jQuery's `bind()` method by prefixing the name of the widget on to the event name, `progressbarchange` in this case.

Progressbar methods

In addition to the common API methods that are exposed by all library components, such as `destroy`, `disable`, `enable`, and `option`, the slider API also exposes the `value` method which is a shortcut for using the `option` method to set the `value` of the progressbar.

For example, we can do exactly the same as we did in the last example, but with less code using the `value` method. Change the final `<script>` element in `progressbar3.html` so that it is as follows:

```
<script type="text/javascript">
  $(function() {

    $("#progress").progressbar();

    $("#increase").click(function() {

      var currentval = $("#progress").progressbar("option", "value"),
      newval = currentval + 10;

      (newval > 90) ? $(this).attr("disabled", "disabled") : null;

      if(currentval < 100) {
        $("#progress").progressbar("value", newval);
        ($("#value").length === 0) ? $("<span>").text(
          newval + "%").attr("id", "value").css({ float: "right",
          marginTop: -28, marginRight:10 }).appendTo("#progress") :
          $("#value").text(newval + "%");
      }
    });
  });
</script>
```

Save this as `progressbar4.html`. We lose the configuration object in this example as it isn't required. All of the logic for determining the current value, increasing the value using the `value` method, and disabling the button has been moved into the click handler for the `<button>` element. After increasing the value to the maximum, the page should appear as shown in the following screenshot:

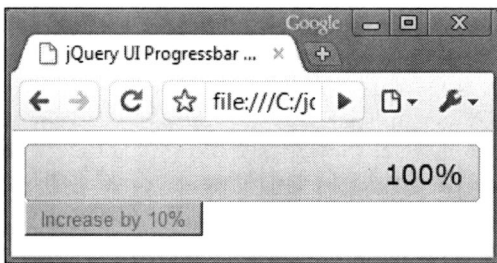

User initiated progress

At its most basic level, we can manually update the progressbar in response to user interaction. For example, we could specify a wizard-style form, which has several steps to complete. In this example, we'll create a form as shown in the following screenshot:

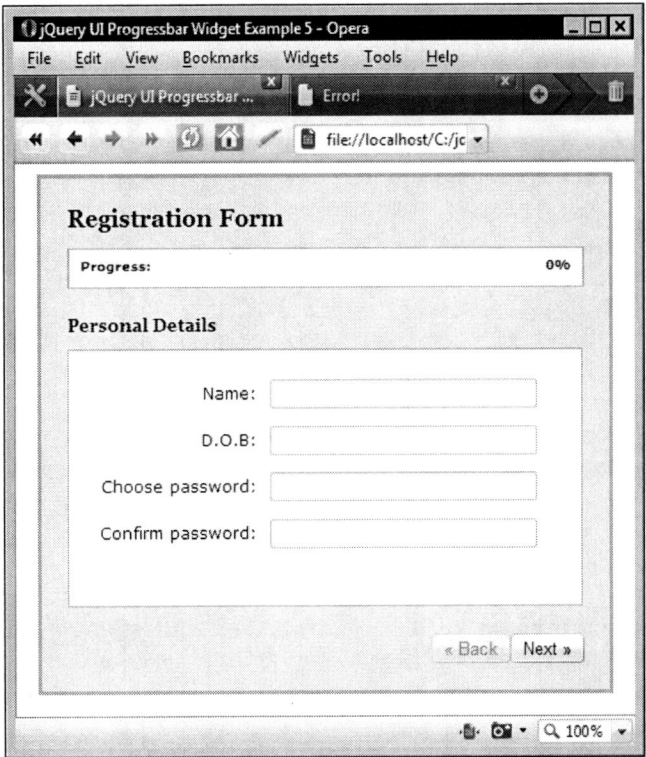

During each step we can increment the progressbar manually to let the user know how far through the process they are. In a new file in your text editor add the following code:

```
<!DOCTYPE HTML PUBLIC "-//W3C//DTD HTML 4.01//EN"
  "http://www.w3.org/TR/html4/strict.dtd">
<html lang="en">
  <head>
    <link rel="stylesheet" type="text/css"
      href="development-bundle/themes/smoothness/ui.all.css">
    <link rel="stylesheet" type="text/css"
      href="css/progressForm.css">
    <meta http-equiv="Content-Type" content="text/html;
      charset=utf-8">
    <title>jQuery UI Progressbar Widget Example 5</title>
  </head>
  <body>
    <div class="form-container ui-helper-clearfix ui-corner-all">
      <h1>Registration Form</h1>
      <p>Progress:</p>
      <div id="progress"></div><label id="amount">0%</label>
```

```
<form action="serverScript.php">
  <div id="panel1" class="form-panel">
    <h2>Personal Details</h2>
    <fieldset class="ui-corner-all">
      <label>Name:</label><input type="text">
      <label>D.O.B:</label><input type="text">
      <label>Choose password:</label><input type="password">
      <label>Confirm password:</label><input type="password">
    </fieldset>
  </div>
  <div id="panel2" class="form-panel ui-helper-hidden">
    <h2>Contact Details</h2>
    <fieldset class="ui-corner-all">
      <label>Email:</label><input type="text">
      <label>Telephone:</label><input type="text">
      <label>Address:</label><textarea rows="3"
                      cols="25"></textarea>
    </fieldset>
  </div>
  <div id="thanks" class="form-panel ui-helper-hidden">
    <h2>Registration Complete</h2>
    <fieldset class="ui-corner-all">
      <p>Thanks for registering!</p>
    </fieldset>
  </div>
  <button id="next">Next &raquo;</button><button id="back"
    disabled="disabled">&laquo; Back</button>
</form>
</div>
<script type="text/javascript"
  src="development-bundle/jquery-1.3.2.js"></script>
<script type="text/javascript"
  src="development-bundle/ui/ui.core.js"></script>
<script type="text/javascript"
  src="development-bundle/ui/ui.progressbar.js"></script>
<script type="text/javascript">

</script>
</body>
</html>
```

Save this as `progressbar5.html`. In the `<head>` section we link to the framework theme files as we have done with the other examples in this chapter, and a custom stylesheet that we'll add in a moment.

The <body> of the page contains a few layout elements and some text nodes, but the main elements are the container for the progressbar and the <form>. The <form> is separated into several different sections using <div> and <fieldset> elements. The reason for this is so that we can hide part of the form to make it appear as if it spans several pages.

We've added a paragraph and a label next to the progressbar. We'll position these so that they appear inside the widget. The paragraph contains a simple text string. The label will be used to show the current progress value.

The outer container is given several class names; the first is so that we can apply some custom styling to the element, but the next two are to target different features of the CSS framework. The ui-helper-clearfix class is used to automatically clear floated elements and is a great way of reducing the clutter of additional and unnecessary <div> elements. Don't forget to make explicit use of this and other framework classes when creating your own widgets.

The ui-corner-all class is used to give the container element (as well as the progressbar itself which has them automatically, and our <fieldset> elements) rounded corners using several proprietary style rules. These are only supported by Gecko and Webkit-based browsers, but in the nature of progressive enhancement it is perfectly acceptable to use them.

We use another class from the CSS framework within the form. Several panels need to be hidden when the page first loads, we can therefore make use of the ui-helper-hidden class to ensure that they are set to display:none, when we want to show them, all we have to do is remove this class name.

Now let's add the JavaScript. In the empty <script> element at the bottom of the page add the following code:

```
$(function() {
   var progressOpts = {
     change: function() {
        $("#amount").text($("#progress").progressbar("option", "value")
          + "%");
     }
   }
   var prog = $("#progress");
   prog.progressbar(progressOpts);
   $("#next").click(function(e) {
      e.preventDefault();
      $(".form-panel").each(function() {
```

```
        var thePanel = $(this);
        (thePanel.attr("id") != "panel1") ? null :
          $("#back").attr("disabled", "");
        (thePanel.hasClass("ui-helper-hidden")) ? null :
          thePanel.fadeOut("fast", function() {
          thePanel.addClass("ui-helper-hidden").next().fadeIn(
            "fast", function() {
            ($(this).attr("id") != "thanks") ? null :
              $("#next").attr("disabled", "disabled");
            $(this).removeClass("ui-helper-hidden");
           prog.progressbar("option", "value",
             prog.progressbar("option", "value") + 50);
        });
      });
    });
  });
```

We first define our configuration object, making use of the change event to specify an anonymous callback function. Each time the event is fired we'll grab the current value of the progressbar using the option method and set it as the text of the label. The event is fired after the change takes place, so the value we obtain will always be the new value.

Following this we have a click handler for the **Next** button. When this button is clicked it will result in the form of the current page changing, via a series of animations, and the value of the progressbar updating. We also need to do a few other things. The default behavior of a <button> inside a form is to submit the form, which we don't want to do at this stage so the first thing our click handler does is prevent the form being submitted using the preventDefault() JavaScript function. This is called on the event object (e), which is automatically passed to the event callback function.

We then look through each of the separate panels in the form to determine the current panel. The first thing we do is check that the current panel is not the first panel and if it isn't, we enable the **Back** button, which is disabled by default. Only one panel will be displayed at one time, so we find the panel that doesn't have the ui-helper-hidden class and fade it out. We specify an anonymous callback function to execute once the fade finishes.

Within this second function we select the next element and show it. If the next element is the final panel, which has an id of thanks, we disable the **Next** button. Although we don't worry about actual submission of the form in this example, this is where we could send the data gathered from the form to the server. We remove the ui-helper-hidden class as the panel is now visible.

Finally we use the option method once again, this time in setter mode, to set the new value of the progressbar. The new value, that we pass to the method as the second parameter is simply the current value plus 50, as there are just two parts of the form. This last part will then trigger the function which updates the label.

Next we need to add a very similar click handler for the **Back** button. The only real differences are that we show the previous panel, and take 50 away from the value:

```
$("#back").click(function(e) {
  e.preventDefault();
  $(".form-panel").each(function() {
    var thePanel = $(this);
    (thePanel.attr("id") != "thanks") ? null :
      $("#next").attr("disabled", "");
    (thePanel.hasClass("ui-helper-hidden")) ? null :
      thePanel.fadeOut("fast", function() {
        thePanel.addClass("ui-helper-hidden").prev().fadeIn(
          "fast", function() {
          ($(this).attr("id") != "panel1") ? null :
            $("#back").attr("disabled", "disabled");
          $(this).removeClass("ui-helper-hidden");
          prog.progressbar("option", "value",
            prog.progressbar("option", "value") - 50);
        });
      });
  });
});
```

This is now all of the code that we'll need, all we have to do now is add some basic CSS to lay the example out; in a new file in your text editor add the following code:

```
h1, h2 { font-family:Georgia; font-size:140%; margin-top:0; }
h2 { font-size:100%; margin:20px 0 10px; text-align:left; }
.form-container {
  width:400px; margin:0 auto; position:relative; font-family:Verdana;
  font-size:80%; padding:20px; background-color:#e0e3e2;
  border:3px solid #abadac;
}
.form-panel { width:400px; height:241px; }
.form-panel fieldset {
  width:397px; height:170px; margin:0 auto; padding:22px 0 0;
  border:1px solid #abadac; background-color:#ffffff;
}
.form-panel label {
  width:146px; display:block; float:left; text-align:right;
  padding-top:2px; margin-right:10px;
```

```
}
.form-panel input, .form-panel textarea {
  float:left; width:200px; margin-bottom:13px;
}
.form-container button { float:right; }
p {
  margin:0; font-size:75%; position:absolute; left:30px; top:60px;
  font-weight:bold;
}
#amount {
  position:absolute; right:30px; top:60px; font-size:80%;
  font-weight:bold;
}
#thanks { text-align:center; }
#thanks p {
  margin-top:48px; font-size:160%; position:relative; left:0; top:0;
}
```

Save this as `progressForm.css` in the `css` directory. We should now have a working page with a wired up progressbar. When we run the page we should find that we can navigate through each panel of the form, and the progressbar will update itself accordingly:

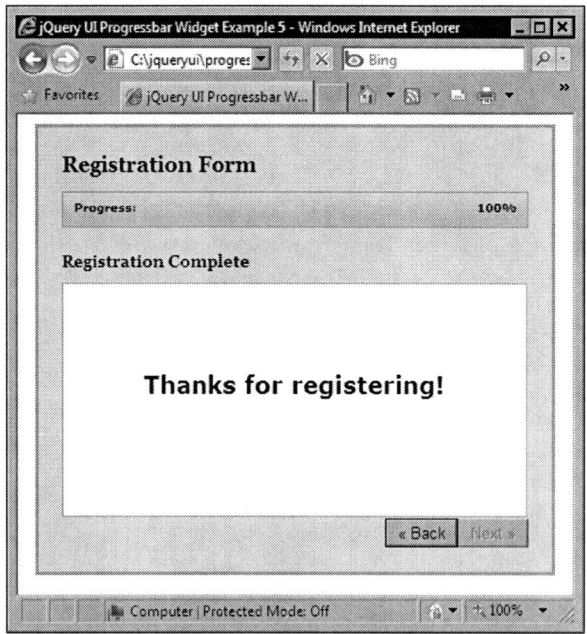

We're still relying on user interaction to set the value of the progressbar in this example, which is driven by the visitor navigating through each of the panels.

Rich uploads with progressbar

Instead of relying on user interaction to increase the value of the progressbar and therefore the completion of the specified task, we can instead rely on the system to update it; deterministic means simply that *something* must be able to update it accurately.

In our final progressbar example we can incorporate the brand-new HTML5 file API in order to upload a file asynchronously, and can use Firefox's propriety `onprogress` event to update the progressbar while the file is uploading. This example will only work in Firefox 3+ at the time of writing, although hopefully more browsers will make use of both the file API and the `onprogress` event in the future.

This example will also only work correctly using a full web server with PHP installed and configured. We won't be looking at the server side of the upload process in this example, we're not interested in what happens to the file once it's been uploaded, only in updating the progressbar based on feedback received from the system.

Begin with the following new HTML page:

```
<!DOCTYPE HTML>
<html lang="en">
  <head>
    <link rel="stylesheet" type="text/css"
      href="development-bundle/themes/smoothness/ui.all.css">
    <link rel="stylesheet" type="text/css"
      href="css/progressUpload.css">
    <meta http-equiv="Content-Type" content="text/html;
      charset=utf-8">
    <title>jQuery UI Progressbar Widget Example 6</title>
  </head>
  <body>
    <h2>AJAX File Upload</h2>
    <input type="file" id="file" />
    <div id="progress"></div>
    <script type="text/javascript"
      src="development-bundle/jquery-1.3.2.js"></script>
    <script type="text/javascript"
      src="development-bundle/ui/ui.core.js"></script>
    <script type="text/javascript"
      src="development-bundle/ui/ui.progressbar.js"></script>
    <script type="text/javascript">
    </script>
  </body>
</html>
```

Save this as `progressbar6.html`. We use the HTML5 DOCTYPE in this example and on the page we have an `<input>` of the type `file` followed by the container for the progressbar. Next let's add the script, in the empty `<script>` element at the end of the `<body>` add the following code:

```
$(function() {
  $("#progress").progressbar();
  $("#file").change(function() {
    var files = $("#file").attr("files"),
      file = files[0],
      xhr = new XMLHttpRequest();

    xhr.upload.onprogress = function updateProgress(e) {
    var loaded = (e.loaded / e.total);
    $("#progress").progressbar("value", Math.round(loaded * 100));
  }
  $("<span>").addClass("filename").text(file.fileName).insertAfter(
    "#progress");

    xhr.open("POST", "progressUpload.php");
    xhr.sendAsBinary(file.getAsBinary());
  });
});
```

First of all we initialize the progressbar in the usual way. Next we add an anonymous function that hooks into the `change` event of the `<input>` which will be triggered when a file is selected (after clicking the **Browse** button that is automatically added next to the `<input>`).

Within this callback we first need to get the file that has been selected, which will be available via the `files` attribute of the `<input>`. Multiple files can be selected, but this example doesn't cover that so we just get the first file from the `files` collection.

Next we create a new `XMLHttpRequest` object and then set an anonymous callback function as the value of the `onprogress` property. The function will be executed each time the event is fired. Within this function, we calculate the percentage of upload by dividing the amount uploaded so far by the total amount to upload. These details are available through the event object (`e`) which is automatically passed to the function.

Once we've established what the percentage of upload is, we can update the value of the progressbar using the `value` method. The value stored in the `loaded` variable will be a number between 0 and 1 so we need to times it by 100 to get the correct percentage. We can also round the number to the nearest decimal point using JavaScript's `Math.round` method.

Next we display the filename of the file being uploaded next to the progressbar. We don't need to do this but it's a good example of how the `file` object can to used to obtain information about the selected file before the upload has even taken place. Finally we can open a POST connection to the server and send the file to the server. Using the `file` API we can send the file as a binary file using the `getAsBinary` and `sendAsBinary` methods.

We also need a tiny bit of CSS for this example; in a new file add the following code:

```
#file { float:left; }
#progress.ui-progressbar {
  height:1em; width:221px; margin-top:5px; float:left;
  clear:left;
}
.filename {
  float:left; margin:7px 0 0 10px; font-family:Verdana;
  font-size:12px;
}
```

This can be saved in the `css` folder as `progressUpload.css`. Mostly the styles just position the different elements and set the `width` of the progressbar.

We link to a PHP file in this example, although this isn't strictly necessary. Even an empty PHP file will prevent 404 errors once he file has been uploaded.

When we run this file in Firefox, we should see that once a file has been selected, it will automatically begin to upload and the progressbar will begin to fill up. If testing locally, it will be pretty quick so it's best tested with reasonably large files. The next screenshot shows the upload in progress.

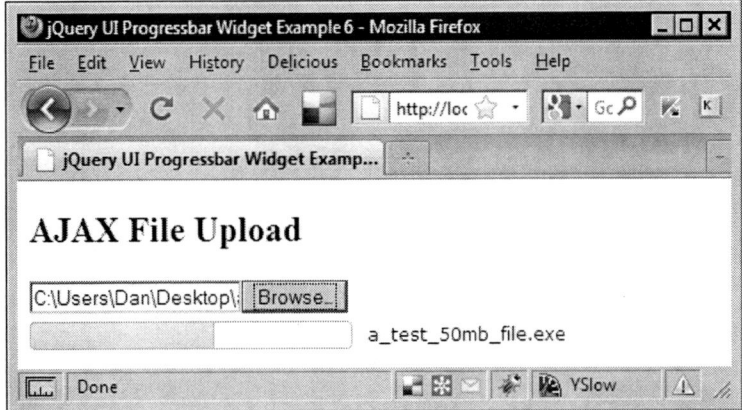

Summary

Despite its compact API, the progressbar widget makes a great addition to the library, providing essential visitor feedback when processes are in progress. The component is useful in any situation where the percentage complete of the process can reliably be updated by the system.

After looking at the default implementation we moved on to take a look at the `value` option and how it can be used; we can set the `value` prior to initialization using a configuration object, and we can set it after initialisation using the `option` method.

Next we looked at the `change` event, which is fired by the widget whenever its `value` is changed. Using the standard way of hooking into the event with an anonymous callback function within our configuration object we can easily react to the amount of progress changing.

We saw that in addition to the standard API methods such as `destroy`, the widget also exposes the `value` method, which can be used as a shortcut to setting the value using the `option` method.

Although the current version of this widget is purely deterministic, a future release will include support for an indeterminate progress indicator for use when the current status of the process cannot be accurately determined. This is currently quite a young widget compared to some of the other components so its API is sure to mature and grow in forthcoming releases.

This now brings us to the end of the section about the widgets of the library. We've now looked at each of the widgets in turn and worked with their APIs to familiarise ourselves with their configuration options, methods, and events. We're now going to move on to look at the interaction helpers.

9
Drag and Drop

So far in this book, we've covered the complete range of fully released interface widgets and over the next four chapters we're going to shift our focus to the core interaction helpers. These components of the library differ from those that we've already looked at in that they are not physical objects or widgets that exist on the page.

Instead, they give an object a set of generic behaviors to suit common implementational requirements for dynamic and engaging websites. You don't actually see these components on the page, but the effects that they add to different elements, and how they cause them to behave can be easily seen. These are low-level components as opposed to the high-level widgets that we looked at in the first part of this book. There are currently five different interaction helpers, each catering for a specific interaction.

They help the elements used on your pages to be more engaging and interactive for your visitors, which adds value to your site and can help make your web applications appear more professional. They also help to blur the distinction between the browser and the desktop as application platforms.

In this chapter, we'll be covering two very closely related components—draggables and droppables. The draggables API transforms any specified element into something that your visitors can pick up with the mouse pointer and drag around the page. Methods are exposed that allow you to restrict the draggables movement, make it return to its starting point after being dropped, and much more.

The droppables API allows you to define a region of the page, or a container of some kind, for people to drop the draggables on to in order to make something else happen. For example, to define a choice that is made or add a product to a shopping basket. A rich set of events are fired by the droppable that lets us react to the most interesting moments of any drag interaction.

The full range of topics we'll be covering in this chapter are:

- How to make elements draggable
- The options available for configuring draggable objects
- How to make an element return to its starting point once the drag ends
- How to use event callbacks at different points in an interaction
- The role of a drag helper
- Containing draggables
- How to control draggability with the component's methods
- Turning an element into a drop target
- Defining accepted draggables
- Working with droppable class names
- Defining drop tolerance
- Reacting to interactions between draggables and droppables

The deal with drag and droppables

Dragging and dropping, as behaviors, go hand-in-hand with each other. Where one is found, the other is invariably close by. Dragging an element around a web page is all very well, but if there's nowhere for that element to be dragged to, then the whole exercise is usually pointless.

You can use the draggable class independently from the droppable class as pure dragging for the sake of dragging can have its uses, such as with the dialog component. However, you can't use the droppable class without the draggable. You don't need to make use of any of draggable's methods of course, but using droppables without having anything to drop onto them is of no value whatsoever.

Like with the widgets, it is possible however to combine some of the interaction helpers, draggables and droppables go together obviously. But draggables can also be used with sortables, as we'll see in *Chapter 12*.

Draggables

The draggables component is used to make any specified element or collection of elements draggable, so that they can be 'picked up' and moved around the page by a visitor. Draggability is a great effect, and is a feature that can be used in numerous ways to improve the interface of our web pages.

Using jQuery UI means that we don't have to worry about all of the tricky differences between browsers that originally made draggable elements on web pages a nightmare to implement and maintain.

A basic drag implementation

Let's look at the default implementation by first making a simple `<div>` element draggable. We won't do any additional configuration. Therefore, all this code will allow you to do is 'pick up' the element with the mouse pointer and drag it around the viewport.

In a new file in your text editor, add the following code:

```
<!DOCTYPE HTML PUBLIC "-//W3C//DTD HTML 4.01//EN"
  "http://www.w3.org/TR/html4/strict.dtd">
<html lang="en">
  <head>
    <link rel="stylesheet" type="text/css" href="css/draggable.css">
    <meta http-equiv="Content-Type"
      content="text/html; charset=utf-8">
    <title>jQuery UI Draggable Example 1</title>
  </head>
  <body>
    <div id="drag"></div>
    <script type="text/javascript"
      src="development-bundle/jquery-1.3.2.js"></script>
    <script type="text/javascript"
      src="development-bundle/ui/ui.core.js"></script>
    <script type="text/javascript"
      src="development-bundle/ui/ui.draggable.js"></script>
    <script type="text/javascript">
      $(function() {
        $("#drag").draggable();
      });
    </script>
  </body>
</html>
```

Save this as `draggable1.html` in your `jqueryui` folder. As with the widget-based components of jQuery UI, the draggable component can be enabled using a single line of code. This invokes the draggable's constructor method `draggable` and turns the specified element into a drag object.

We need the following files from the library to enable draggability:

- `jquery-1.3.2.js`
- `ui.core.js`
- `ui.draggable.js`

We're using a plain `<div>` with a background image specified in the CSS file that we're linking to in the `<head>` of the page. Use the following stylesheet for the drag element:

```css
#drag {
    background:url(../img/drag-drop/draggable.png) no-repeat;
    width:114px;
    height:114px;
    cursor:move;
}
```

Save this as `draggable.css` in the `css` folder. When you view the page in a browser, you'll see that the image can be moved around to your heart's content, as shown in the following screenshot:

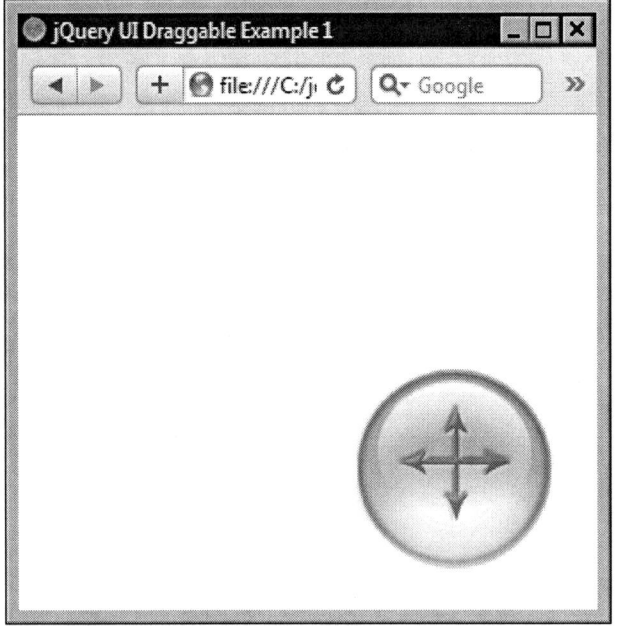

Configuring draggable options

The draggable component has a wide range of configurable options, giving you a very fine degree of control over the behavior that it adds. The following table lists the options that we can manipulate to configure and control our drag elements.

Option	Default	Usage
addClasses	true	Adds the ui-draggable class to the drag object. Set to false to prevent this class being added.
appendTo	"parent"	Specifies a container element for drag objects with a helper attached.
axis	false	Constrains drag objects to one axis of motion. Accepts the strings x and y as values, or the Boolean false.
cancel	":input, option"	Prevents certain elements from being dragged if they match the specified element selector.
connectToSortable	false	Allows the drag object to be dropped on to a sortable list and become one of the sort elements. Accepts a jQuery selector that matches a sortable list.
containment	false	Prevents drag objects from being dragged out of the bounds of its parent element.
cursor	"auto"	Specifies a CSS cursor to be used while the pointer is over the drag object.
cursorAt	false	Specifies a default position at which the cursor appears relative to the drag object while it is being dragged.
delay	0	Specifies a time in milliseconds that the start of the drag interaction should be delayed.
distance	1	Specifies the distance in pixels that the pointer should move with the mouse button held down on the drag object before the drag begins.
grid	false	Makes the drag object snap to an imaginary grid on the page. Accepts an array containing x and y pixel values of the grid.
handle	false	Defines a specific area of the drag object that is used to hold the pointer on in order to drag.
helper	"original"	Defines a pseudo-drag element that is dragged in place of the drag object. Can accept the string values original, or clone, or can accept a function that returns the helper element.

Option	Default	Usage
iframeFix	false	Applies a shim to all `<iframe>` elements on the page to prevent them from capturing mouse events while a drag is in progress. Can also accept a selector, in which case only matching `<iframe>` elements will have the shim applied.
opacity	false	Sets the opacity of the helper element.
refreshPositions	false	Calculates the positions of all drop objects while the drag is in progress. Can impact performance.
revert	false	Makes the drag object return to its start position once the drag ends when set to true. Can also accept the strings valid and invalid where revert only applies if the drag object is dropped on a drop object or vice-versa respectively.
revertDuration	500	Sets the number of milliseconds it takes for the drag object to return to its starting position.
scope	"default"	Sets the scope of the drag object with respect to the drop objects that are valid for it. Supply a selector to set the scope.
scroll	true	Makes the viewport automatically scroll when the drag object is moved within the threshold of the viewport's edge.
scrollSensitivity	20	Defines how close in pixels the drag object should get to the edge of the viewport before scrolling begins.
scrollSpeed	20	Sets the speed at which the viewport scrolls.
snap	false	Causes drag objects to snap to the edges of specified elements.
snapMode	"both"	Can be set to either inside, outside, or both, and refers to the edges of the element to which the drag object will snap.
snapTolerance	20	The distance from snapping elements that drag objects should reach before snapping occurs.
stack	false	When set ensures the current drag object is always on top of other drag objects in the same group. Accepts an object containing group and/or min options.
zIndex	false	Sets the zIndex of the helper element.

Using the configuration options

Let's put some of these options to use. They can be configured in exactly the same way as the options exposed by the widgets that we looked at in previous chapters, and also usually have both getter and setter modes.

In the first example a moment ago, we used CSS to specify that the move cursor should be used when the pointer hovers over our draggable <div>. Let's change this and use the cursor option of the draggables component instead.

Remove cursor:move from draggable.css and resave it as draggableNoCursor. css. Also change the <link> tag in draggable1.html to the following:

```
<link rel="stylesheet" type="text/css"
  href="css/draggableNoCursor.css">
```

Then change the final <script> element to the following:

```
<script type="text/javascript">
  $(function() {
    var dragOpts = {
      cursor: "move"
    };
    $("#drag").draggable(dragOpts);
  });
</script>
```

Save this as draggable2.html and try it out in your browser. An important point to note about this option is that the move cursor we have specified is not applied until we actually start the drag. When using this option in place of simple CSS, we should perhaps provide some other visual cue that the element is draggable on mouseover.

Let's look at a few more of draggable's many properties. Change the configuration object in draggable2.html to the following:

```
var dragOpts = {
  cursor: "move",
  axis: "y",
  distance: "30",
  cursorAt: {
    top: 0,
    left: 0
  }
};
```

This can be saved as `draggable3.html`. The first new option that we've configured is the `axis` option, which has restricted the draggable to moving only up or down the page, but not side-to-side.

Next, we've specified `30` as the value of the `distance` option. This means that the cursor will have to travel 30 pixels across the drag object, with the mouse button held down, before the drag will begin.

The final option, `cursorAt`, is configured using an object literal whose properties can be `top`, `right`, `bottom`, or `left`. The values supplied to the properties we choose to use are the values relative to the drag object that the cursor will assume when a drag occurs.

However, you'll notice in this example that the value for the `left` option seems to be ignored. The reason for this is that we have configured the `axis` option. When we begin the drag, the drag object will automatically move so that the cursor is at `0` pixels from the `top` of the element, but it will not move so that the cursor is `0` pixels from the `left` edge as we have specified because the drag object cannot move left.

 Let's look at some more of draggable's options in action. Change `draggable3.html` so that the configuration object appears as follows:

```
var dragOpts = {
    delay: "1000",
    grid: [100,100]
};
```

Save the file as `draggable4.html`. The `delay` option that takes a value in milliseconds, configures the time that the mouse button must be held down with the cursor over the drag object before the drag will begin.

The `grid` option is similar in usage to the `steps` option of the slider widget. It is configured using an array of two values representing the number of pixels along each axis the drag element should jump when it is dragged. This option can be used safely in conjunction with the `axis` option.

Resetting dragged elements

It is very easy to configure drag objects to return to their original starting position on the page once they've been dropped, and there are several options that can be used with this behavior. Change the configuration object we used with `draggable4.html` so that it appears as follows:

```
var dragOpts = {
    revert: true
};
```

Save this as `draggable5.html`. By supplying `true` as the value of the `revert` option, we've caused the drag object to return to its starting position at the end of any drag interaction. However, you'll notice that the drag element doesn't just pop back to its starting position instantly. Rather, it's smoothly animated back with no additional configuration required.

Another revert-related option is the `revertDuration` option, which we can use to control the speed of the revert animation. Change the configuration object in `draggable5.html` so that it appears as follows:

```
var dragOpts = {
    revert: true,
    revertDuration: 100
};
```

Save this as `draggable6.html`. The default value for the `revertDuration` is 500 milliseconds, so by lowering it to 100, the relative speed of the animation is considerably increased.

The actual speed of the animation will always be determined on the fly, based on the distance from the drop point to the starting point. The `revertDuration` option simply defines a target for the animation length.

Drag handles

The `handle` option allows us to define a region of the drag object that can be used to drag the object. All other areas cannot be used to drag the object. A simple analogy is the dialog widget. You can drag the dialog around only if you click and hold on the title bar. The title bar is the drag handle.

In the following example, we'll add a simple drag handle to our drag object. Put a new empty `<div>` element inside the drag element.

```
<div id="drag"><div id="handle"></div></div>
```

Then change the configuration object to this:

```
var dragOpts = {
    handle: "#handle"
};
```

Save this as `draggable7.html`. We've given the new `<div>` an `id` attribute. We have then specified this `id` as the value of the `handle` option in our configuration object.

The handle is styled with a few simple style rules. Create a new stylesheet and add to it the following code:

```css
#drag {
  background:url(../img/drag-drop/draggable.png) no-repeat;
  width:114px; height:114px;
}
#handle {
  border-bottom:2px solid #ff0000;
  border-left:2px solid #ff0000;
  position:absolute;
  right:10px; top:10px;
  width:30px; height:30px;
  cursor:move;
}
```

Save this as `dragHandle.css` in the `css` folder. When we run the page in a browser, we see that the original drag object is still draggable, but only when the handle is selected with the pointer as seen in the following figure:

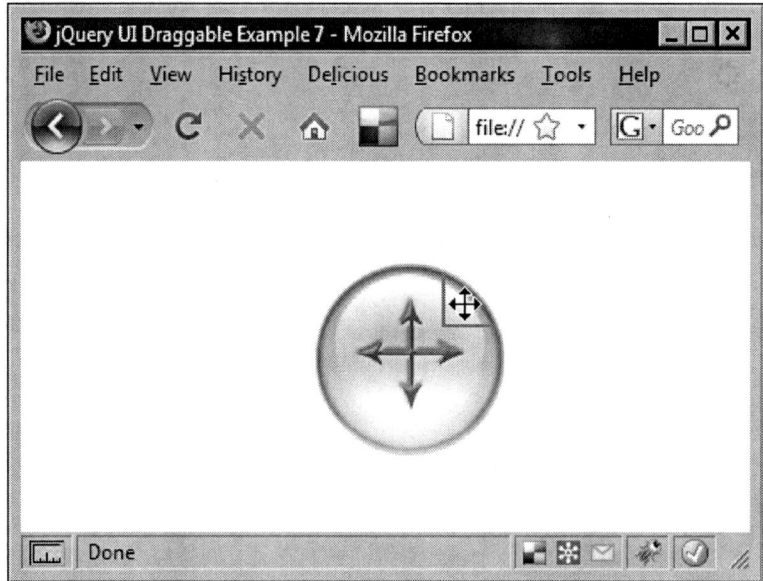

Helper elements

Several configuration options are directly related to drag helpers. A **helper** is a substitute element that is used to show where the object is on screen while the drag is in progress, instead of moving the actual draggable.

A helper can be used with a very simple object in place of the actual drag object. This can help cut down on the intensity of the drag operation, lessening the load on the visitor's computer. Once the drag has completed, the actual element can be moved to the new location.

Let's look at how helpers can be used in the following example. Change the configuration object in `draggable7.html` to the following:

```
var dragOpts = {
   helper: "clone"
};
```

Save this file as `draggable8.html`. The value `clone` for the `helper` option causes an exact copy of the original drag object to be created and used as the draggable. Therefore, the original object stays in its starting position at all times. Don't forget to remove the `<div>` element we added as the handle in the previous example.

This also causes the clone object to revert back to its starting position, an effect which cannot be changed, even by supplying `false` as the value of the `revert` option. The following screenshot shows the `clone` option in action:

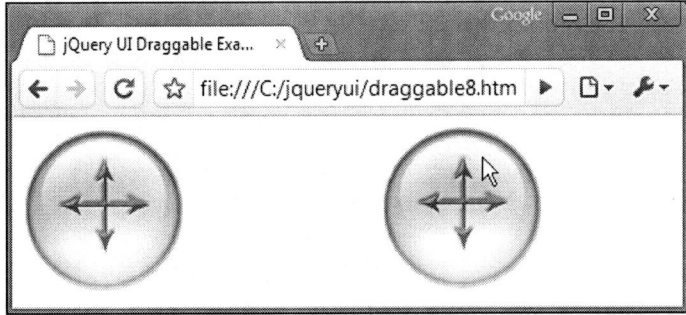

Using the clone value will not help reduce the intensity of the drag operation, but it does have other uses. For example, the drag object may be a product that can be dragged into a shopping basket. The visitor may want several instances of the same product, so using `clone` means that we don't have to create a new drag object each time a product is added to the basket.

In addition to the `clone` string and the default string value of `original`, we can also use a function as the value of this option. This allows us to specify our own custom element to use as the helper. Change the final `<script>` element in `draggable8.html` to the following:

```
<script type="text/javascript">
   $(function() {
      function helperMaker() {
```

```
        return $("<div>").css({
          border: "4px solid #cccccc",
          opacity: "0.5",
          height: "110px",
          width: "120px"
        });
      }

      var dragOpts = {
        helper:helperMaker
      };
      $("#drag").draggable(dragOpts);
    });
  </script>
```

Save this file as `draggable9.html`. Our `helperMaker()` function creates a new `<div>` element using standard jQuery functionality, and then sets some CSS properties on it to define its physical appearance. It then, importantly, returns the new element. When supplying a function as the value of the `helper` option, the function must return an element.

Now, when the drag begins, it is our custom helper that becomes the drag object. Because our custom element is much simpler than the original drag object, it can help improve the responsiveness and performance of the application it is used in. The following screenshot shows our custom helper:

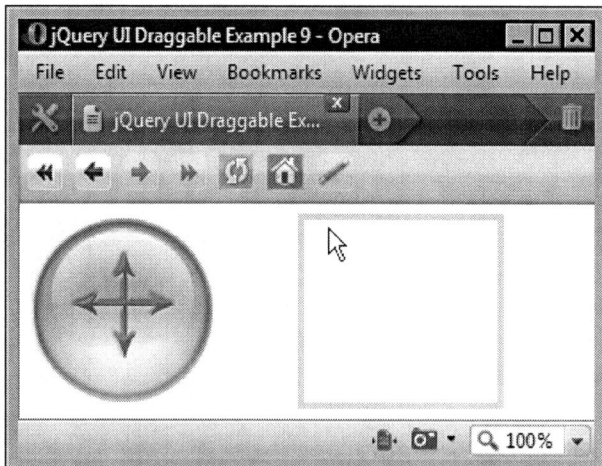

Helper opacity

We used the css jQuery method in this example during the creation of the custom helper. However, we can also use the opacity option of the drag object to set the opacity of helper elements as a cross-platform solution.

Constraining the drag

Another aspect of drag scenarios is that of containment. In our examples so far, the `<body>` of the page has been the container of the drag object. There are also options that we can configure to specify how the drag object behaves with regard to another container element.

We'll look at these in the following examples, starting with the `container` option which allows us to specify a container element for the drag object. In the `<head>` of `draggable9.html` add a link to the stylesheet we'll be using in this example.

```
<link rel="stylesheet" type="text/css"
  href="css/draggableContainer.css">
```

Then wrap the drag element within a container `<div>` as follows:

```
<div id="container"><div id="drag"></div></div>
```

Then change the configuration object to the following:

```
var dragOpts = {
  containment: "parent"
};
```

Save this variant as `draggable10.html`. On the page, we've added a new `<div>` element as the parent of the existing drag element. In the code, we've used the value `parent` for the `containment` option, so the element that is the direct parent of the drag object (the `<div>` with the `id` of `container` in this example) will be used as the container.

The parent `<div>` needs some basic styling to give it dimensions and so it can be seen on the page. Add the following line of code to `draggable.css` and resave the file as `draggableContainer.css`.

```
#container {
  height:250px; width:250px;
  border:2px solid #ff0000;
}
```

When you run the page in your browser, you'll see that the drag object cannot exceed the boundary of its container.

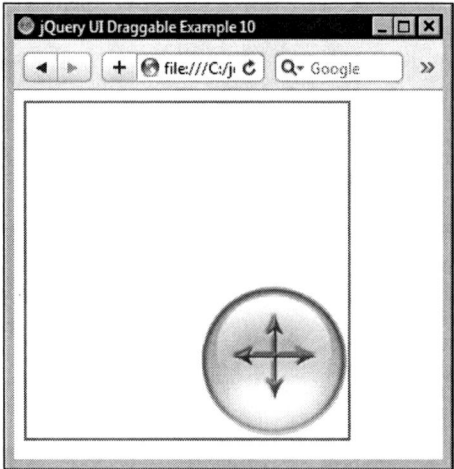

Along with the string parent that we used in this example, we could also specify a selector, like the following:

```
var dragOpts = {
   containment: "#container"
};
```

There are three additional options related to drag objects within containers and these are all related to scrolling. However, you should note that these are only applicable when the document is the container.

The default value of the `scroll` option is `true`, but when we drag the `<div>` to the edge of the container, it does not scroll. You may have noticed in previous examples, where the drag object was not within a specified container, the viewport automatically scrolled. We can fix this by setting the CSS `overflow` option to `auto` in a stylesheet if necessary.

Snapping

Drag elements can be given an almost magnetic quality by configuring snapping. This feature causes dragged elements to align themselves to specified elements while they are being dragged. There are three options related to snapping. They are:

- snap
- snapMode
- snapTolerance

In the next example, we'll look at the effects that these options have on the behavior of the drag object when they are configured. Get rid of the container we added in the previous example, and add a new empty `<div>` element directly after the drag element like as follows:

```
<div id="drag"></div>
<div id="snapper"></div>
```

Then change the configuration object so that it appears as follows:

```
var dragOpts = {
    snap: "#snapper",
    snapMode: "inner",
    snapTolerance: 50
};
```

Save this as `draggable11.html`. We've supplied the selector `#snapper` as the value of the `snap` option, and have added a `<div>` element with a matching `id` to the page. Therefore, our drag object will snap to this element on the page while the object is being dragged.

We also set the `snapMode` option to `inner` (the other possible values are `outer` and `both`), so snapping will occur on the inside edges of our snapper element. If you drag the element towards the outer edge of the snapper element and get within the tolerance range, the element will snap to the inner edge.

Finally, we've set the `snapTolerance` to `50`, which is the maximum distance (in pixels) the drag object will need to get to the snapper element before snapping will occur. As soon as a drag object is within this range it will snap to the element.

Now, when you drag the image within `50` pixels of an edge of the snapper element, the drag object will automatically align itself to that edge, as shown in the following screenshot:

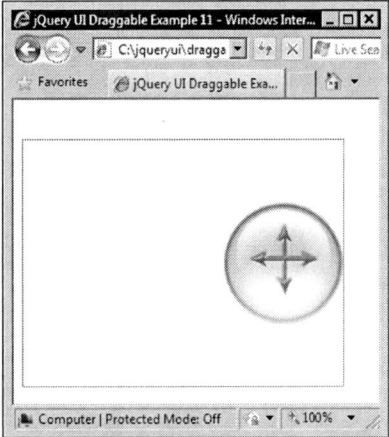

Draggable event callbacks

In addition to the options that we have already looked at, there are three more that can be used as callback functions to execute code after specific custom events, defined by the draggables component, occur. These events are listed below.

Option	Triggered
drag	When the mouse is moved while dragging.
start	When dragging starts.
stop	When dragging stops.

When defining callback functions to make use of these events, the functions will always receive two arguments automatically. The original event object as the first argument and a second object containing the following properties:

Option	Usage
helper	A jQuery object representing the helper element.
position	A nested object with properties top and left of the helper element relative to the original drag element.
absolutePosition	A nested object with properties top and left of the helper element relative to the page.

Using the callbacks, and the two objects that are passed as arguments, is extremely easy. We can look at a brief example to highlight their usage. Remove the snapper `<div>` in `draggable11.html` and change the final `<script>` element to as follows:

```
<script type="text/javascript">
  $(function() {
      function setShadow() {
        $("#drag").css({ background:
          "url(img/drag-drop/draggable_on.png)",
          width:"120px", height:"121px" });
      }
      function unsetShadow() {
        $("#drag").css({ background:
          "url(img/drag-drop/draggable.png)",
          width:"114px", height:"114px" });
      }
    var dragOpts = {
      start: setShadow,
      stop: unsetShadow
    };
    $("#drag").draggable(dragOpts);
  });
</script>
```

Save this as `draggable12.html`. In this example, our configuration object contains just two options—the `start` and `stop` callbacks. We set these values to our callback function names.

All the functions do in this example are simple image swaps. When the `start` callback is invoked, the background image of the drag object is switched for one containing a drop shadow. When the `stop` callback is invoked, the image is swapped back to the original image with no shadow. The following screenshot shows the drop shadow:

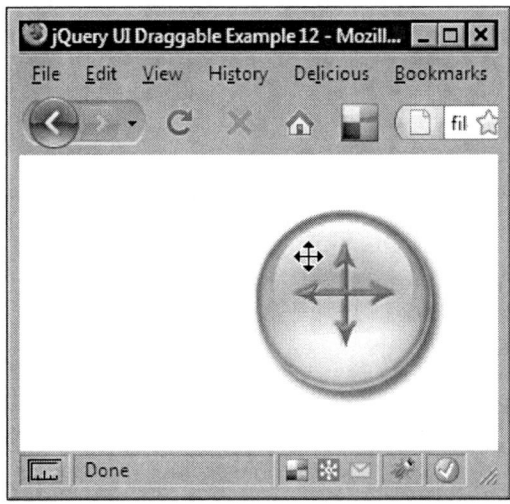

Using the callbacks in this way is just one example of how the usability of the drag object is improved with a visual cue that indicates the object is currently in a draggable state.

Let's move on to a slightly more complex example where we can make use of the second object passed to our callbacks. We need a couple of new elements on the page, change the `<body>` of the page so that it appears as follows:

```
<div id="container">
  <div id="drag"></div>
</div>
<div id="results"></div>
    <script type="text/javascript">
      $(function() {
        var dragOpts = {
          stop: getNewPos
        };
        function getNewPos(e, ui) {
          e.stopPropagation();
```

```
              var relativeP = $("<p>").attr("id", "test").text("The
                 helper was moved to " + ui.position.top + "px down, and "
                 + ui.position.left + "px to the left of its original
                 position.");
              var offset = $("<p>").attr("id", "test").text("The helper
                 was moved to " + ui.offset.top + "px from the top, and "
                 + ui.offset.left + "px to the left relative to the
                 viewport.");
              $("#results").empty().append(relativeP).append(offset);
           }
           $("#drag").draggable(dragOpts);
        });
      </script>
   </body>
</html>
```

Save this as `draggable13.html`. We've defined the `getNewPos` callback function as
the value of the `stop` option, so it will be executed each time a drag interaction stops.

Our callback function receives an object `e` that is the event object (which we don't
need but must specify in order to access the second object), and `ui` for the jQuery UI
object containing useful information about the drag object.

All our callback function does is create two new paragraphs, concatenating
the values found in the object passed to the function as the second argument-
`ui.position.top`, `ui.position.left`, `ui.offset.top`, and `ui.offset.left`.
It then inserts the new `<p>` elements into the results `<div>`.

This examples requires the following simple stylesheet:

```
#container {
  width:450px; height:250px;
  position:relative; top:50px; left:50px;
  border:1px solid #ff0000;
}
#drag {
  width:114px; height:114px; cursor:move;
  background:url(../img/drag-drop/draggable.png) no-repeat;
}
#results { position:relative; top:50px; left:50px; }
p { font-size:80%; }
```

This should be saved as `draggableIndented.css` in the `styles` folder. We've
positioned the drag objects container away from the edge of the page to highlight
the differences between the `position` and `offset` properties of the `ui` object. Here's
how it should look after dragging to the bounds of the container.

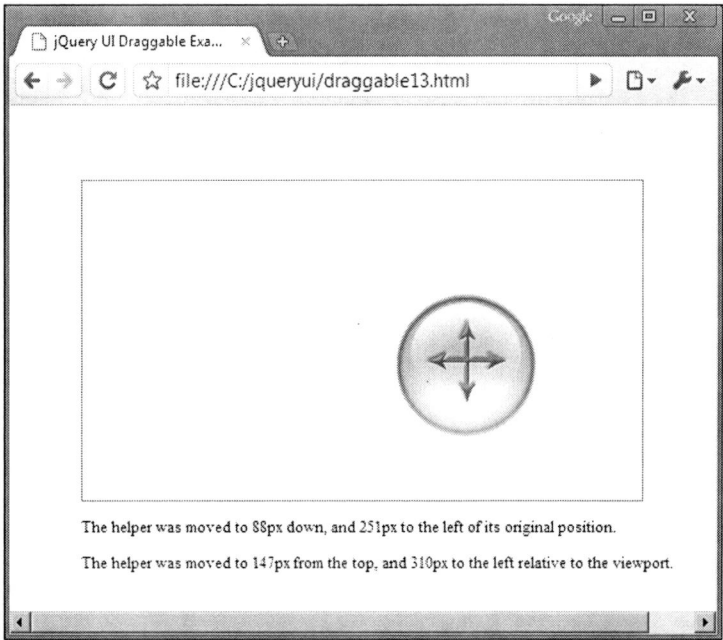

The helper was moved to 88px down, and 251px to the left of its original position.

The helper was moved to 147px from the top, and 310px to the left relative to the viewport.

Using draggable's methods

Draggable uses only the four common API methods:

- `destroy`
- `disable`
- `enable`
- `option`

These methods are used in the same way as the methods for the widgets that we've already used, for clarification of how these methods work, see Chapter 1.

Droppables

In a nutshell, the droppables component of jQuery UI gives you a place for drag objects to be dropped. A region of the page is defined as a droppable and when a drag object is dropped onto that region, something else is triggered. You can react to drops on a valid target very easily using the extensive event model.

Let's start with the default droppable implementation. In a new file in your text editor, add the following page:

```html
<!DOCTYPE HTML PUBLIC "-//W3C//DTD HTML 4.01//EN"
  "http://www.w3.org/TR/html4/strict.dtd">
<html lang="en">
  <head>
    <link rel="stylesheet" type="text/css" href="css/droppable.css">
    <meta http-equiv="Content-Type" content="text/html;
      charset=utf-8">
    <title>jQuery UI Droppable Example 1</title>
  </head>
  <body>
    <div id="drag"></div>
    <div id="target"></div>
    <script type="text/javascript"
      src="development-bundle/jquery-1.3.2.js"></script>
    <script type="text/javascript"
      src="development-bundle/ui/ui.core.js"></script>
    <script type="text/javascript"
      src="development-bundle/ui/ui.draggable.js"></script>
    <script type="text/javascript"
      src="development-bundle/ui/ui.droppable.js"></script>
    <script type="text/javascript">
      $(function() {
        $("#drag").draggable();
        $("#target").droppable();
      });
    </script>
  </body>
</html>
```

Save this as droppable1.html. The extremely basic stylesheet that is linked to in this example is simply an updated version of draggable.css and appears as follows:

```css
#drag {
  background:url(../img/drag-drop/draggable.png) no-repeat;
  width:114px; height:114px;
  cursor:move; margin-bottom:5px;
  z-index:2;
}
#target {
  width:200px; height:200px;
  border:3px solid #000;
  position:absolute;
  right:20px; top:20px;
  z-index:1;
}
```

Save this as `droppable.css` in the `css` folder. When run the page in a browser, the page should look like the following screenshot:

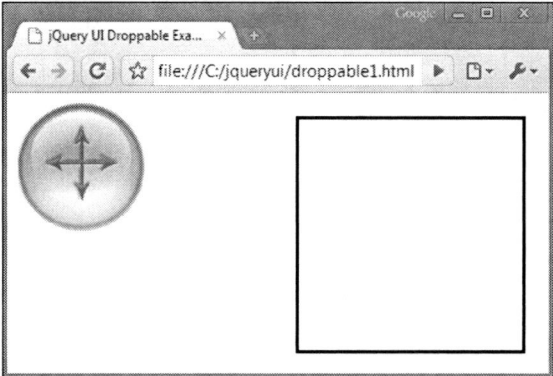

In this example, the droppable is created (we can see this with the class name `ui-droppable` that is added to the specified element when the page loads).

Even though we haven't added any additional logic to our script, events are firing throughout the interaction on both the drag object and the drop target. A little later in the chapter we'll look at these events in more detail to see how we can hook into them to react to successful drops.

The files we used for this basic droppable implementation are:

- `jquery-1.3.2.js`
- `ui.core.js`
- `ui.draggable.js`
- `ui.droppable.js`

As you can see, the droppables component is an extension of draggables, rather than a completely independent component. Therefore, it requires the `ui.draggable.js` file in addition to its own source file. The reason our droppable does nothing is that we haven't configured it, so let's do that next.

Configuring droppables

The droppable class is considerably smaller than the draggables class and there are less configurable options for us to play with. The following table lists those options available to us:

Option	Default	Usage
accept	'*'	Sets the element(s) that the droppable will accept.
activeClass	false	The class that is applied to the droppable while an accepted drag object is being dragged.
addClasses	true	Adds the ui-droppable class to the droppable.
greedy	false	Used to stop drop events from bubbling when a drag object is dropped onto nested droppables.
hoverClass	false	The class that is applied to the droppable while an accepted drag object is within the boundary of the droppable.
scope	'default'	Defines sets of drag objects and drop targets.
tolerance	intersect	Sets the mode that triggers an accepted drag object being considered over a droppable.

In order to get a visible result from configuring the droppable, we're going to use a couple of these options together in the following example that will highlight the drag object that is accepted by the droppable. Change the elements on the page in droppable1.html so that they appear as follows:

```
<div class="drag" id="drag1"></div>
<div class="drag" id="drag2"></div>
<div id="target"></div>
```

Next change the final `<script>` element to this:

```
<script type="text/javascript">
  $(function() {
    $(".drag").draggable();
    var dropOpts = {
      accept: "#drag1",
      activeClass: "activated"
    };
    $("#target").droppable(dropOpts);
  });
</script>
```

Save this as droppable2.html. The accept option takes a selector. In this example, we've specified that only the drag object that has an id of drag1 should be accepted by the droppable.

We've also specified the class name `activated` as the value of the `activeClass` option. This class name will be applied to the droppable when the accepted drag object starts to be dragged. The `hoverClass` option can be used in exactly the same way to add styles when an accepted drag object is over a droppable.

We need a new stylesheet for this example, modify `droppable.css` so that it appears as follows:

```
#drag, .drag {
  width:114px; height:114px;
  background:url(../img/drag-drop/draggable.png) no-repeat;
  cursor:move; margin-bottom:5px; z-index:2;
}
#target {
  width:200px; height:200px; border:3px solid #000;
  position:absolute; right:20px; top:20px; z-index:1;
}
.activated {
  border:3px solid #339900; background-color:#ccffcc;
}
```

Save this in the `css` folder as `droppableActive.css` and link to it in the `<head>` of the page.

```
<link rel="stylesheet" type="text/css"
  href="css/droppableActive.css">
```

When we view this page in a browser, we should find that as we move the first drag object that is defined as accepted, the droppable picks up the `activated` class and turns green. However, when the second drag object is moved, the drop target does not respond. The following screenshot shows how the page should look whilst the first drag object is being dragged:

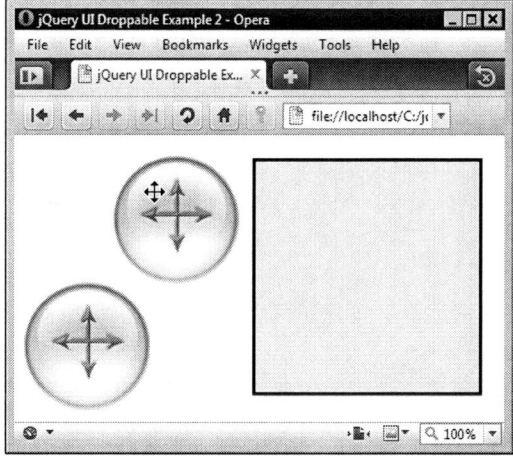

In addition to a string value, the `accept` option can also take the name of a function as its value. This function will be executed once for every drag object that is on the page. The function must return either `true`, to indicate that the drag object is accepted, or `false` to indicate that it's not.

To see the function value of the `accept` option in action change the final `<script>` element in `droppable2.html` to the following:

```
<script type="text/javascript">
  $(function() {
    $(".drag").draggable();
    function dragEnrol(el) {
      return (el.attr("id") == "drop1") ? true : false;
    }
    var dropOpts = {
      accept: dragEnrol,
      activeClass: "activated"
    };
    $("#target").droppable(dropOpts);
  });
</script>
```

Save this variation as `droppable3.html`. On the surface, the page works exactly the same as it did in the previous example. But this time, acceptability is being determined by the JavaScript ternary statement within the `dragEnrol` function, instead of a simple selector.

Note that the function is automatically passed an object containing useful data about the drag object as an argumental. This makes it is easy to obtain information about it, like its `id` as in this example. This callback can be extremely useful when advanced filtering, beyond a simple selector, is required.

Tolerance

Drop tolerance refers to the way a droppable detects whether a drag object is over it or not. The default value is `intersect`. The following table lists the modes that this option may be configured with:

Mode	Implementation
fit	The drag object must be completely within the boundary of the droppable for it to be considered over it.
intersect	At least 25% of the drag object must be within the boundary of the droppable before it is considered over it.
pointer	The mouse pointer must touch the droppable boundary before the drag object is considered over the droppable.
touch	The drag object is over the droppable as soon as an edge of the drag object touches an edge of the droppable.

So far, all of our droppable examples have used `intersect`, the default value of the `tolerance` option. Let's see what difference the other values for this option make to an implementation of the component. Revert back to the drag and target elements from `droppable1.html` and then use the following configuration object:

```
var dropOpts = {
  hoverClass: "activated",
  tolerance: "pointer"
};
```

Save this as `droppable4.html` and don't forget to link to the `droppableActive.css` stylesheet that we used in the previous two examples. This time we use the `hoverClass` option to specify the class name that is added to the droppable. We then use the `tolerance` option to specify which tolerance mode is used (see previous table).

The part of the drag object that is over the droppable is irrelevant in this example, it is the mouse pointer that must cross the boundary of the droppable while a drag is in progress for our `over` class to be activated.

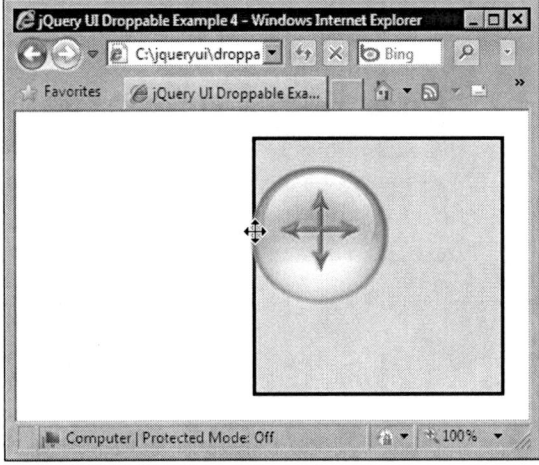

For good measure, the following screenshot shows how the `touch` mode works. Here, the drag element itself need only to touch the edge of the droppable before triggering our `over` class:

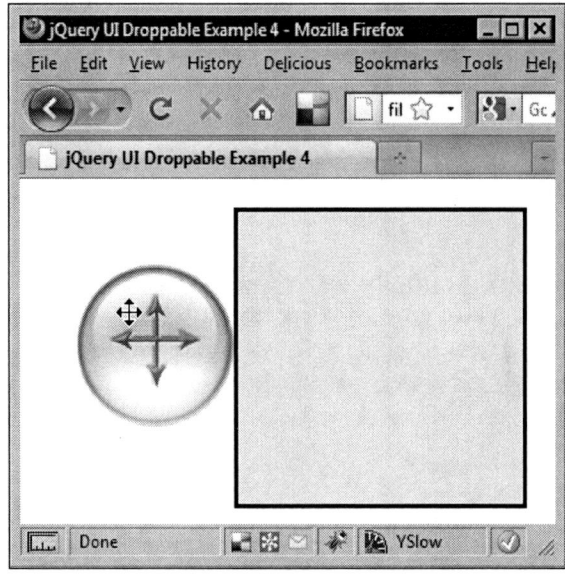

Droppable event callbacks

The options that we've looked at so far configure various operational features of the droppable. In addition to these, there are almost as many callback options so that we can define functions that react to different things occurring to the droppable and its accepted drag objects. These options are listed below.

Callback option	Invoked
activate	When an accepted drag object begins dragging.
deactivate	When an accepted drag object stops being dragged.
drop	When an accepted drag object is dropped onto a droppable.
out	When an accepted drag object is moved out of the bounds (including the tolerance) of the droppable.
over	When an accepted drag object is moved within the bounds (including the tolerance) of the droppable.

Let's put together a basic example that makes use of these callback options. We'll add a status bar to our droppable that reports the status of different interactions between the drag object and the droppable. In `droppable4.html` add the following new element directly after the `target` element.

```
<div id="status"></div>
```

Then change the final `<script>` element to this:

```
<script type="text/javascript">
  $(function() {
    $("#drag").draggable();
    var eventMessages = {
      dropactivate: "A draggable is active",
      dropdeactivate: "A draggable is no longer active",
      drop: "An accepted draggable was dropped on the droppable",
      dropout: "An accepted draggable has been moved out of the
        droppable",
      dropover: "An accepted draggable is over the droppable"
    };
    function eventCallback(e) {
      var message = $("<p>").attr("id",
        "message").text(eventMessages[e.type]);
      $("#status").empty().append(message);
    }
    var dropOpts = {
      accept: "#drag",
      activate: eventCallback,
      deactivate: eventCallback,
      drop: eventCallback,
      out: eventCallback,
      over: eventCallback
    };
    $("#target").droppable(dropOpts);
  });
</script>
```

Save this file as `droppable5.html`. The `<body>` of the page contains, along with the droppable, a new status bar, which in this case is a simple `<div>` element.

Next we define an object literal in which the key for each property is set to one of the event types that may be triggered. The value of each property is the message that we want to display for any given event.

We then define our callback function. Like other components, the callback functions used in the droppables component are automatically passed two objects — the `event` object and an object representing the drag element.

We use the `type` property of the event object to retrieve the appropriate message from the `eventMessages` object. This is the same way we would access an associative array. We then use standard jQuery element creation and manipulation methods to add the message to the status bar.

Our configuration object has all of the callback options defined, and for efficiency, they all point to the same function.

We also need some new styles for this example. Create a new stylesheet in your text editor and add the following selectors and rules:

```css
#drag {
    background:url(../img/drag-drop/draggable.png) no-repeat;
    width:114px;  height:114px;
    cursor:move;
    margin-bottom:5px;
    z-index:2;
}
#target {
    width:250px;  height:200px;
    border:3px solid #000;
    position:absolute;
    right:20px;  top:20px;
    z-index:1;
}
#status {
    width:230px;
    border:3px solid #000;
    position:absolute;
    top:223px;  right:20px;
    color:#000;
    padding:10px;
}
#message {
    margin:0px;
    font-size:80%;
}
```

Here's how the status bar should look like following an interaction:

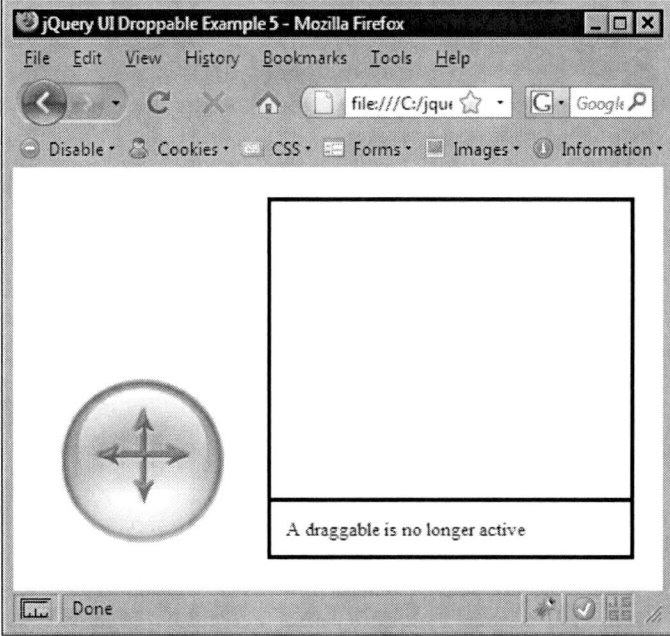

After playing around with the page for some time, we see that one of our messages does not appear to be working. When the drag object is dropped onto the droppable, our `drop` message does not appear.

Actually, the message does appear, but because the `deactivate` event is fired immediately after the `drop` event, the `drop` message is overwritten right away. There are a number of ways we could work around this, the simplest would be not to define the `deactivate` option.

Although we only make use of the event object in this example, a second object is also passed automatically to our callback functions. This object contains information relevant to the droppable such as:

Option	Value
ui.draggable	The current drag object.
ui.helper	The current drag helper.
ui.position	The current relative position of the helper.
ui.offset	The current absolute position of the helper.

Scope

Both the draggables and droppables feature the `scope` configuration option that allows us to easily define groups of drag objects and drop targets. In this next example we can look at how these options can be configured and the effect that configuring them has. We'll link to another new stylesheet in this example, so in the `<head>` of `droppable5.html` add the following code:

```
<link rel="stylesheet" type="text/css" href="css/droppableScope.css">
```

We need a number of new elements for this example. Change the `<body>` of the page in `droppable5.html` so that it contains the following elements:

```
<div id="target_a">A</div>
<div id="target_b">B</div>
<div id="group_a">
  <p>A</p>
  <div id="a1" class="group_a">a1</div>
  <div id="a2" class="group_a">a2</div>
  <div id="a3" class="group_a">a3</div>
</div>
<div id="group_b">
  <p>B</p>
  <div id="b1" class="group_b">b1</div>
  <div id="b2" class="group_b">b2</div>
  <div id="b3" class="group_b">b3</div>
</div>
```

To make these elements behave correctly change the final `<script>` element to the following:

```
<script type="text/javascript">
  $(function() {
    var dragOpts_a = {
      scope: "a"
    }
    var dragOpts_b = {
      scope: "b"
    }
    $(".group_a").draggable(dragOpts_a);
    $(".group_b").draggable(dragOpts_b);
    var dropOpts_a = {
      hoverClass: "over",
      scope: "a"
    }
    var dropOpts_b = {
      hoverClass: "over",
      scope: "b"
    }
    $("#target_a").droppable(dropOpts_a);
```

```
        $("#target_b").droppable(dropOpts_b);
    });
  </script>
 </body>
</html>
```

Save this file as `droppable6.html`. The page has two drop targets and two groups of three drag objects, all of which are labeled to show the group they belong to. In the script we define two configuration objects for the two groups of draggables, and two configuration objects for the drop targets. Within each object we set the `scope` option.

The values we set for the scope of each drop target matches the scopes of each drag object. Therefore, if we want to use scope, it must be defined for both the drag object and drop target. If we try to set the `scope` of a droppable but don't give at least one drag object the same `scope` an error is thrown.

Setting the scope gives us another technique for defining which drag objects are accepted by which drop targets, but it is provided as an alternative to the accept option—the two options should not be used together. Next we need to create the CSS file, so in a new page in your text editor add the following code:

```css
#target_a, #target_b, #group_a, #group_b {
  width:150px; height:150px; float:left;
  border:2px solid black; margin:0 20px 20px 0;
  font-family:Georgia; font-size:100px; color:red;
  padding:50px; text-align:center;
}
#group_a, #group_b {
  width:518px; height:115px; margin-bottom:20px; clear:both;
  padding:5px 0 5px 5px;
}
p { float:left; margin:0 20px 0; }
.group_a, .group_b {
  width:94px; height:94px;
  background:url(../img/drag-drop/draggable.png) no-repeat;
  float:left; margin-right:20px; font-family:arial;
  font-size:14px; color:red; text-align:left;
  padding:20px 0 0 20px;
}
.over { background-color:#ccffcc; }
```

Save this as `droppableScope.css` in the `css` folder.

The following screenshot shows how the page should appear:

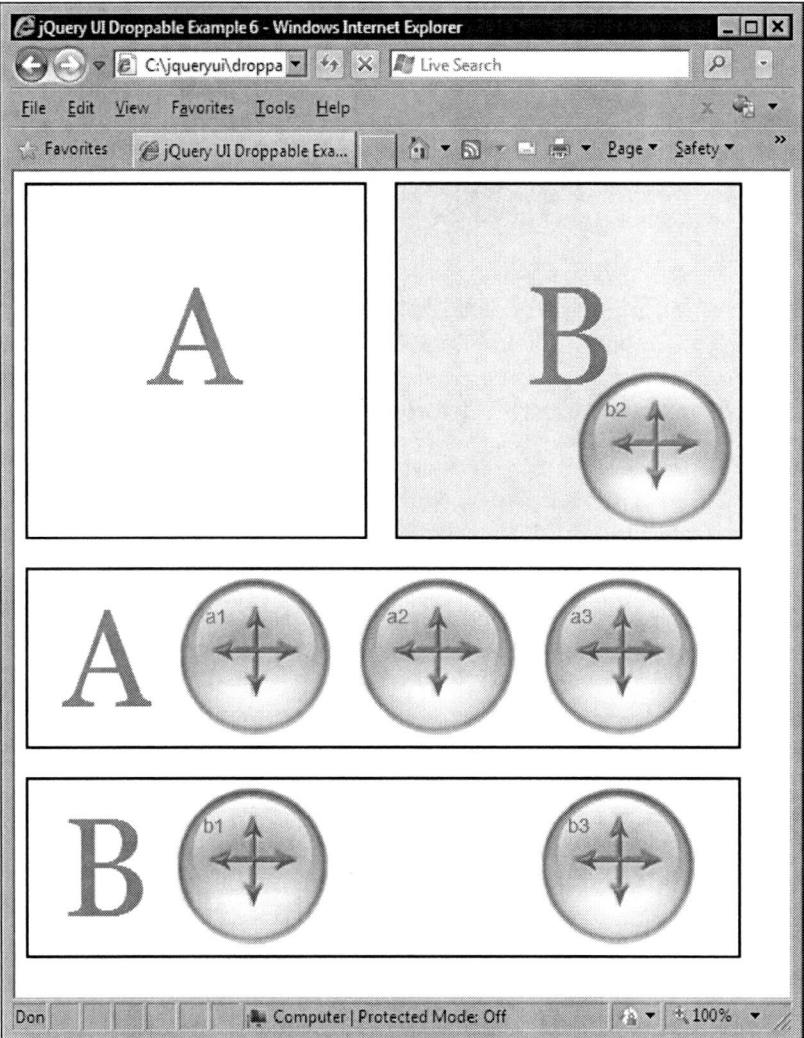

Greedy

The final option that we are going to look at in connection with the droppable component is the `greedy` option. This option can be useful in situations where there is a droppable nested within another droppable. If we don't use this option, both droppables will fire events during certain interactions.

The `greedy` option is an easy way to avoid event-bubbling problems in an efficient and cross-browser manner. Let's take a closer look at this option with an example. Create a new page in your text editor and add the following code to it:

```
<!DOCTYPE HTML PUBLIC "-//W3C//DTD HTML 4.01//EN" "http://www.w3.org/
TR/html4/strict.dtd">
<html lang="en">
  <head>
    <link rel="stylesheet" type="text/css"
      href="css/droppableNesting.css">
    <meta http-equiv="Content-Type" content="text/html;
      charset=utf-8">
    <title>jQuery UI Droppable Example 6</title>
  </head>
  <body>
    <div id="drag"></div>
    <div class="target" id="outer">
      <div class="target" id="inner"></div>
    </div>
    <div id="status"></div>
    <script type="text/javascript"
      src="development-bundle/jquery-1.3.2.js"></script>
    <script type="text/javascript"
      src="development-bundle/ui/ui.core.js"></script>
    <script type="text/javascript"
      src="development-bundle/ui/ui.draggable.js"></script>
    <script type="text/javascript"
      src="development-bundle/ui/ui.droppable.js"></script>
    <script type="text/javascript">
      $(function() {
        $(".target").css({ opacity:"0.5" });
        var dragOpts = {
          zIndex: 3
        };
        $("#drag").draggable(dragOpts);
        function dropCallback(e) {
          var message = $("<p>").attr("id", "message").text("The
            firing droppable was " + e.target.id);
          $("#status").append(message);
        }
        var dropOpts = {
          drop:dropCallback,
          greedy:true
        };

        $(".target").droppable(dropOpts);
      });
    </script>
  </body>
</html>
```

Save this example as `droppable7.html`. In this example, we have a smaller droppable nested in the center of a larger droppable. Their opacity is set using the standard jQuery library's `css()` method. In this example, this is necessary because if we alter the `zIndex` of the elements, so that the drag object appears above the nested droppables, the target element is not reported correctly.

We didn't get to see the `zIndex` option of the draggables component in the first part of this chapter, but we can see it in action in this example instead. The drag object will have the specified `zIndex` applied to it whilst it is being dragged. Once it has been dropped, it will appear to be under the droppables.

The `dropCallback` function is used to add a simple message to the status bar notifying us which droppable was the `target` of the drop.

Our droppables configuration object uses the `drop` option to wire up our callback function. However, the key option is the `greedy` option that makes whichever target the draggable is dropped on to stop the event from escaping into other targets.

The CSS for this example is simple and builds on the CSS of previous examples.

```css
#drag {
  background:url(../img/drag-drop/draggable.png) no-repeat;
  width:114px; height:114px;
  cursor:move;
  margin-bottom:5px;
}
#outer {
  width:300px; height:300px;
  border:3px solid #000;
  position:absolute;
  right:20px; top:20px;
  background-color:#99FF99;
}
#inner {
  width:100px; height:100px;
  border:3px solid #000;
  position:relative;
  top:100px; left:100px;
  background-color:#FFFF99;
}
#status {
  width:280px;
  border:3px solid #000;
  position:absolute;
  top:323px; right:20px;
  color:#000;
```

```
      padding:10px;
  }
  #message {
    margin:0px;
    font-size:80%;
  }
```

Save this as `droppableNesting.css` in the `css` folder. If you run the page, and drop the drag object onto one of the droppables, you should see something as shown in the following screenshot:

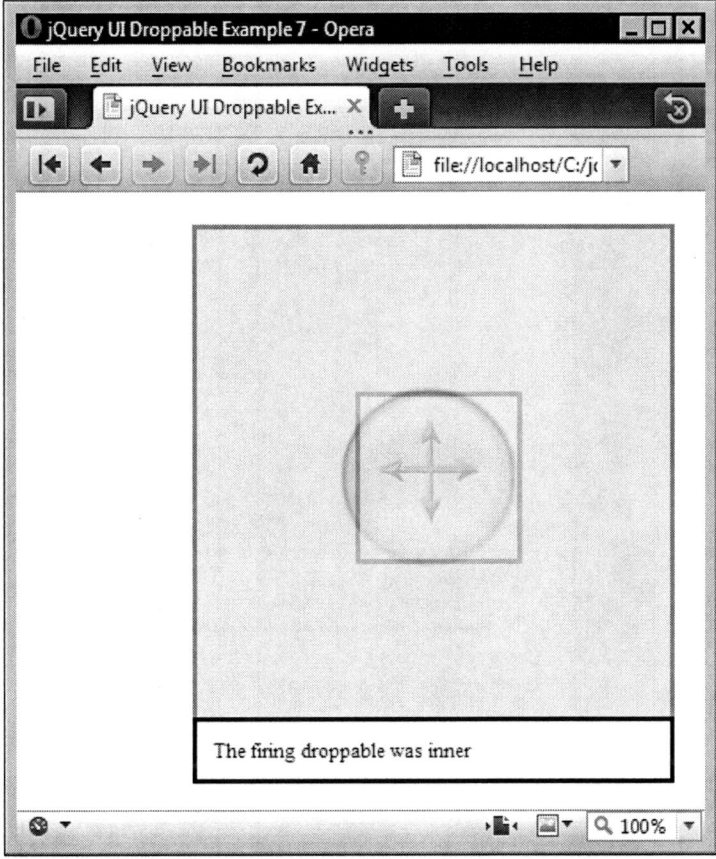

The net effect of setting the `greedy` option to `true` is that the inner droppable prevents the event from propagating into the outer droppable and firing again. If you comment out the `greedy` option and drop the draggable onto the inner droppable, the status message will be inserted twice, once by the inner droppable and once by the outer droppable. Without this option set, the page would look like this following a drop on the inner target:

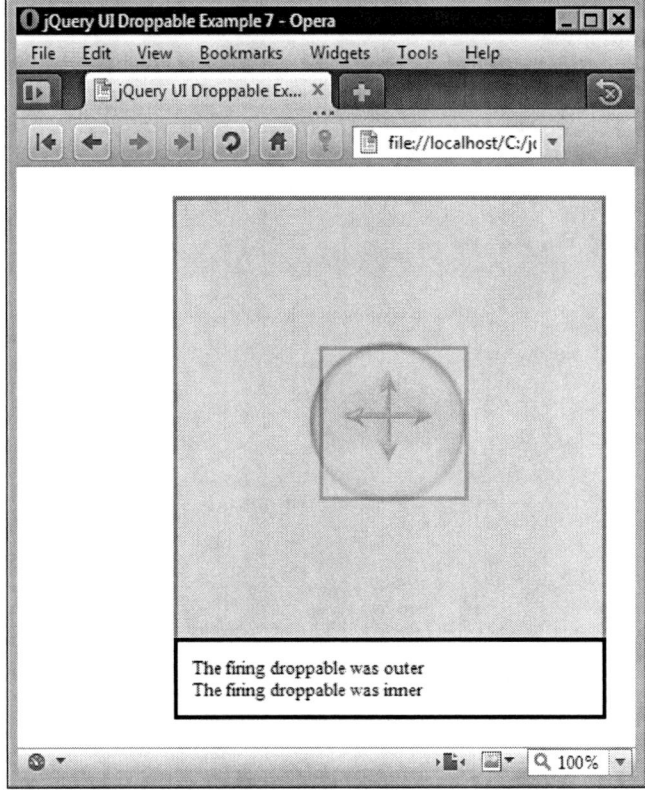

Droppable methods

Like the draggable component, droppable has only the common API methods shared by all library components. This is another component that is primarily option-driven. The methods available to us are the same ones exposed by draggable:

- `destroy`
- `disable`
- `enable`
- `option`

They function, and are used in exactly the same way as the methods exposed by draggables. We can temporarily disable the droppable using the `disable` method, re-enable the droppable with `enable`, and permanently remove (at least for the duration of the session) functionality with `destroy`. The `option` method is again used to get or set any option after initialization.

A drag and drop game

We've now reached the point where we can have a little fun by putting what we've learned about these two components into a fully working example. In our final drag and drop example, we're going to combine both of these components to create a simple maze game. The game will consist of a draggable marker that will need to be navigated through a simple maze to a specified droppable at the other end of the maze. We can make things a little more challenging, so that if any of the maze walls are touched by the marker it will return to the starting position.

The following screenshot shows what we're going to build:

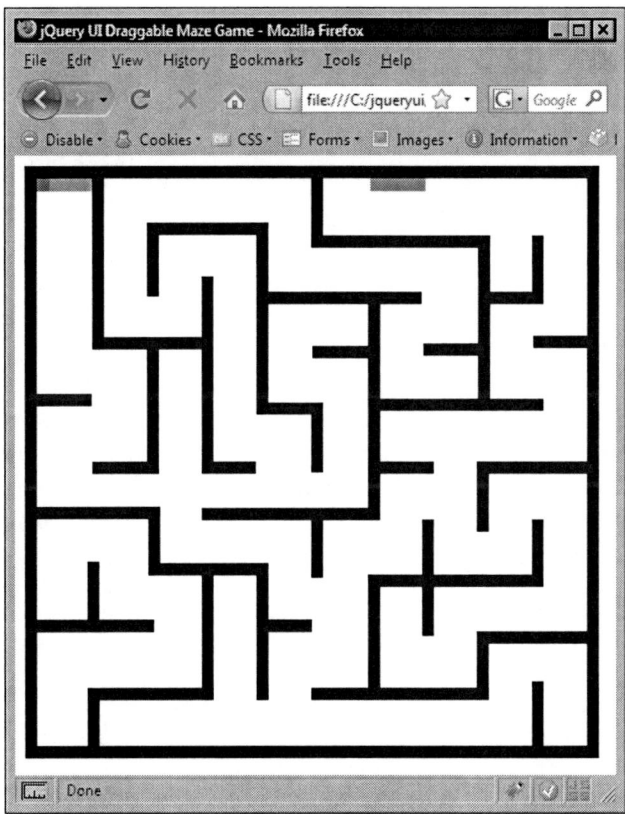

Let's start with the markup. In a new page in your text editor, add the following code:

```
<!DOCTYPE HTML PUBLIC "-//W3C//DTD HTML 4.01//EN"
  "http://www.w3.org/TR/html4/strict.dtd">
<html lang="en">
  <head>
    <link rel="stylesheet" type="text/css"
      href="css/dragMaze.css">
    <meta http-equiv="Content-Type" content="text/html;
      charset=utf-8">
    <title>jQuery UI Draggable Maze Game</title>
  </head>
  <body>
    <div id="maze">
      <div id="drag"></div>
      <div id="start"></div>
      <div id="end"></div>
    </div>
    <script type="text/javascript"
      src="development-bundle/jquery-1.3.2.js"></script>
    <script type="text/javascript"
      src="development-bundle/ui/ui.core.js"></script>
    <script type="text/javascript"
      src="development-bundle/ui/ui.draggable.js"></script>
    <script type="text/javascript"
      src="development-bundle/ui/ui.droppable.js"></script>
    <script type="text/javascript">

    </script>
  </body>
</html>
```

Save this file as `dragMaze.html`. On the page we have our outer container that we've given an id of maze. We have `<div>` elements for the starting and ending positions as well as for the drag marker. Our map will need walls. Rather than handcoding the 46 required walls for the map pattern that we're going to use, I thought we could use jQuery to do this for us instead.

We left an empty `<script>` element at the bottom of our page. Let's fill that up next with the following code:

```
$(function() {
  for (var x = 1; x < 47; x++) {
    $("<div>").attr({
      id: "a" + x,
```

```
      class: "wall"
    }).appendTo("#maze");
  }
  var dragOpts = {
    containment: "#maze"
  };
  $("#drag").draggable(dragOpts);
  var dropOpts = {
    tolerance: "touch",
    over: function(e, ui) {
      $("#drag").draggable("destroy").remove();
      $("<div>").attr("id", "drag").css({ left:0,
        top:0 }).appendTo("#maze");
      $("#drag").draggable(dragOpts);
    }
  };
  var endOpts = {
    over: function(e, ui) {
      $("#drag").draggable("destroy").remove();
      alert("Woo!, you did it!");
    }
  };
  $(".wall").droppable(dropOpts);
  $("#end").droppable(endOpts);
});
```

Let's review what the new code does. First, we use a simple `for` loop to add the walls to our maze. We use the plain-vanilla `for` loop in conjunction with standard jQuery to create 46 `<div>` elements and add `id` and `class` attributes to each one before appending them to the `maze` container.

We then define a simple configuration object for the drag object. The only option we need to configure is the `container` option that constrains the draggable marker element within the maze. We can then go ahead and create the draggable behavior with the `draggable` constructor method.

Next, we can define the configuration object for the walls. Each wall is treated as a droppable. We specify `touch` as the value of the `tolerance` option and add a callback function to the `over` option. Therefore, whenever the drag object touches a wall, the function will be executed.

All we do in this function is destroy the current drag object and remove it from the page. We then create a new drag object back at the starting position and make it draggable once more. There is no `cancelDrag` method that causes the drag object to act as if it had been dropped and revert to its starting position, but we can easily replicate this behavior ourselves.

We then add another droppable configuration object that configures the ending point of the maze. All we configure for this droppable is a function to execute when the draggable is over this droppable. In this function, we remove the drag object again and present the user with an alert congratulating them.

Finally, we make the walls and the end target droppables. So far, this is probably the simplest JavaScript game ever written, but we also need to add some CSS for the maze and the draggable along with the start and end points.

We also need to style up the walls of the maze, but we can't use any simple JavaScript pattern for this. Unfortunately, we have to hardcode them. In another new file in your text editor, add the following selectors and rules:

```css
#maze {
  width:441px; height:441px; border:10px solid #000000;
  background-color:#ffffff; position:relative;
}
#drag {
  width:10px; height:10px;
  background-color:#0000FF; z-index:1;
}
#start {
  width:44px; height:10px; background-color:#00CC00;
  position:absolute; top:0; left:0; z-index:0;
}
#end {
  width:44px; height:10px; background-color:#FF0000;
  position:absolute; top:0; right:130px;
}
.wall { background-color:#000000; position:absolute; }
#a1 { width:10px; height:133px; left:44px; top:0; }
#a2 { width:44px; height:10px; left:0; top:167px; }
#a3 { width:44px; height:10px; left:44px; top:220px; }
#a4 { width:89px; height:10px; left:0; bottom:176px; }
```

```
#a5  { width:94px;  height:10px;  left:0;     bottom:88px;  }
#a6  { width:10px;  height:41px;  left:40px;  bottom:0;     }
#a7  { width:10px;  height:48px;  left:88px;  top:44px;     }
#a8  { width:78px;  height:10px;  left:54px;  top:123px;    }
#a9  { width:10px;  height:97px;  left:88px;  top:133px     }
#a10 { width:10px;  height:45px;  left:40px;  bottom:98px;  }
#a11 { width:88px;  height:10px;  left:89px;  bottom:132px; }
#a12 { width:10px;  height:97px;  left:132px; bottom:35px;  }
#a13 { width:10px;  height:44px;  left:89px;  bottom:142px; }
#a14 { width:92px;  height:10px;  left:40px;  bottom:35px;  }
#a15 { width:89px;  height:10px;  left:88px;  top:34px;     }
#a16 { width:10px;  height:145px; left:132px; top:76px;     }
#a17 { width:44px;  height:10px;  left:132px; top:220px;    }
#a18 { width:133px; height:10px;  left:132px; bottom:175px; }
#a19 { width:10px;  height:107px; left:176px; bottom:35px;  }
#a20 { width:10px;  height:150px; left:176px; top:34px;     }
#a21 { width:35px;  height:10px;  left:186px; top:174px     }
#a22 { width:35px;  height:10px;  left:186px; bottom:88px;  }
#a23 { width:122px; height:10px;  left:186px; top:88px;     }
#a24 { width:10px;  height:44px;  left:220px; top:0px;      }
#a25 { width:10px;  height:55px;  left:220px; top:174px;    }
#a26 { width:10px;  height:45px;  left:220px; bottom:130px; }
#a27 { width:133px; height:10px;  right:88px;  top:44px;    }
#a28 { width:10px;  height:168px; right:166px; top:98px;    }
#a29 { width:44px;  height:10px;  right:176px; top:130px;   }
#a30 { width:10px;  height:98px;  right:166px; bottom:35px; }
#a31 { width:133px; height:10px;  right:88px;  bottom:35px; }
#a32 { width:10px;  height:133px; right:78px;  top:44px;    }
#a33 { width:44px;  height:10px;  right:88px;  top:128px;   }
#a34 { width:131px; height:10px;  right:35px;  top:171px;   }
#a35 { width:43px;  height:10px;  right:123px; top:220px;   }
#a36 { width:10px;  height:91px;  right:123px; bottom:85px; }
#a37 { width:131px; height:10px;  right:35px;  bottom:123px; }
#a38 { width:10px;  height:55px;  right:79px;  top:220px;   }
#a39 { width:44px;  height:10px;  right:0;     top:122px;   }
#a40 { width:10px;  height:54px;  right:79px;  bottom:35px; }
#a41 { width:79px;  height:10px;  right:0;     bottom:79px; }
#a42 { width:10px;  height:45px;  right:35px;  top:44px;    }
#a43 { width:43px;  height:10px;  right:35px;  top:88px;    }
#a44 { width:79px;  height:10px;  right:0;     top:220px;   }
#a45 { width:10px;  height:44px;  right:35px;  bottom:132px; }
#a46 { width:10px;  height:50px;  right:35px;  bottom:0;    }
```

Save this file as `dragMaze.css` in the `css` folder. These two new files now form our simple game. It's limited, but you can see how well the drag and drop components work in this particular scenario.

We can now attempt to navigate the marker from the starting point to the finish by dragging it through the maze walls. If any wall is touched, the marker will return to the starting point. We could make it harder (by adding additional obstacles to navigate, and so on), but for the purpose of having fun with jQuery UI draggables and droppables, our work here is complete.

Summary

We looked at two very useful library components in this chapter—the draggable and droppable components. Draggables and droppables, as we saw, are very closely related and have been designed to be used with each other, allowing us to create advanced and highly-interactive interfaces.

We've covered a lot of material in this chapter, so let's recap on what we have learned. We saw that the draggable behavior can be added to any element on the page with zero configuration. There may be implementations where this is acceptable, but usually we'll want to use one or more of the component's extensive range of configurable options.

In the second part of this chapter, we saw that the droppables class allows us to easily define areas on the page that draggables can be dropped onto, and can react to things being dropped on them. We can also make use of a smaller range of configurable droppable options to implement more advanced droppable behavior.

Both components feature an effective event model for hooking into the interesting moments of any drag and drop interaction. We also saw that each component has a simple set of methods for enabling or disabling drag or drop, and also a `destroy` method for removing the functionality (but not the underlying elements) from the page.

Our final example showed how both the draggables and droppables components can be used together to create a fun and interactive game. Although the game was very basic by modern gaming standards, it nevertheless provides a sound base that we can easily build upon to add additional features.

10
Resizing

We have already seen resizables in action briefly when we looked at the dialog widget earlier in the book. This time, we're going to focus directly on this utility instead of looking at it incidentally. However, the dialog is a perfect example of how useful the resizable component can be in a real-world implementation.

The resizable is a flexible component that can be used with a wide range of different elements. For example, `<textarea>` elements that may have different amounts of user-entered text in them could be styled so the `<textarea>` would be quite small initially. Users could then resize it as they saw fit depending on how much text they entered into it.

Throughout the examples in this chapter, we'll mostly be using simple `<div>` elements so that the focus remains on the component and not on the underlying HTML. We will also look at some brief examples using `<img>` and `<textarea>` elements towards the end of the chapter.

In this chapter, we'll be looking at the following aspects of the component:

- Implementing basic resizability
- The configurable options available for use
- Specifying which resize handles to add
- Managing the resizable's minimum and maximum sizes
- The role of resize helpers and ghosts
- A look at the built-in resize animations
- How to react to resize events

The resizables component works well with other components and is very often used in conjunction with draggables. However, while you can easily make draggable components resizable (think dialog), the two classes are in no way related.

A basic resizable

Let's implement the basic resizable so we can see just how easy making elements resizable is when you use jQuery UI as the driving force behind your pages. In a new file in your text editor add the following code:

```
<!DOCTYPE HTML PUBLIC "-//W3C//DTD HTML 4.01//EN"
  "http://www.w3.org/TR/html4/strict.dtd">
<html lang="en">
  <head>
    <link rel="stylesheet" type="text/css"
      href="development-bundle/themes/smoothness/ui.all.css">
    <link rel="stylesheet" type="text/css"
      href="css/resize.css">
    <meta http-equiv="Content-Type" content="text/html;
      charset=utf-8">
    <title>jQuery UI Resizable Example 1</title>
  </head>
  <body>
    <div id="resize"></div>
    <script type="text/javascript"
      src="development-bundle/jquery-1.3.2.js"></script>
    <script type="text/javascript"
      src="development-bundle/ui/ui.core.js"></script>
    <script type="text/javascript"
      src="development-bundle/ui/ui.resizable.js"></script>
    <script type="text/javascript">
      $(function() {
        $("#resize").resizable();
      });
    </script>
  </body>
</html>
```

Save this as `resizable1.html`. The basic widget method, used with no arguments for the default implementation, uses the same simplified syntax as the rest of the library. This requires just one line of specific code for the example to work.

Along with the CSS framework files that we need for any resizables implementation, we also use a custom stylesheet to add basic dimension and borders to our `<div>`. Use the following CSS in a new file in your text editor:

```
#resize {
  width:200px; height:200px; margin:30px 0 0 30px;
  border:1px solid #7a7a7a;
}
```

Save this file as `resize.css` in the `css` folder. We've given the resizable element dimensions in our CSS because without them the `<div>` will stretch the width of the screen. We've also specified a border to clearly define it as the default implementation only adds a single resize handle to the bottom-right corner of the targeted element. The following screenshot shows how our basic page should look after the `<div>` has been resized:

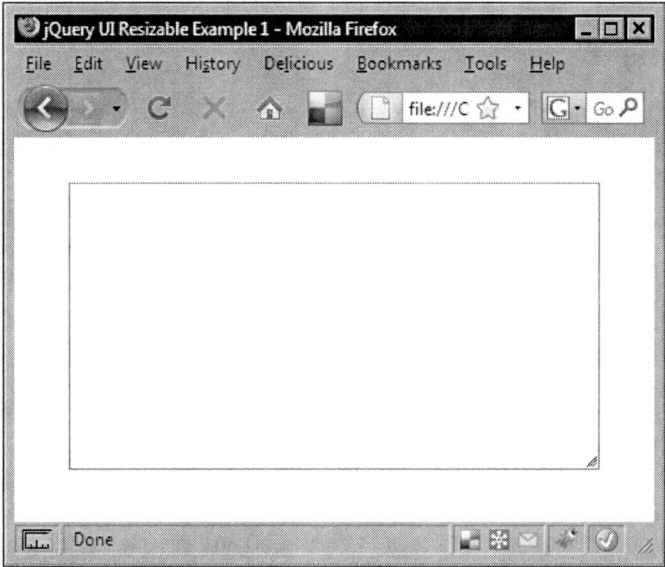

The library files we use in this example are as follows:

- `ui.all.css`
- `jquery-1.3.2.js`
- `ui.core.js`
- `ui.resizable.js`

The component automatically adds the three required elements for the drag handles. Although the only visible resize handle is the one in the bottom-right corner, both the bottom and right edges also allow for resizing.

Resizable options

The following table lists the configurable options we have at our disposal when working with the resizable component:

Option	Default value	Usage
alsoResize	false	Automatically resizes specified elements in sync with the resizable.
animate	false	Animates the resizable element to its new size.
animateDuration	slow	Sets the speed of the animation. Values can be integers specifying the number of milliseconds, or one of the string values slow, normal, or fast.
animateEasing	swing	Adds easing effects to the resize animation.
aspectRatio	false	Maintains the aspect ratio of the element. Accepts numerical custom aspect ratios in addition to Boolean values.
autoHide	false	Hides the resize handles until the resizable is hovered over with the mouse pointer.
cancel	':input,option'	Stops specified elements from being resizable.
containment	false	Constrains the resizable within the boundary of the specified container element.
delay	0	Sets a delay in milliseconds from when the pointer is clicked on a resizable handle to when the resizing begins.
distance	1	Sets the number of pixels the mouse pointer must move with the mouse button held down before resizing begins.
ghost	false	Shows a semi-transparent helper element while the resizing is taking place.

Option	Default value	Usage
grid	false	Accepts an object specifying x and y coordinates to snap the resize to while resizing is taking place.
handles	'e, se, s'	Defines which handles to use for resizing. Accepts a string containing any of the following values: n, ne, e, se, s, sw, w, nw, or all. The string could also be an object where the properties are any of the above and the values are jQuery selectors matching the elements to use as handles.
helper	false	Used to add a class name to the helper element that is applied during resizing.
maxHeight	null	Sets the maximum height the resizable may be changed to.
maxWidth	null	Sets the maximum width the resizable may be set to.
minHeight	null	Sets the minimum height the resizable may be changed to.
minWidth	null	Sets the minimum width the resizable may be set to.

Configuring resize handles

Thanks to the handles configuration option, specifying which handles we would like to add to our target element is exceptionally easy. In resizable1.html change the final <script> element so that it appears as follows:

```
<script type="text/javascript">
  $(function() {

    var resizeOpts = {
      handles: "all"
    }

    $("#resize").resizable(resizeOpts);

  });
</script>
```

Save this as `resizable2.html`. When you run the example in a browser, you'll see that although the component looks exactly as it did before, we can now use any edge or corner to resize the `div`, as shown in the following screenshot:

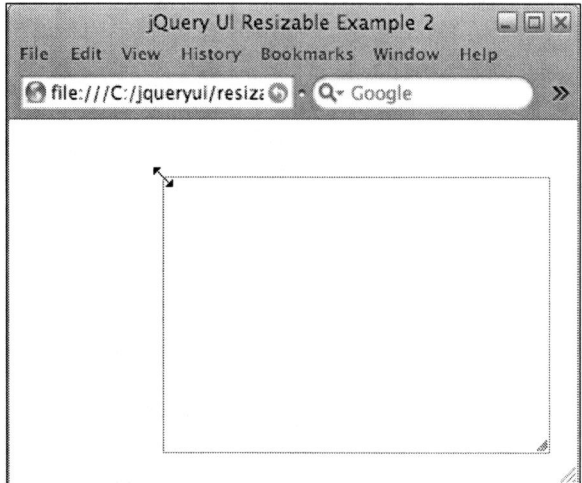

Adding additional handle images

One thing you'll notice straight away is that although the element is resizable along any axis, there's no visual cue to make this obvious; the component will automatically add the resize stripes to the bottom-right corner, but it's up to us to add the rest.

There are several different ways to do this. Although the method doesn't add images to the other three corners, it does insert DOM elements with class names, so we can easily target these with CSS and provide our own images. In a new page in your text editor, add the following style rules:

```css
#resize { width:200px; height:200px; margin:30px 0 0 30px; border:1px
solid #7a7a7a; }
.ui-resizable-sw, .ui-resizable-nw, .ui-resizable-ne {
  background:url(../img/resizable/handles.png) no-repeat 0 0;
  width:12px; height:12px;
}
.ui-resizable-sw { left:0; bottom:0; }
.ui-resizable-nw {
  left:0; top:0; background-position:0 -12px;
}
.ui-resizable-ne {
  right:0; top:0; background-position:0 -24px;
}
```

Save this file in the `css` folder as `resizeHandles.css`. We provide our own image for this example, which is a sprite file containing copies of the standard bottom-right image flipped and reversed (this can be found in the code download).

Our selectors target the class names that are automatically added to the handle elements by the control. Link to the new stylesheet in the `<head>` of `resizable2.html` and resave it as `resizable3.html`. The new stylesheet should give our element the following appearance:

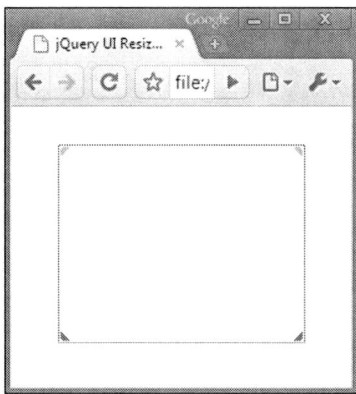

Another configuration option related to resize handles and how they are displayed is `autoHide`. Let's take a quick look at this option next. Change the configuration object in `resizable3.html` to the following:

```
var resizeOpts = {
   handles: "all",
   autoHide: true
}
```

Save this version as `resizable4.html`. We've added the `autoHide` option and set its value to `true` in this example. Configuring this option hides all of the resize handles until the mouse pointer moves onto the resizable element. This is great for a minimal intrusion of the additional DOM elements when there is pictorial content inside the resizable element.

Defining size limits

Restricting the minimum or maximum sizes that the target element can be resized to is made exceptionally easy with four configurable options, which we will see in action in the next example. It's better to have some content in the container for this example, so add some layout text in a `<p>` element within our resizable in `resizable4.html`:

```
<p>Lorem ipsum...</p>
```

Change the configuration object we used in `resizable4.html` to as follows:

```
var resizeOpts = {
  maxWidth: 500,
  maxHeight: 500,
  minWidth: 100,
  minHeight: 100
};
```

Save this as `resizable5.html`. This time, the configuration object uses the dimension-boundary options to specify minimum and maximum heights and widths that the resizable may be adjusted to. These options take simple integers as their values, which are then converted to pixels by the component.

As we can see when we run this example, the resizable now adheres to the sizes we have specified, whereas in previous examples, the resizable element's minimum size was the combined size of its resize handles and it had no maximum.

So far our resizable has been an empty `<div>` and you may be wondering how the resizable handles minimum and maximum sizes when there is content within the target element. The restrictions are maintained, but we'll need to add `overflow:hidden;` to the CSS. Otherwise the content may overflow the resizable if there is too much for the minimum size to handle.

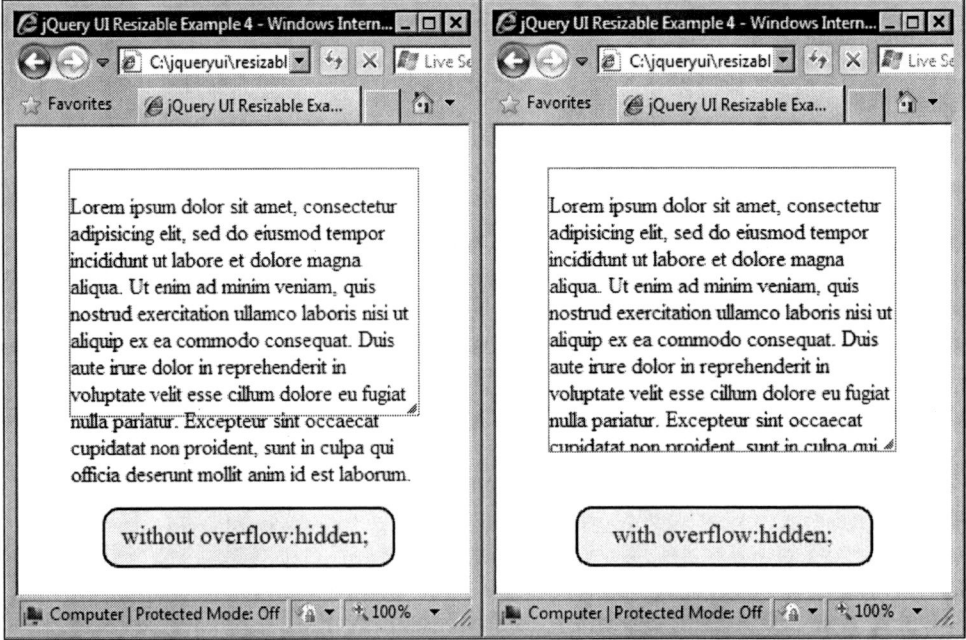

Of course, we can also use `scroll:auto` as well to add a scrollbar when there is too much content, which would sometimes be the desired behavior, such as when used with a `<textarea>` element.

Resize ghosts

Ghost elements are very similar to the proxy element we used when we looked at the draggables component in the previous chapter. A ghost element can be enabled with the configuration of just one option. Let's see how this is done.

Change the configuration object we used in `resizable5.html` to this:

```
var resizeOpts = {
  ghost: true
};
```

Save this file as `resizable6.html`. All that is needed to enable a resize ghost is to set the `ghost` option to `true`. The effect of the resizable ghost is very subtle. It is basically a clone of the existing resizable element but is only a quarter of the opacity. This is why we've left the layout text from the previous example within the resizable element.

We're also linking to a new stylesheet in this example, which is exactly the same as `resize.css` with a `background-color` specified.

```
#resize {
  width:200px; height:200px; margin:30px 0 0 30px;
  border:1px solid #7a7a7a; overflow:hidden;
  background-color:#999999;

}
```

Save this as `resizeGhosts.css` in the `css` folder. The next screenshot shows how the resizable ghost will appear while it is visible.

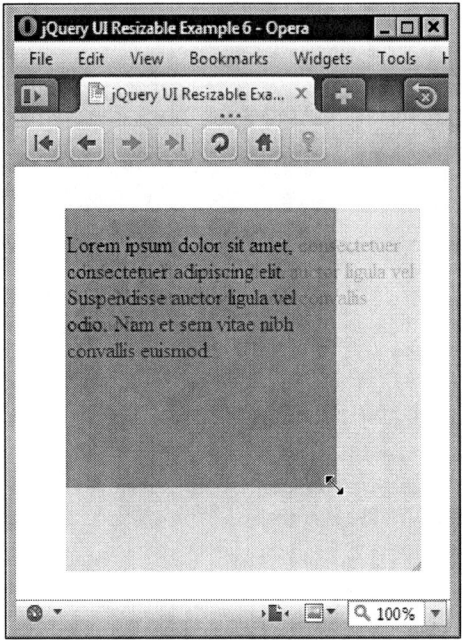

 Note that in some versions of Internet Explorer ghost elements may cause issues when transparent PNGs are within the resizable.

The ghost element is just a helper element that has been made transparent. If this is not suitable and further control over the appearance of the helper element is required, we can use the `helper` option to specify a class name to be added to the helper element, which we can then use to style it. Change the configuration object in `resizable6.html` so that it appears as follows:

```
var resizeOpts = {
   helper: "my-ui-helper"
};
```

Save this revision as `resizable7.html`. We've simply specified the class name that we'd like added as the value of the `helper` option. We can target the new class name from a CSS file, open `resize.css` and add the following code to it:

```
.my-ui-helper { background-color:#FFFF99; }
```

Save the new stylesheet as `resizeHelper.css` and don't forget to link to it at the top of `resizable7.html`. The only thing we do in this example is give the helper a simple `background-color`. This is how it looks when the new page is run.

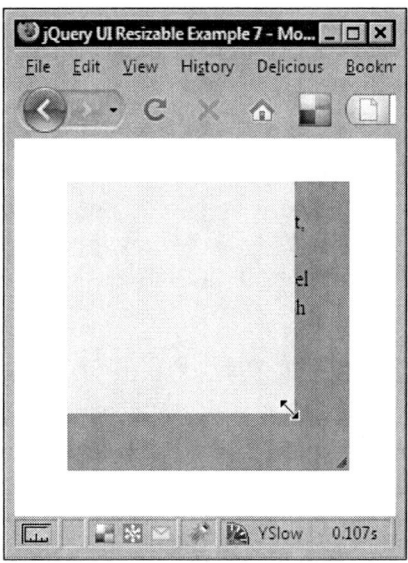

Containing the resize

The resizable component makes it easy to ensure that a resized element is contained within its parent element. This is great if we have other content on the page that we don't want moving around all over the page during a resize interaction. In `resizable7.html` change the `<link>` in the `<head>` of the page from `resizeHelper.css` to a new stylesheet.

```
<link rel="stylesheet" type="text/css" href="css/resizeContainer.css">
```

Then change the elements on the page to as follows:

```
<div class="container">
  <img id="resize" src="img/resizable/moon.jpg" alt="Moon Landing">
</div>
```

Finally, change the configuration object to use the `containment` option:

```
var resizeOpts = {
  containment: ".container"
};
```

Save this as `resizable8.html`. On the page we've added a container element for the resizable and have switched from using a `<div>` to an image as the resizable element.

Once again, we need some slightly different CSS for this example, in a new file in your text editor add the following code:

```
.container {
  width:600px; height:600px; border:1px solid #7a7a7a;
  padding:1px 0 0 1px;
}
#resize { width:300px; height:300px; }
```

Save this as `resizeContainer.css` in the `css` folder. The `containment` option allows us to specify a container for the resizable, which will limit how large the resizable can be made, forcing it to stay within its boundaries. We specify a jQuery selector as the value of this option. When we view the page, we should see that the image cannot be resized to larger than its container.

Handling the aspect ratio

The 1.7 release of jQuery UI gives us not only the ability to maintain the aspect ratio of the resizable element, but also to define it. Let's see what control over the resize interaction this gives us. Change the configuration object used in `resizable8.html` to the following:

```
var resizeOpts = {
  containment: ".container",
  aspectRatio: true
};
```

Save this file as `resizable9.html`. Setting the `aspectRatio` option to `true` ensures our image will maintain its original aspect ratio, so in this example, the image will always be a perfect square:

For a greater degree of control, we can also specify the actual aspect ratio that the resizable should maintain:

```
var resizeOpts = {
  containment: ".container",
  aspectRatio: 0.5
};
```

By specifying the floating-point value of 0.5 we're saying that when the image is resized, the x axis of the image should be exactly half of the y axis.

 Care should be taken when deviating from the aspect ratio of any images.

Resizable animations

The resizable API exposes three configuration options related to animations—
`animate`, `animateDuration`, and `animateEasing`. By default, animations are switched off in resizable implementations. However, we can easily enable them to see how they enhance this component. Also change the markup from the previous example so that the resizable element goes back to a plain `<div>`:

```
<div id="resize"></div>
```

Now change the configuration object to use the following options:

```
var resizeOpts = {
  ghost: true,
  animate: true,
  animateDuration: "fast"
};
```

Save this as `resizable10.html`. The configuration object we use in this example starts with the `ghost` option. When using animations, the resizable element is not resized until after the interaction has ended, so it's useful to show the ghost as a visual cue that the element will be resized.

All we need to do to enable animation is set the `animate` option to `true`. That's it, no further configuration is required. Another option we can change is the speed of the animation, which we have done in this example, by setting the `animateDuration` option. This can either be an integer to represent the number of milliseconds the animation should last for, or using one of the strings `slow`, `normal`, or `fast`.

The code for the new stylesheet used in this example is as follows:

```
#resize {
  width:400px; height:200px; display:block; position:relative;
  border:2px solid #000000;
}
```

Save this file in the `css` folder as `resizeAnimate.css`.

Simultaneous resizing

We can easily make several elements on the same page resizable by individually passing references to them, to the resizable constructor. But, as well as doing this, we can also make use of the `alsoResize` property to specify additional elements that are to be resized whenever the actual resizable element is resized. Let's see how. First we'll need to reference to a different stylesheet once again.

```
<link rel="stylesheet" type="text/css"
  href="css/resizeSimultaneous.css">
```

Next we'll need to change the elements in the `<body>` of the page to as follows:

```
<div id="mainResize">
  <p>I am the main resizable!</p>
</div>
<div id="simultaneousResize">
  <p>I will also be resized when the main resizable is resized!</p>
</div>
```

Then change the configuration object to this:

```
var resizeOpts = {
   alsoResize: "#simultaneousResize"
};
```

The `id` of our resizable element has also changed in this example, so be sure to update the selector accordingly:

```
$("#mainResize").resizabl(resizeOpts);
```

Save this file as `resizable11.html`. We provide a selector as the value of the `alsoResize` option in order to target the second `<div>` element. The secondary element will automatically pick up the resizable attributes of the actual resizable, so if we limit the resizable to having just an `e` handle, the secondary element will also only resize in this direction. We also need a little bit of CSS, so create the following stylesheet:

```
#mainResize {
   width:100px; height:100px; margin:0 0 30px;
   border:2px solid #7a7a7a; text-align:center;
}
#simultaneousResize {
   width:150px; height:150px; border:2px solid #7a7a7a;
   text-align:center;
}
p { font-family:arial; font-size:15px; }
```

Save this file as `resizeSimultaneous.css` in the `css` folder. When we run the file, we should see that the second `<div>` element is resized along with the first.

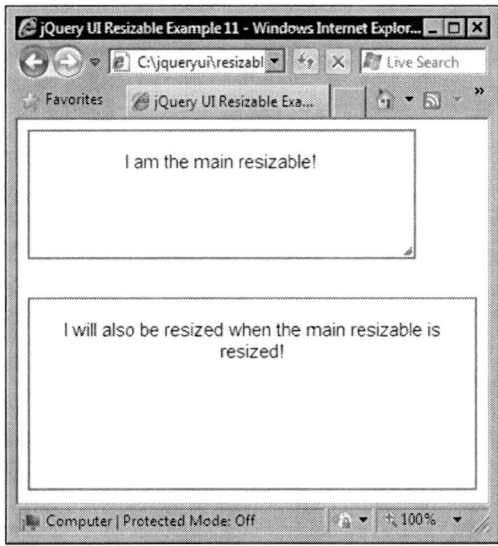

Preventing unwanted resizes

There may be times when we'd like to make an element resizable, but it also has other functionality, perhaps it listens for click events too. In this situation it may be desirable to prevent the resize unless it is definitely required, enabling us to easily differentiate between clicks and true drags. We can use two options to achieve this, in `resizable11.html` revert back to the original stylesheet `resize.css`.

```
<link rel="stylesheet" type="text/css" href="css/resize.css">
```

We can also return to the simple empty resizable `<div>`.

```
<div id="resize"></div>
```

Then change the configuration object to this:

```
var resizeOpts = {
   delay: 1000
};
```

Save this version as `resizable12.html`. The `delay` option accepts an integer that represents the number of milliseconds that need to pass while the mouse button is held down after clicking on a resize handle.

We've used `1000` as the value in this example that is equal to one second. Try it out and you'll see that if you click on a resize handle and release the mouse button too soon, the resize won't take place.

Along with delaying the resize, we could also use the `distance` option instead to specify that the mouse pointer must move a certain number of pixels, with the button held down after clicking on a resize handle, before the resize occurs. Change the configuration object in `resizable12.html` so that it appears as follows:

```
var resizeOpts = {
   distance: 30
};
```

Save this as `resizable13.html`. Now when the page is run, instead of having to wait with the mouse button held down the mouse pointer will need to travel 30 pixels with the mouse button held down before the resize occurs.

Resizable callbacks

Like other components of the library, resizable defines a selection of custom events and allows us to easily execute functions when these events occur. This makes the most of interactions between your visitors and the elements on your pages. Resizable defines the following callback options:

Option	Triggered
resize	When the resizable is in the process of being resized
start	When the resize interaction begins.
stop	When the resize interaction ends.

Hooking into these custom methods is just as easy for resizables as it has been for the other components of the library we have looked at. Let's explore a basic example to highlight this fact. In `resizable13.html` change the second `<link>` to point to a new stylesheet as follows:

```
<link rel="stylesheet" type="text/css" href="css/resizeStop.css">
```

Then change the final `<script>` element so that it appears as follows:

```
<script type="text/javascript">
  $(function() {

    function reportNewSize() {

      function goAway() {
        setTimeout("$('.tip').fadeOut('slow')", 2000);
      }

      $("<div>").addClass("tip").text("The resizable is now " +
        $(this).height() + " pixels high, and " + $(this).width() +
        "pixels wide").width($(this).width()).appendTo(
        "body").fadeIn("slow", goAway);

    var resizeOpts = {
      stop: reportNewSize
    };

    $("#resize").resizable(resizeOpts);

  });
</script>
```

Save this as `resizable14.html`. We have an outer function called `reportNewSize`, a reference to this function is then passed to the `stop` callback option, so the function will be executed each time an interaction ends.

Within this function we first define another function called `goAway`, which is used to fade the tooltip out after a specified length of time. We then create a new `<div>` element that will act as a tooltip, which appears below the resizable. We give it a class name and set its inner text to report the current size of the resizable. We set its width to equal the resizable's width and then append it to the `<body>` of the page.

Once appended we fade it in using jQuery's `fadeIn` method and specify our `goAway` function as a callback to be executed once the animation finishes, which will fade the tip from view.

We also need to style the tooltip as well, in `resize.css` add the following selector and rules:

```
.tip {
  border:1px solid #7a7a7a; fontSize:80%; font-weight:bold;
  text-align:center; position:absolute; left:38px;
  display:none; margin-top:5px;
}
```

Save this as `resizeStop.css` in the `css` folder. The following screenshot shows how our page looks before the `<div>` fades away:

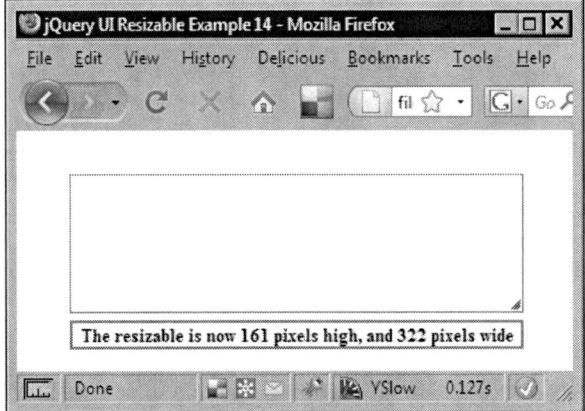

Resizable methods

This component comes with the four basic methods found with all of the interaction components of the library, namely the `destroy`, `disable`, `enable`, and `option` methods. Unlike most of the other components, the resizables component has no custom methods unique to it. For clarification on these basic API methods, see the *API introduction* section in *Chapter 1*.

Resizable tabs

In our final resizable example let's look at combining this component with one of the widgets that we looked at earlier. This will help us see how compatible it is with the rest of the library. We'll be working with the tabs component in the following example. The following screenshot shows the page we will end up with:

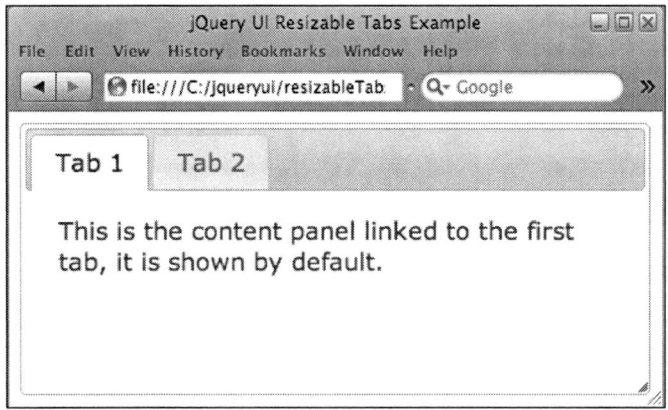

In your text editor, add the following code:

```
<!DOCTYPE HTML PUBLIC "-//W3C//DTD HTML 4.01//EN"
  "http://www.w3.org/TR/html4/strict.dtd">
<html lang="en">
  <head>
    <link rel="stylesheet" type="text/css"
      href="development-bundle/themes/smoothness/ui.all.css">
    <link rel="stylesheet" type="text/css"
      href="css/resizableTabsTheme.css">
    <meta http-equiv="Content-Type" content="text/html;
      charset=utf-8">
    <title>jQuery UI Resizable Tabs Example</title>
  </head>
  <body>
    <div id="myTabs">
      <ul>
        <li><a href="#0"><span>Tab 1</span></a></li>
        <li><a href="#1"><span>Tab 2</span></a></li>
      </ul>
      <div class="tab" id="0">This is the content panel linked to the
        first tab, it is shown by default.</div>
      <div class="tab" id="1">This content is linked to the second
        tab and will be shown when its tab is clicked.</div>
    </div>
    <script type="text/javascript"
      src="development-bundle/jquery-1.3.2.js"></script>
    <script type="text/javascript"
      src="development-bundle/ui/ui.core.js"></script>
    <script type="text/javascript"
      src="development-bundle/ui/ui.resizable.js"></script>
    <script type="text/javascript"
      src="development-bundle/ui/ui.tabs.js"></script>
    <script type="text/javascript">
```

```
$(function(){
    var tabs = $("#myTabs").tabs();
    var resizeOpts = {
        autoHide: true,
        minHeight: 170,
        minWidth: 400
    };
    tabs.resizable(resizeOpts);
});
    </script>
  </body>
</html>
```

Save this as `resizableTabs.html`. We also link to a new stylesheet for this example. It's extremely simple and just contains the following selector:

```
#myTabs { width:400px; height:170px; }
```

This can be saved as `resizableTabsTheme.css` in the `css` folder. Making the tabs widget resizable is extremely easy and only requires calling the `resizable` method on tab's underlying `<ul>`.

We're using a single configuration object in this example. The tabs component can be initialized with zero configuration. Apart from setting the `autoHide` option for the resizable in our configuration object, we also define `minWidth` and `minHeight` values for usability purposes.

Summary

In this chapter we covered resizables. This is a component that allows us to easily resize any onscreen element. It dynamically adds resize handles to the specified sides of the target element and handles all of the tricky DHTML resizing for us, neatly encapsulating the behavior into a compact, easy-to-use class.

We then looked at some of the configurable options we can use with the widget, such as how to specify which handles to add to the resizable, and how the minimum and maximum sizes of the element can be limited.

We briefly looked at how to maintain an image's aspect ratio, or how to work with custom ratios, while it is being resized. We also explored how to use ghosts, helpers, and animations to improve the usability and appearance of the resizable component.

We looked at the event model exposed by the component's API and how we can react to elements being resized in an easy and effective way. Our final example explored resizable's compatibility with another component of the library.

11
Selecting

The selectables component allows you to define a series of elements that can be 'chosen' by dragging a selection square around them or by clicking them, as if they were files on the desktop. In this way, elements on the page can be treated as file-like objects, allowing either single or groups of them to be selected.

A selection square has been a standard part of modern operating systems for a long time. For example, if you wanted to select some of the icons on your desktop, you could hold the mouse button down on a blank part of the desktop and drag a square around the icons you wanted to select.

The selectables interaction helper adds this same functionality to our web pages, which allows us to build more user-friendly interfaces without needing to use external environments like Flash or Silverlight. This is yet another example of how the Web is increasingly becoming less distinct from the desktop as an application platform.

Topics that will be covered in this section include:

- Creating the default implementation
- How selectable class names reflect the state of selectables
- Filtering selectable elements
- Working with selectable's built-in callback functions
- A look at selectable's methods

Basic implementation

A demonstration that you can play with will tell you more about the functionality provided by this library component than merely reading about it. The first thing we should do is invoke the default implementation to get a glimpse of the basic functionality provided by this component. In a new file in your text editor, add the following code:

```
<!DOCTYPE HTML PUBLIC "-//W3C//DTD HTML 4.01//EN"
  "http://www.w3.org/TR/html4/strict.dtd">
<html lang="en">
  <head>
    <meta http-equiv="Content-Type" content="text/html;
      charset=utf-8">
    <title>jQuery UI Selectable Example 1</title>
  </head>
  <body>
    <ul id="selectables">
      <li>This list item can be selected</li>
      <li>This list item can be selected</li>
      <li>This list item can be selected</li>
      <li>This list item can be selected</li>
      <li>This list item can be selected</li>
    </ul>
    <script type="text/javascript"
      src="development-bundle/jquery-1.3.2.js"></script>
    <script type="text/javascript"
      src="development-bundle/ui/ui.core.js"></script>
    <script type="text/javascript"
      src="development-bundle/ui/ui.selectable.js"></script>
    <script type="text/javascript">
      $(function() {
        $("#selectables").selectable();
      });
    </script>
  </body>
</html>
```

Save this as `selectable1.html` in the `jqueryui` folder. We simply call the `selectable` widget method on the parent list element and then all of its child `<li>` elements are made selectable. This allows selection by clicking on them or using the selection square (like you would on your desktop).

Note that there is no styling associated with the selectables component. Default behavior includes clicking on individual elements, causing them only to be selected and clicking outside of the selected elements will deselect them. Holding down the *Ctrl* key will enable multi-select. The following screenshot shows the selection square enclosing the list items:

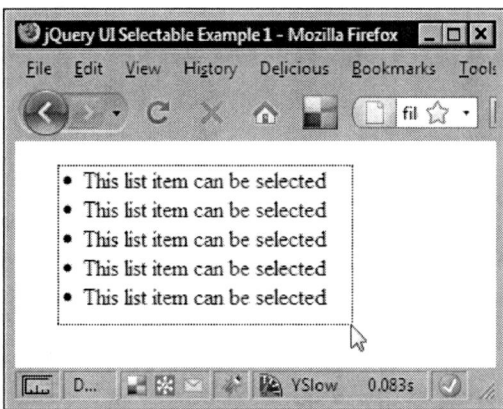

The minimum set of library files we need for a selectable implementation is:

- `jquery-1.3.2.js`
- `ui.core.js`
- `ui.selectable.js`

Along with building selectables from list items, we can also build them from other elements, such as a collection of `<div>` elements. Add the following link to the `<head>` of the `selectable1.html`:

```
<link rel="stylesheet" type="text/css"
  href="css/selectable.css ">
```

Also replace the list elements in `selectable1.html` with the following code.

```
<div id="selectables">
  <div>This div can be selected</div>
  <div>This div can be selected</div>
  <div>This div can be selected</div>
  <div>This div can be selected</div>
  <div>This div can be selected</div>
</div>
```

Save this as `selectable2.html`. Everything is essentially the same as before. We're just basing the example on different elements. However, due to the nature of these elements, we should add a little basic styling so that we can see what we're working with.

In a new file in your text editor, add the following code:

```
#selectables div {
  width:160px; height:25px;
  padding:5px 0 0 10px; margin:10px 0 0 10px;
  border:1px solid #000;
}
```

Save this as `selectable.css` in the `css` folder. It's not much, but it helps to clarify the individual selectables in the example, as shown in the following screenshot:

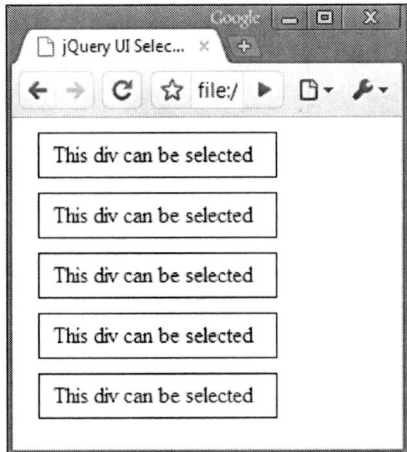

Selectee class names

The elements that are made selectable are all initially given the class `ui-selectee`, and the parent element that contains the selectables is given the class `ui-selectable`. While elements are selected they are given the class `ui-selected`.

While the selecting square is around selectable elements, they are given the class `ui-selecting`, and for a brief moment, when an element is deselected it is given the class `ui-unselecting`. These class names are added purely for our benefit, so that we can highlight different states that the selectable may be in.

This extensive class system makes it very easy to add custom styling to show when elements are either in the process of being selected or have been selected. Let's add some additional styling now to reflect the *selecting* and *selected* states. Add the following new selectors and rules to `selectable.css`:

```
#selectables div.ui-selecting {
  border:1px solid #66CC00;
}
#selectables div.ui-selected {
  background:#66CC00; color:#000000;
}
```

Save this `selectableVisual.css` in the `css` folder and link to it from the `<head>` of `selectable2.html`, then save this file as `selectable3.html`. With the addition of this very simple CSS, we can add visual cues to elements which are part of the current selection, both during and following a select interaction. The following screenshot shows some elements that have been selected:

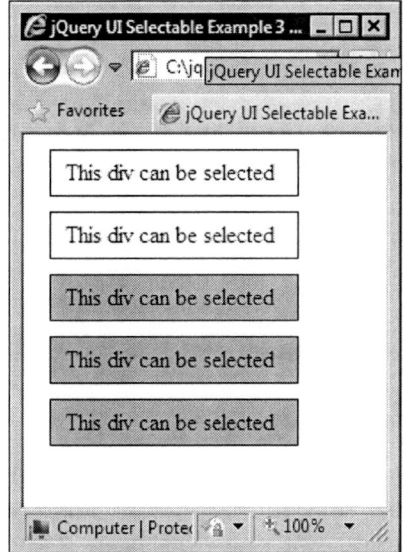

Configurable options of the selectable component

The selectable class is quite compact, with relatively few configurable options compared to some of the other components that we've looked at. The following options are available for configuration:

Option	Default value	Usage
autoRefresh	true	Automatically refreshes the size and position of each selectable at the start of a select interaction.
cancel	":input,option"	Prevents the specified elements from being selected with a click. The default string contains the :input jQuery filter, which matches all <input>, <textarea>, <select>, and <button> elements along with the standard option element selector.
delay	0	Sets the delay in milliseconds before the element is selected. The mouse button must be held down on the element for this length of time before the selection will begin.
distance	0	Sets the distance the mouse pointer must travel, with the mouse button held down, before selection will begin.
filter	"*"	Used to specify child elements to make selectable.
tolerance	"touch"	Sets the tolerance of the selection square. Possible values are touch or fit. If fit is specified the element must be completely within the selection square before the element will be selected.

Filtering selectables

There may be situations when we don't want to allow all of the elements within the targeted container to be made selectable. In this situation, we can easily make use of the filter option to nominate specific elements, based on a CSS selector, that we want selecting to be enabled on. In selectable3.html change the collection of <div> elements so that it appears as follows:

```
<div id="selectables">
    <div class="unselectable">This div can't be selected</div>
    <div class="selectable">This div can be selected</div>
    <div class="selectable">This div can be selected</div>
    <div class="selectable">This div can be selected</div>
    <div class="selectable">This div can be selected</div>
</div>
```

Then change the final `<script>` element to this:

```
<script type="text/javascript">
  $(function() {
    var selectableOpts = {
      filter: ".selectable"
    }
    $("#selectables").selectable(selectableOpts);
  });
</script>
```

Save this version as `selectable4.html`. In the underlying markup, we have given a different class name to the first element. In the JavaScript, we define a configuration object containing the `filter` option. The value of this option is the class selector of the elements that we want to be selectable, elements without this class name are filtered out.

We also used a new stylesheet in this example to give the unselectable element its own styling. This new stylesheet is the same as the `selectableVisual.css` stylesheet with the addition of the following selector and rules:

```
.unselectable { background-color:#999999; color:#666666; }
```

The new stylesheet is saved as `selectableFiltered.css`. The following screenshot shows what the page should look like:

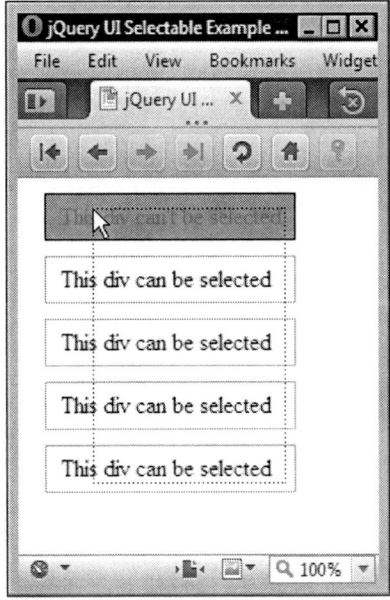

As you can see in this screenshot, the selection square is over the unselectable element, but it's not picking up the `ui-selecting` class like the others. The component completely ignores the filtered selectable and it does not become part of the selection.

Cancelling the selection

Along with indirectly making elements unselectable using the `filter` option, we can also directly make elements unselectable using the `cancel` option. This option was also exposed by the interaction helper we looked at in the last chapter, **Resizable**, although we didn't look at it in any detail. Now is the perfect opportunity to have a play with it.

Change the configuration object from the last example so that it uses the `cancel` option.

```
var selectableOpts = {
    cancel: ".unselectable"
}
```

Save this as `selectable5.html`. Instead of passing the class name of the selectable elements to the configuration object, we pass the class name of the unselectable element to it. But as we see when we run the example, it is only unselectable in certain situations.

The first element, with the class name `unselectable`, is still given the class `ui-selectee`. However, it is only selectable with the selection square, it cannot be selected by clicking, even with the *Ctrl* key held down.

Selectable callbacks

In addition to the standard configurable options of the selectable API, there are also a series of event callback options that can be used to specify functions that are executed at specific points during a select interaction. These options are as listed below.

Option	Triggered when
selected	The select interaction ends and each element added to the selection triggers the callback.
selecting	Each selected element triggers the callback during the select interaction.
start	A select interaction begins.
stop	This is fired once, regardless of the number of items selected, as the select interaction ends.
unselected	Any elements that are part of the selectable but are not selected during the interaction will fire this callback.
unselecting	Unselected elements will fire this during the select interaction.

Selecting really only becomes useful when something happens to the elements once they have been selected, which is where this event model comes into play. Let's put some of these callbacks to work so that we can appreciate their use. Add a reference to the default theme file (smoothness in this example) to the <head> of the page.

```
<link rel="stylesheet" type="text/css"
  href="css/smoothness/jquery-ui-1.7.1.custom.css">
```

Then change the underlying markup for the selectables to as follows:

```
<div id="selectables">
  <div id="selectabl1" class="selectable">This div can be
    selected</div>
  <div id="selectabl2" class="selectable">This div can be
    selected</div>
  <div id="selectabl3" class="selectable">This div can be
    selected</div>
  <div id="selectabl4" class="selectable">This div can be
    selected</div>
  <div id="selectabl5" class="selectable">This div can be
    selected</div>
</div>
```

Next change the final <script> element so that it contains the following code:

```
<script type="text/javascript">
  $(function() {

    var selectableOpts = {
      selected: function(e, ui) {
        $("#" + ui.selected.id).text("I have been selected!");
      },
      unselected: function(e, ui) {
```

```
        $("#" + ui.unselected.id).text("This div was selected");
    },
    start: function(e) {
    if ($("#tip").length == 0) {

        $("<div>").addClass("
            ui-corner-all ui-widget ui-widget-header").attr("id",
            "tip").text("Drag the lasso around elements, or click to
            select").css({
            position: "absolute",
            padding: 10,
            left: e.pageX,
            top: e.pageY - 30,
            display: "none"
        }).appendTo($("body")).fadeIn();
        }
    },
    stop: function() {
        $("#tip").fadeOut("slow", function() {
            $(this).remove();
        });
    }
    }
    $("#selectables").selectable(selectableOpts);
});
</script>
```

Save this as `selectable6.html`. To the HTML elements, we've added `id` attributes so that we can easily target specific elements. In the `<script>`, we've added functions to the `selected`, `unselected`, `start`, and `stop` options. These will be executed at the appropriate times during an interaction.

As with other components, these functions are automatically passed two objects. The first is the original browser event object and the other is an object containing useful properties of the selected element. However, not all callbacks can successfully work with the second object—`start` and `stop` for example.

When a `<div>` is selected, we change its inner text to reflect the selection using the `selected` event callback. We are able to get the `id` of the element that has been selected using the `selected.id` property of the second object that is passed to our function. When an element is unselected, we set the text back to its original value using the same technique. We can also alter the inner text of any selectable that was previously selected using the `unselected` function.

At the start of any interaction, we create a little tool tip that is appended to the `<body>` of the page, slightly offset from the mouse pointer, using the `start` anonymous function. We use a basic conditional to check that the tool tip does not already exist to prevent duplicate tips. We're linking to the theme stylesheet, so we can make use of the framework classes `ui-corner-all`, `ui-widget`, and `ui-widget-header` to do most of the styling for us. The few styles we require that are not provided by the theme are added using the `css()` method.

We can get the pointer coordinates using the `e` (event) object, which is passed as the first argument to our callbacks, in order to position the tool tip. At the end of the selection, we remove the tool tip using the `stop` property. The following screenshot shows the results of different interactions:

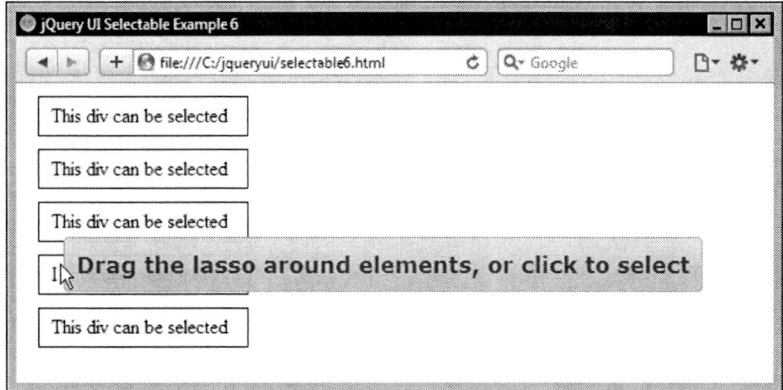

The `selecting` and `unselecting` callbacks work in exactly the same way as those we just looked at but are fired as elements that are added and removed to the selection. To see them in action change the final `<script>` element in `selectable6.html` so that it appears as follows:

```
<script type="text/javascript">
  $(function() {
    var selectableOpts = {
      selecting: function(e, ui) {
        $("#" + ui.selecting.id).text("I am part of the selection");
      },
      unselecting: function(e, ui) {
        $("#" + ui.unselecting.id).text("I was part of the
          selection");
      }
    }
    $("#selectables").selectable(selectableOpts);
  });
</script>
```

Also remove the `<link>` that we added to `selectable6.html`. Save this as `selectable7.html`. This time we use the `selecting` and `unselecting` properties to specify callback functions, which again change the inner text of the elements at certain times during an interaction.

We repeat the procedure, using the same techniques as well. This time, we're just using different callbacks and properties of the objects passed to them. The effects of these callbacks are shown in the following screenshot:

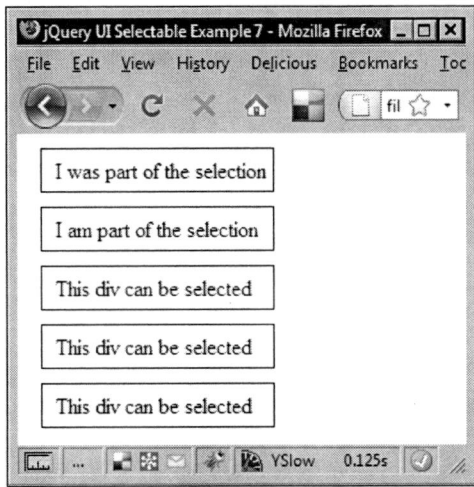

The second object passed to any of the selectable callbacks contains a property relating to the type of custom event. For example, the `selected` callback receives an object with a `selected` property, which can be used to gain information about the element that was added to the selection. All callbacks have a matching property that can be used in this way.

Working with vast amounts of selectables

The jQuery UI library, like jQuery itself, is already extremely efficient. It uses the ultra effective Sizzle selector engine (via jQuery) and each component has been optimized as much as possible.

However, there is only so much that the creators of the library can do. In our examples so far, we've used a maximum of five selectable elements, which isn't really many at all. What if we were to use 500 instead?

When working with great numbers of selectables there is still something we can do to make sure select interactions are as efficient as possible. The `autoRefresh` option is set to `true` by default, which causes the sizes and positions of all selectable elements on the page to be recalculated at the beginning of every interaction.

This can cause delays on pages with many selectable elements on it, so the `autoRefresh` option can be set to `false`. We can also use the `refresh` method to manually refresh the selectables at appropriate times in order to improve the speed and responsiveness of the interactions. On most pages we would not need to worry about configuring this option and can leave it enabled.

Let's take a look, in the `<head>` of the page add a link to the following theme files:

```
<link rel="stylesheet" type="text/css"
  href="css/smoothness/jquery-ui-1.7.1.custom.css">
<link rel="stylesheet" type="text/css"
  href="css/selectable.css ">
```

Then change the selectables container element so that it appears as follows:

```
<div id="selectables" class="ui-helper-clearfix">
    <div class="selectable">Selectable</div>
    <!-- 199 more selectables! -->
</div>
```

Then change the configuration object as follows:

```
<script type="text/javascript">
  $(function() {

    var selectOpts = {
      autoRefresh: false
    }
    $("#selectables").selectable(selectOpts);

  });
</script>
```

Save this as `selectable8.html`. Our page should now contain 200 individual selectables within the selectables container. We're using the default smoothness theme file in this example, specifically so that we can make use of the `ui-helper-clearfix` class to clear the floated selectables. We can't use the selection square in this example if the parent does not clear the float properly. We also need a new stylesheet in this example that consists of the following code:

```
#selectables div {
 width:70px; height:25px; padding:5px 0 0 10px; border:1px solid #000;
 margin:10px 0 0 10px; float:left;
}
.ui-selected { background-color:#00FF66; }
```

Save this in the `css` folder as `selectableMany.css`. It's purely for layout purposes and isn't important in this discussion.

We can use Firebug to profile a selection of all 200 selectables with and without the `autoRefresh` option enabled (remember, it's enabled by default, so our example will disable it). The following screenshot shows the results of a few selections with and without the option enabled:

The results will probably vary between tests, but you should find that the profile (in both milliseconds and the number of calls) is consistently lower with `autoRefresh` set to `disabled`.

Selectable methods

The methods that we can use to control the selectables component from our code are similar to the methods found in other interaction helpers and follow the same pattern of usage. The only unique method exposed by the selectables component is listed below:

Method	Usage
refresh	Manually refreshes the positions and sizes of all selectables. Should be used when autoRefresh is set to false.

Setting the `autoRefresh` property to `false` can yield performance gains when there are many selectables on the page, especially in IE. However, there will still be times when you will need to refresh the size and positions of the selectables, such as when this component is combined with the draggables component.

Let's take a look at the `refresh` method as it leads on perfectly from the last example. Add the following new `<button>` element directly after the selectables container:

```
<button id="refresh">Refresh</button>
```

We'll also need to link to the draggable source file for this example.

```
<script type="text/javascript"
  src="development-bundle/ui/ui.draggable.js"></script>
```

Then change the configuration object as follows:

```
$(function() {
  $("#selectables div").draggable();
```

Finally we can add the following new click handler directly after the call to the `selectable()` method:

```
$("#refresh").click(function() {
  $("#selectables").selectable("refresh");
});
```

Save this as `selectable9.html`. We've added a new button to the page and we now link to the draggable source file as well as selectable's. Each of the 200 elements are made draggable and selectable.

Our click handler that is attached to the `<button>` will simply call the `refresh` method manually on the selectables container. When we run the page in a browser we should first make a selection of a group, but not all, of the selectable. We should then deselect the elements and move some of them around. We can maybe move other elements that weren't selected into the selection group as well. Really shuffle them up!

When we try to select the same group again, we find that the wrong elements are somehow being selected:

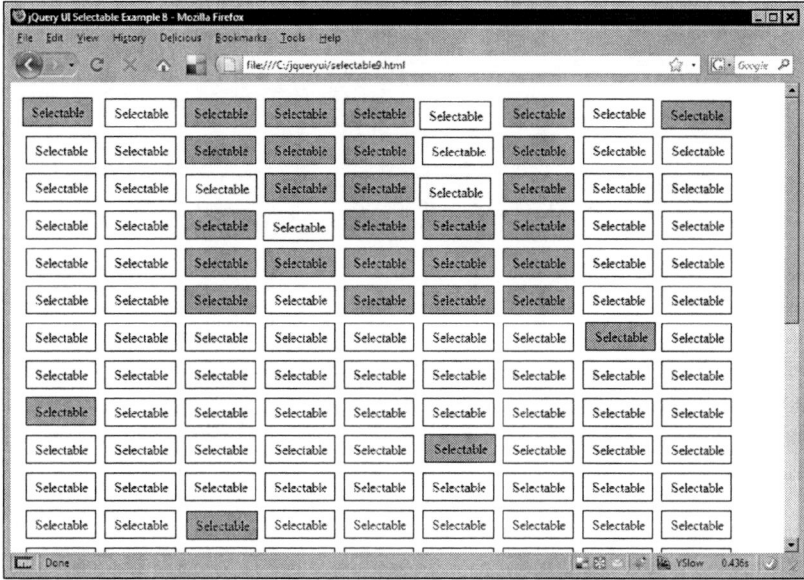

The component hasn't refreshed the positions of the selectables, so it still thinks that all of the selectables are in the same place they were when the first selection was made. If we now click the refresh <button> and make a third selection, the correct elements will be selected.

A selectable image viewer

In our final selectable example, we're going to make a basic image viewer. Images can be chosen for viewing by selecting the appropriate thumbnail. Although this sounds like a relatively easy achievement, in addition to the actual mechanics of displaying the selected image, we'll also need to consider how to handle multiple selections. The following screenshot shows an example of what we'll end up with:

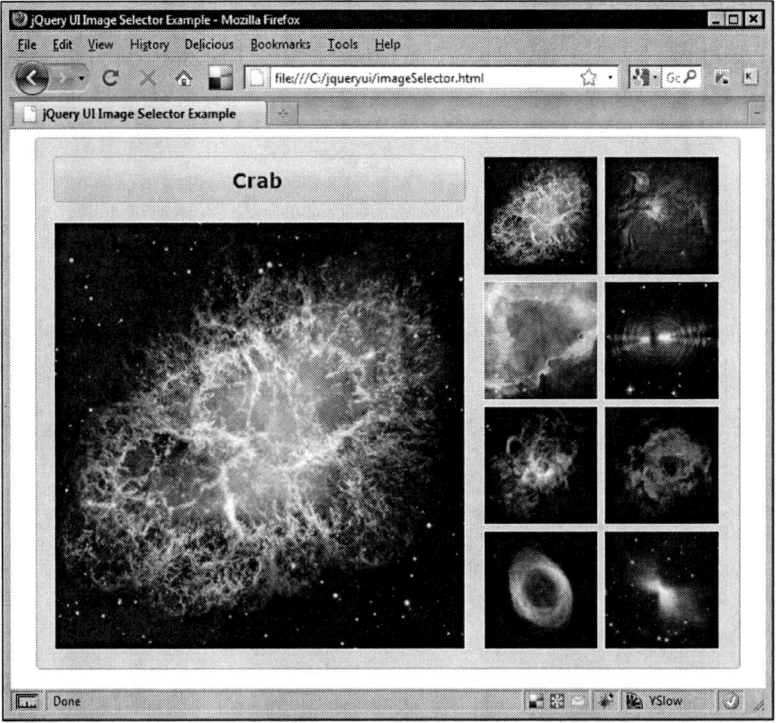

The images used in this example are provided in the code download because they need to be the correct size for this example to look right. There should be eight of both the large and thumbnail versions of each image, and the sizes of each are 110 by 110 pixels for the thumbnails and 400 by 400 pixels for the large versions.

Create a new directory called `selectable` within our `img` directory, then create a new folder called `image-selector` inside this. Next create two new folders inside the previous one called `large` and `thumbs`. You should place the thumbnail images from the code download, or an equivalent number of equally sized images, in the `thumbs` folder and the full-sized images from the code download, or larger versions of your own thumbnails, into the `large` folder.

Let's get started with the code. In a fresh page in your text editor, add the following page:

```
<!DOCTYPE HTML PUBLIC "-//W3C//DTD HTML 4.01//EN"
  "http://www.w3.org/TR/html4/strict.dtd">
<html lang="en">
  <head>
    <link rel="stylesheet" type="text/css"
      href="development-bundle/themes/base/ui.core.css">
    <link rel="stylesheet" type="text/css"
      href="development-bundle/themes/base/ui.theme.css">
    <link rel="stylesheet" type="text/css"
      href="development-bundle/themes/base/ui.tabs.css">
    <link rel="stylesheet" type="text/css"
      href="css/imageSelector.css">
    <meta http-equiv="Content-Type" content="text/html;
      charset=utf-8">
    <title>jQuery UI Image Selector Example</title>
  </head>
  <body>
  <div id="status" class="ui-widget-header ui-corner-all">Crab</div>
    <div id="viewer"><img
      src="img/selectable/image-selector/large/crab.jpg"></div>
    <div id="thumbs">
      <img class="ui-selected" id="crab"
        src="img/selectable/image-selector/thumbs/crab.jpg">
      <img class="right" id="orion"
        src="img/selectable/image-selector/thumbs/orion.jpg">
      <img id="omega"
        src="img/selectable/image-selector/thumbs/omega.jpg">
      <img class="right" id="egg"
        src="img/selectable/image-selector/thumbs/egg.jpg">
      <img id="triangulum"
        src="img/selectable/image-selector/thumbs/triangulum.jpg">
      <img class="right" id="rosette"
        src="img/selectable/image-selector/thumbs/rosette.jpg">
      <img id="ring"
        src="img/selectable/image-selector/thumbs/ring.jpg">
      <img class="right" id="boomerang"
```

```
            src="img/selectable/image-selector/thumbs/boomerang.jpg">
      </div>
   </div>
   <script type="text/javascript"
     src="development-bundle/jquery-1.3.2.js"></script>
   <script type="text/javascript"
     src="development-bundle/ui/ui.core.js"></script>
   <script type="text/javascript"
     src="development-bundle/ui/ui.selectable.js"></script>
   <script type="text/javascript"
     src="development-bundle/ui/ui.tabs.js"></script>
  </body>
</html>
```

Save this as `imageSelector.html`. On the page we have a parent `<div>` with an id of `imageSelector` into which all of our other elements go.

Within the parent, we have a `<div>` that will act as a status bar and display the names of individually selected images, and a `<div>` that will act as the viewing panel and will display the full-sized version of the image. Finally, we have our thumbnail images, which will be made selectable.

Next we need to add the script that make the image selector work, so directly after the final `<script>` element add the following code:

```
<script type="text/javascript">
  $(function() {
    function singleSelect() {
      var id = $(".ui-selected", "#thumbs").attr("id");
      $("<div>").attr("id", "status").text(id).addClass("
        ui-widget-header ui-corner-all").insertBefore("#viewer")
      $("<img>").attr({src: "img/selectable/image-selector/large/" +
        id + ".jpg", id: id }).appendTo("#viewer");
    }
    function multiSelect() {
      $("<div>").attr("id", "tabs").insertBefore("#viewer");
      var tabList = $("<ul>").attr("id",
        "tabList").appendTo("#tabs");
      $(".ui-selected", "#thumbs").each(function() {
        var id = $(this).attr("id"),
          tabItem = $("<li>").appendTo(tabList),
          tabLink = $("<a />").text(id).attr("href", "#tabpanel_" +
            id).appendTo(tabItem),
```

```
            panel = $("<div>").attr("id", "tabpanel_" +
                id).appendTo("#viewer");

          $("<img>").attr({ src: "img/selectable/image-selector/large/"
              + id + ".jpg", id: id }).appendTo(panel);

        });

        $("#viewer").css("left", -1).appendTo("#tabs");

        $("#tabs").tabs();
      }
      var selectOpts = {
        stop: function(e, ui) {
          $("#imageSelector").children().not("#thumbs").remove();

          $("<div>").attr("id", "viewer").insertBefore("#thumbs");

          ($(".ui-selected", "#thumbs").length == 1) ? singleSelect() :
            multiSelect();
        }
      };
      $("#thumbs").selectable(selectOpts);
    });
  </script>
```

The first thing we do in our document.ready function (`$(function(){ }`) is define the two functions `singleSelect()` and `multiSelect()`. One of these functions will be invoked every time a selection is made. If a single thumbnail image is selected the first function is called, if more than one of the elements are selected the second function will be called.

In the `singleSelect()` function we first cache the id of the selected element; we'll be referring to this several times so it's more efficient to store it in a variable. Next we create a new status bar and set its `innerText` to the id value that was cached a moment ago; remember this will be the id attribute of whichever thumbnail is selected. We give the new element some of the framework classes to style the element and then insert it into the image selector container.

The last thing we do in this function is create the full-sized version of the thumbnail. To do this we create a new image, set its `src` attribute to match the large version of the thumbnail that was selected (both the large and thumbnail versions of each image have the same filename). The full-size image is then inserted into the `viewer` container.

Next we define the `multiSelect()` function. This time we start by creating a new `<div>` element, give it an `id` of `tabs` and append it to the `viewer` container. Following this we create a new `<ul>` element as this is a required component of the tabs widget (that we looked at in *Chapter 3*). This element is appended to the `tabs` container we created a moment ago.

We then use jQuery's `each()` method to iterate over each of the thumbnails that were selected. For each item we create a series of variables, which will hold the different elements that make up the tab headings. We cache the `id` attribute of each image, create a new `<li>` and a new `<a>` element. The link will make the clickable tab heading and is given the `id` of the thumbnail as its `innerText`.

We then create the new tab panel that will match the tab heading that we just created. Notice that we create a unique `id` for the content panel based on the thumbnail's `id` attribute and some hardcoded text. Note that the `id` will precisely match the `href` attribute that we set on the `<a>` element. Each new image is created in the same way as in the `singleSelect()` function.

After the `each()` method, we set a CSS property on the viewer container to tidy up its appearance and then append it to the `tabs` container. Finally the `tabs()` method is called on the `tabs` container, transforming it into the tabs widget.

Next we define the configuration object for the selectables. We use the stop callback function to do some prep work such as removing the contents of the image selector container (except for the thumbnails) and creating an empty `viewer` container. We then use the JavaScript ternary conditional to call either the `singleSelect()` or `multiSelect()` functions. Lastly the thumbnails are made selectable.

Styling the image selector

Our example is also heavily reliant on CSS to provide its overall appearance. In a new file in your text editor, create the following stylesheet:

```
#imageSelector {
  width:684px; height:497px; position:relative; margin:0 auto;
  background-color:#dfdede; border:1px solid #adadad;
}
#status {
  width:380px; height:21px; position:absolute; left:17px;
  top:17px; padding:7px 0 0; font-size:19px;
  text-align:center; background-color:#adadad; padding:10px;
  border:1px solid #adadad; text-transform:capitalize;
}
#viewer {
  width:400px; height:400px; position:absolute; left:17px;
```

```
    top:78px; border:1px solid #ffffff;
}
#thumbs {
    width:231px; height:460px; position:absolute; right:17px;
    top:17px;
}
#thumbs img {
    float:left; margin:0 5px 5px 0; cursor:pointer; border:1px solid
#ffffff;
}
#thumbs img.right { margin-right:0; }
#thumbs img.ui-selected { border:1px solid #99ff99; }
#tabs {
    position:absolute; left:17px; background:none; border:none;
    padding:0;
}
#tabs .ui-tabs-panel { padding:0; }
#tabs .ui-tabs-nav {
    padding:0; border:none; background:none; top:54px;
}
#tabs .ui-tabs-nav li { margin:0; }
#tabs .ui-tabs-nav li a {
    padding:5px 4px; font-size:50%; text-transform:capitalize;
}
#tabs .ui-tabs-nav li.ui-tabs-selected a,
#tabs .ui-tabs-nav li.ui-state-disabled a,
#tabs .ui-tabs-nav li.ui-state-processing a {
    font-weight:bold;
}
```

Save this in the css folder as imageSelector.css. Most of the styles are arbitrary and are required purely for layout or very basic styling such as fonts, and background-colors. We're using some of the framework classes in our markup in order to add the rounded corners so the amount of CSS we need to write is minimal. The last few selectors are required in order to override some of the tab widget's default styling.

When we run the example in a browser, we should see something like what is shown in the previous screenshot. When a single thumbnail is selected the full-size version of the image will be displayed. When multiple images have been selected, tabs are created at the top of the viewer, which allow all of the selected images to be shown.

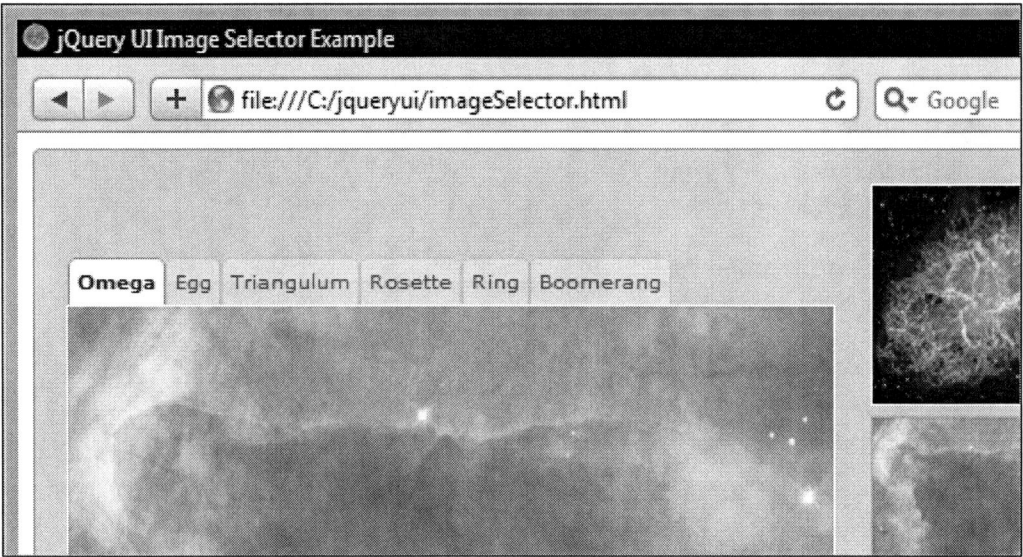

Summary

The selectables component provides a powerful set of behaviors for related items. This enables us to easily provide users with a better means of selecting and manipulating sets of objects.

We first looked at the default implementation and then moved on to look at the two standard properties, along with the numerous callback properties, which can be used to perform different actions at different points in an interaction.

Finally, we looked at the methods exposed by this component's API. We saw that it had the usual range of methods for enabling, disabling, and removing functionality. It also contains a `toggle` method, which reduces the amount of code by allowing us to do one of two things based on the current state of the component.

12
Sorting

The final interaction helper that we're going to look at is the sortables component. This component allows us to define one or more lists of elements (not necessarily actual `<ul>` or `<ol>` elements) where the individual items in the list(s) can be reordered by dragging.

The sortables component is like a specialized implementation of drag-and-drop, with a very specific role. It has an extensive API which caters for a wide range of behaviors. We'll be looking at the following aspects of the component in this chapter:

- The default sortable implementation
- Basic configurable properties
- Working with placeholders
- Sortable helpers
- Sortable items
- Connected sortables
- Sortable's wide range of built-in event handlers
- A look at sortable's methods
- Submitting the sorted result to a server
- Adding drag elements to a sortable

The default implementation

A basic sortable list can be enabled with no additional configuration. Let's do this first so you can get an idea of the behavior enabled by this component. In a new file in your text editor, add the following code:

```html
<!DOCTYPE HTML PUBLIC "-//W3C//DTD HTML 4.01//EN"
  "http://www.w3.org/TR/html4/strict.dtd">
<html lang="en">
  <head>
    <meta http-equiv="Content-Type" content="text/html;
      charset=utf-8">
    <title>jQuery UI Sortable Example 1</title>
  </head>
  <body>
    <p>Put these DJ's in order of your preference:</p>
    <ul id="sortables">
      <li>BT</li>
      <li>James Zabiela</li>
      <li>Sasha</li>
      <li>John Digweed</li>
      <li>Pete Tong</li>
    </ul>
    <script type="text/javascript"
      src="development-bundle/jquery-1.3.2.js"></script>
    <script type="text/javascript"
      src="development-bundle/ui/ui.core.js"></script>
    <script type="text/javascript"
      src="development-bundle/ui/ui.sortable.js"></script>
    <script type="text/javascript">
      $(function() {

        $("#sortables").sortable();
      });
    </script>
  </body>
</html>
```

Save this as `sortable1.html`. On the page, we have a simple unordered list with five list items. There is no default styling associated with this component, so we don't need to link to any stylesheets in this basic example.

Code-wise, the default implementation is the same as it has been for each of the other components. We simply call the `sortable` constructor method on the parent `<ul>` element of the list items we want to make sortable.

Thanks to the sortables component, we should find that the individual list items can be dragged to different positions in the list, as in the following screenshot:

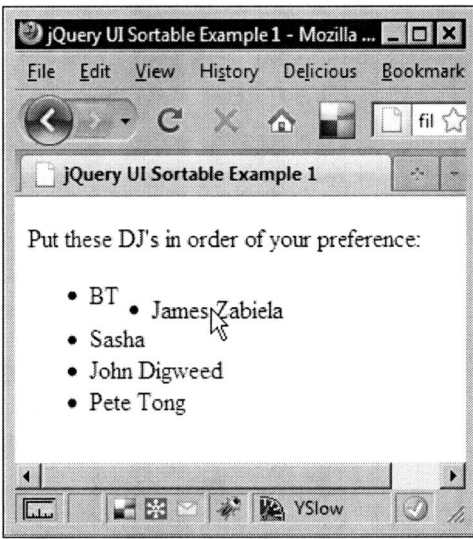

A lot of behaviors are added to the page to accommodate this functionality. As we drag one of the list items up or down in the list, the other items automatically move out of the way creating a slot for the item that is currently being sorted to be dropped on.

Additionally, when a sortable item is dropped, it will slide quickly but smoothly into its new position in the list. The library files that were needed for the basic implementation are as follows:

- `jquery-1.3.2.js`
- `ui.core.js`
- `ui.sortable.js`

As I mentioned earlier, the sortables component is a flexible addition to the library that can be applied to many different types of elements. For example, instead of using a list, we could use a series of `<div>` elements as the sortable list items in place of the `<ul>` element in the previous example.

```
<div id="sortables">
  <div>BT</div>
  <div>James Zabiela</div>
  <div>Sasha</div>
  <div>John Digweed</div>
  <div>Pete Tong</div>
</div>
```

This can be saved as `sortable2.html`. As you can see, the behavior exhibited by this version is exactly the same as it was before. All that's changed is the underlying markup. We can also easily improve its appearance with some basic CSS. In a new file in your text editor, add the following code:

```
#container {
  width:272px; height:322px;
  background:url(../img/sortable/sortable_bg.gif) no-repeat;
  position:relative;
}
#container p {
  font-family:Arial; font-size:11px; position:absolute;
  width:100%; text-align:center; margin-top:20px;
}
#sortables { position:relative; top:45px; height:255px; }
#sortables div {
  height:35px; width:120px; margin-left:80px;
  padding-top:16px;
}
```

Save this in the `css` folder as `sortable.css`. Link to the CSS file in the `<head>` of `sortable2.html` and wrap the existing markup for the sortables in a new container as follows:

```
<div id="container">
  <p>Put these DJs in order of your preference:</p>
  <div id="sortables">
    <div>BT</div>
    <div>James Zabiela</div>
    <div>Sasha</div>
    <div>John Digweed</div>
    <div>Pete Tong</div>
  </div>
</div>
```

Save the change as `sortable3.html`. The underlying HTML and the JavaScript that drives it are identical, but with just a few CSS selectors and rules we can dramatically change the appearance of our example, as shown in the following screenshot:

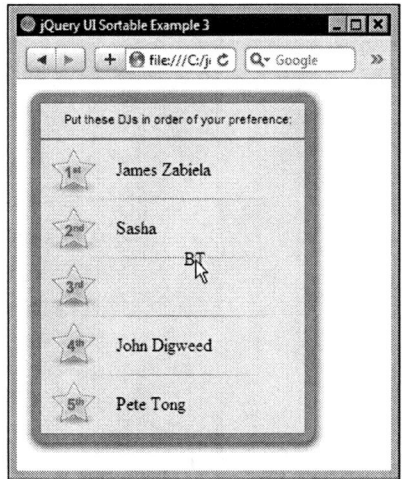

In this example we use a simple background image on top of which the sortable elements are positioned.

Configuring sortable options

The sortables component has a huge range of configurable options, much more than any of the other interaction components (but not as many as some of the widgets). The table below illustrates the range of options at our disposal.

Option	Default value	Usage
appendTo	"parent"	Sets the element that helpers are appended to during a sort.
axis	false	Constrains sortables to one axis of movement. Possible values are the strings x or y.
cancel	":input, button"	Specifies elements that cannot be sorted if they are the elements being sorted.
connectWith	false	Accepts the selector of another list of sortables to enable one-way sorting from the current list to the specified list.

Option	Default value	Usage
containment	false	Constrains sortables to their container while they are being dragged. Values can be the strings parent, window, or document, or can be a jQuery selector, or element node.
cursor	"auto"	Defines the CSS cursor to apply while dragging a sortable element.
cursorAt	false	Accepts an object specifying the coordinates that the mouse pointer should be at while a sort is taking place. The keys in the object may be top, right, bottom, or left and the values should be integers.
delay	0	Sets the time delay in milliseconds before the sort begins once a sortable item has been clicked (with the mouse button held down).
distance	1	Sets how far in pixels the mouse pointer should move while the left button is held down before the sort begins.
dropOnEmpty	true	Allows linked items from linked sortables to be dropped onto empty slots.
forceHelperSize	false	Forces the helper to have a size when set to true.
forcePlaceholderSize	false	Forces the placeholder to have a size if set to true. The placeholder is the empty space that a sortable can be dropped on to.
grid	false	Sets sortables to snap to a grid while being dragged. Accepts an array with two items — the x and y distances between gridlines.
handle	false	Specifies an element to be used as the drag handle on sortable items. Can be a selector or an element node.

Option	Default value	Usage
helper	"original"	Specifies a helper element that will be used as a proxy element while the element is being sorted. Can accept a function that returns an element.
items	">*"	Specifies the items that should be made sortable. The default makes all children sortable.
opacity	false	Specifies the CSS opacity of the element being sorted. Value should be an integer from 0.01 to 1 with 1 being fully opaque.
placeholder	false	Specifies a CSS class to be added to empty slots.
revert	false	Enables animation when moving sortables into their new slots once they have been dropped.
scroll	true	Enables page scrolling when a sortable is moved to the edge of the viewport.
scrollSensitivity	20	Sets how close a sortable must get, in pixels, to the edge of the viewport before scrolling should begin.
scrollSpeed	20	Sets the distance in pixels that the viewport should scroll when a sortable is dragged within the sensitivity range.
tolerance	"intersect"	Controls how much of the element being sorted must overlap other elements before the placeholder is moved. Other possible value is the string pointer.
zIndex	1000	The CSS z-index of the sortable/ helper while being dragged.

Let's work some of these properties into our previous example to get a feel for the effect they have on the behavior of the component.

Change the final `<script>` element in `sortable3.html` so that it appears as follows:

```
<script type="text/javascript">
  $(function() {
    var sortOpts = {
      axis: "y",
      containment: "#container",
      cursor: "move",
      distance: 30
    };
        $("#sortables").sortable(sortOpts);
  });
</script>
```

Save this as `sortable4.html`. We use four options in our configuration object; the `axis` option is set to `y` to constrain the motion of the sortable currently being dragged to just up and down.

The `containment` option specifies the element that the sortables should be contained within. Care should be taken with this option. If we had specified `#sortables` as the container, we would have not been able to move items into the top or bottom positions. This is because the first sortable element is flush against the top of the container and the last element is flush against the bottom. In order to be able to push a sortable element out of the way, there must be some space above or below it.

We also specify the `cursor` option that automatically adds the CSS `move` icon. Like with the draggable component that we looked at in *Chapter 9*, the CSS `move` icon is not actually displayed until the sort begins.

Finally, we configure the `distance` option with a value of `30`, which specifies that the mouse pointer should move 30 pixels before the sort begins. The `distance` option works in the same way with sortables as it did with draggables and is great for preventing unwanted sorts, but in practice we'd probably use a much lower threshold than 30 pixels.

The effects of these options can easily be seen when the page is run in a browser.

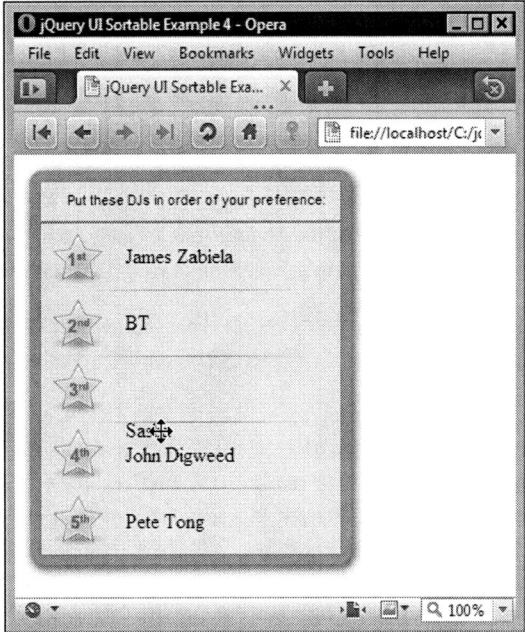

 Note that Google Chrome can have problems displaying the correct cursor when the cursor option is used, although this doesn't prevent the interaction from working. We could set the cursor using CSS instead, but then Chrome will only display the move cursor while the pointer hovers over the sortables, not while a sort is actually taking place.

Let's look at some more options. Change the underlying `<div>` elements in `sortable4.html` so that they appear as follows:

```
<div id="sortables">
  <div>BT<div class="handle"></div></div>
  <div>James Zabiela<div class="handle"></div></div>
  <div>Sasha<div class="handle"></div></div>
  <div>John Digweed<div class="handle"></div></div>
  <div>Pete Tong<div class="handle"></div></div>
</div>
```

Then change the configuration object to as follows:

```
var sortOpts = {
  revert: "slow",
  handle: ".handle",
  delay: 1000,
  opacity: 0.5
};
```

Save this as `sortable5.html`. We've made a slight change to the page. Within each sortable element is a new `<span>` element that will be used as the sort handle.

The `revert` option has a default value of `true`, but can also take one of the speed string values (`slow`, `normal`, or `fast`) that we've seen in other animation options in other components.

The `delay` option accepts a value in milliseconds that the component should wait before allowing the sort to begin. If the mouse pointer is moved away from the handle while the left-button is held down the sort will still occur after the specified time. If the mouse-button is let go of however, the sort will be cancelled.

The value of the `opacity` option is used to specify the CSS opacity of the element that is being sorted while the sort takes place. The value should be a floating-point number between `0` and `1`, with `1` corresponding to full opacity and `0` specifying no opacity. Note that the `opacity` property can affect the way that IE renders text.

One of the properties we've used is the `handle` option that allows us to define a region within the sortable, which must be used to initiate the sort. Dragging on other parts of the sortable will not cause the sort to begin.

The handles have been styled with some CSS, so we'll need to update `sortable.css` as well. We need to add `position:relative` to the `#sortables div` selector, and then add the highlighted new selector and rules to the end of the file:

```
#container {
  width:272px; height:322px;
  background:url(../img/sortable/sortable_bg.gif) no-repeat;
  position:relative;
}
#container p {
  font-family:Arial; font-size:11px; position:absolute;
  width:100%; text-align:center; margin-top:20px;
}
#sortables { position:relative; top:45px; height:255px; }
#sortables div {
  height:35px; width:120px; margin-left:80px;
```

```
    padding-top:16px;
    position:relative;
}

#sortables div.handle {
    border:1px solid #003399; position:absolute; top:20px;
    margin-left:20px; width:7px; height:7px; background-color:#66FF66;
}
```

Save the changes as `sortableHandle.css` in the `css` folder. You can see how the handle will appear in the following screenshot:

Note that Opera positions any sortables that have been moved incorrectly due to the relative positioning of the sortable elements.

Placeholders

A placeholder defines the empty space or slot, that is left while one of the sortables is in the process of being moved to its new position. The placeholder isn't rigidly positioned, it will dynamically move to whichever sortable has been displaced by the movement of the sortable that is being sorted.

There are two options that are specifically concerned with placeholders—the very aptly named `placeholder` option and the `forcePlaceholderSize` property.

The `placeholder` option allows you to define a CSS class that should be added to the placeholder while it is empty. This is a useful property that we can use often in our implementations.

The `forcePlaceholderSize` option, set to `false` by default, is an option that we'll probably use less often. The placeholder will automatically assume the size of the sortable item while a sort is in progress, which in most cases is fine.

Let's take a look at the `placeholder` option, remove the `<span>` elements from the sortable `<div>` elements in `sortable5.html` and then change the configuration object so that it appears as follows:

```
var sortOpts = {
  placeholder: "empty"
};
```

Save this as `sortable6.html`. We've specified the name of the class that we want to add to the placeholder. Remember this is a class name, not a class selector, so no period is used at the start of the string.

Next, we should add the selector and rules to our CSS file. The CSS file we use is exactly the same as our base CSS file (not the one from the previous example) with the following code added to the end:

```
.empty { background-color:#cdfdcd; }
```

Save this as `sortablePlaceholder.css` in the `css` folder. When we run the new HTML file in a browser, we should be able to see the specified styles applied to the placeholder while the sort is taking place.

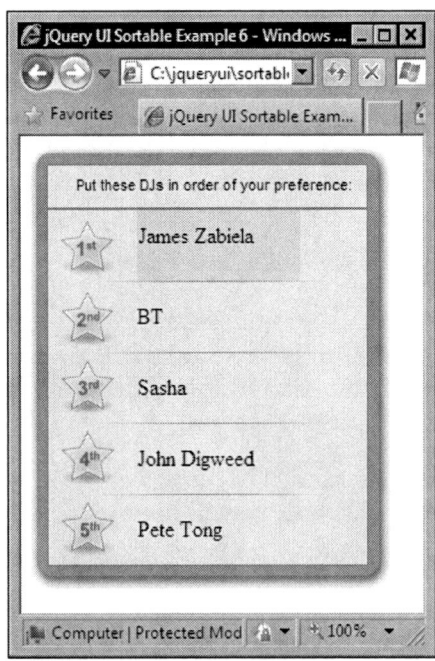

Sortable helpers

We looked at helper/proxy elements back when we looked at the draggables component earlier in the book. Helpers can also be defined for sortables that function in a similar way to those of the draggable component, although there are some subtle differences in this implementation.

With sortables, the original sortable is hidden when the sort interaction begins and a clone of the original element is dragged instead. So with sortables, helpers are an inherent feature.

Like with draggables, the `helper` option of sortables may take a function as its value. The function, when used, will automatically receive the `event` object and an object containing useful properties from the sortable element as arguments.

The function must return the element to use as the helper. Although it's very similar to the draggable helper example, let's take a quick look at it when used in conjunction with sortables. In `sortable6.html`, change the last `<script>` block so that it appears as follows:

```
<script type="text/javascript">
  $(function() {
    function helperMaker(e, ui) {
      return $("<div>").text($(ui).text()).css({
        opacity: 0.5,
        border: "4px solid #cccccc",
        textAlign: "center"
      });
    }
    var sortOpts = {
      helper: helperMaker
    };

    $("#sortables").sortable(sortOpts);
  });
</script>
```

Save this file as `sortable7.html`. We have our `helperMaker` function that creates and returns the element to be used as the helper while the sort is in progress. We can set some basic CSS properties on the new element so that we don't need to provide additional rules in the stylesheet (additionally you may want to switch back to `sortable.css`).

The following screenshot shows how the helper will appear while a sort is taking place:

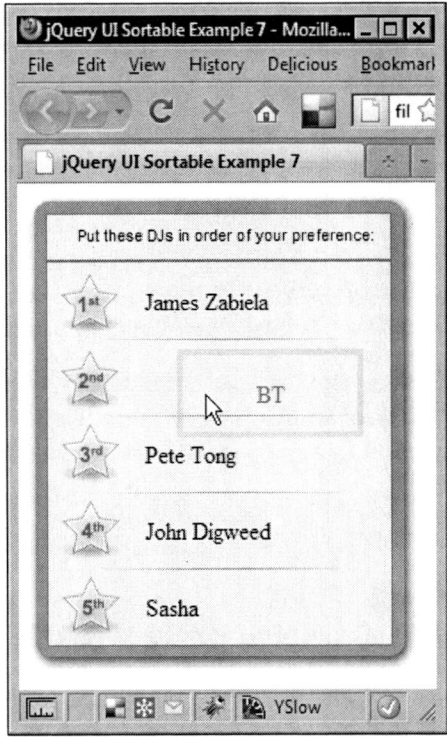

Sortable items

By default, all children of the element that the `sortable` method is called on are turned into sortables. While this is a useful feature of the component, there may be times when we don't necessarily want all child elements to become sortable.

The `items` option controls which child elements of the specified element should be made sortable. It makes all child elements sortable using the string `>*` as its default value, but we can alter this to specify only the elements we want. Change the sortable `<div>` elements in `sortable7.html` so that they appear as follows:

```
<div id="sortables">
  <div>BT</div>
  <div>James Zabiela</div>
  <div>Sasha</div>
  <div>John Digweed</div>
  <div class="unsortable">Pete Tong</div>
</div>
```

Then change the configuration object to make use of the `items` option.

```
$(function() {
  var sortOpts = {
    items: ">:not(.unsortable)"
  };
```

Save this as `sortable8.html`. We've added a class name of `unsortable` to the last sortable element in the underlying markup.

In our `<script>`, we've specified the selector `">:not(.unsortable)"` as the value of the `items` option, so our last `<div>` element with the class name `unsortable` will not be made sortable, while the rest of the `<div>` elements will.

The new CSS used to style the `unsortable` element can be as simple as the following selector and rules, which should be added to `sortable.css`.

```
#sortables div.unsortable {
  border:1px solid #000; background-color:#CCCCCC;
  height:26px; padding:4px 0 0 5px; margin-top:8px;
  color:#adabab;
}
```

Save this as `sortableItems.css` in the `css` folder. Try the new page out, the following screenshot shows what you should see:

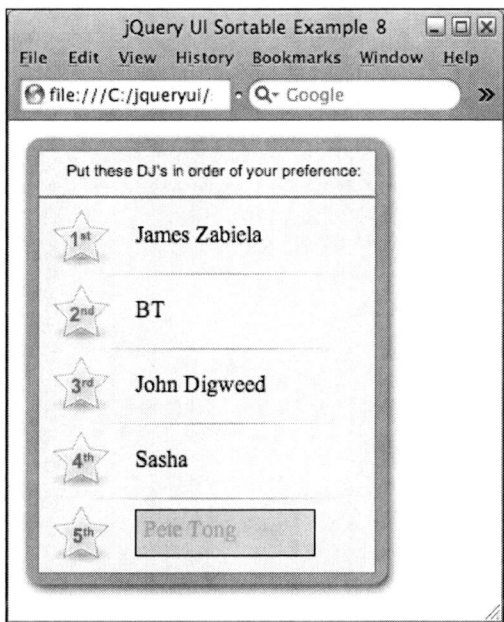

Connected lists

So far, the examples that we have looked at have all centered on a single list of sortable items. What happens when we want to have two lists of sortable items, and more importantly, can we move items from one list to another?

Having two sortable lists is of course extremely easy and involves simply defining two containers and their child elements, and then passing each container to the `sortable()` method.

Allowing separate lists of sortables to exchange and share sortables is also extremely easy. This is thanks to the `connectWith` option that allows us to define an array of sortable containers whose sortables can move between the specified lists. Let's look at this in action. In a new file in your text editor, add the following page:

```html
<!DOCTYPE HTML PUBLIC "-//W3C//DTD HTML 4.01//EN"
  "http://www.w3.org/TR/html4/strict.dtd">
<html lang="en">
  <head>
    <link rel="stylesheet" type="text/css"
      href="css/sortableConnected.css">
    <meta http-equiv="Content-Type" content="text/html;
      charset=utf-8">
    <title>jQuery UI Sortable Example 9</title>
  </head>
  <body>
    <p>Tell us what music you like and don't like:</p>
    <div id="likes">
      <p>Likes</p>
      <div>House</div>
      <div>Hip Hop</div>
      <div>Breaks</div>
      <div>Drum and Bass</div>
      <div>Rock</div>
    </div>
    <div id="dislikes">
      <p>Dislikes</p>
      <div>Folk</div>
      <div>Country</div>
      <div>Pop</div>
      <div>Classical</div>
      <div>Opera</div>
    </div>
    <script type="text/javascript"
      src="development-bundle/jquery-1.3.2.js"></script>
    <script type="text/javascript"
      src="development-bundle/ui/ui.core.js"></script>
    <script type="text/javascript"
      src="development-bundle/ui/ui.sortable.js"></script>
```

```
<script type="text/javascript">
  $(function() {
    var sortOpts = {
      items: "div",
      connectWith: ["#likes", "#dislikes"]
    };
    $("#likes, #dislikes").sortable(sortOpts);
  });
</script>
</body>
</html>
```

Save this as `sortable9.html`. Everything on the page is pretty similar to what we have worked with before. There are just two simple collections of nested `<div>` elements with some explanatory text instead of one. However, within our final `<script>` tag we have some new, although still very simple, code.

We still define a single configuration object, which can be shared between both sets of sortable elements. We're using the `items` option once again to ensure that the `<p>` elements that form the box headings within our sortable containers aren't sortable themselves.

The `connectWith` option is able to accept multiple selectors if they are passed in as an array and it's this option that allows us to share individual sortables between the two sortable containers.

This configuration option only provides a one-way transmission of sortables, so if we were to only use the configuration object in the `likes` sortable and specify just the `id` of the `dislikes` sortable, we would only be able to move items from `likes` to `dislikes`, not the other way.

Specifying both sortables' `id` attributes in the option and selecting both of the containers when calling the `sortable()` method allows us to move items between both elements, and allows us to cut down on coding. Note that we could also have used the following `<script>` to achieve the same result:

```
<script type="text/javascript">
  $(function() {
    var sortOpts = {
      items: "div",
      connectWith: "#dislikes"
    };
    var sortOpts2 = {
      items: "div",
      connectWith: "#likes"
    };
```

```
    $("#likes, #dislikes").sortable(sortOpts);
  });
</script>
```

Our example code will work completely as it is with no styling whatsoever, but for aesthetic purposes, we may use any arbitrary CSS to make things look as we wish. The following CSS for example is more than adequate in giving an impression of how the two sets could look:

```css
p { position:relative; left:10px; }
#likes, #dislikes {
  width:180px;
  border:1px solid #000;
  float:left;
  margin-left:10px; padding-bottom:5px;
}
#likes p, #dislikes p {
  margin:0px 0 5px;
  text-align:center; font-weight:bold;
  border-bottom:1px solid #000;
  color:#fff;
  left:0px;
}
#likes p { background-color:#66CC66; }
#dislikes p { background-color:#FF0000; }
#likes div, #dislikes div { margin-left:10px; }
```

Save this as `sortableConnected.css` in the `css` folder. When you run the page in your browser, you should find that not only can the individual items be sorted in their respective elements, but that items can also be moved between elements, as shown in the following screenshot:

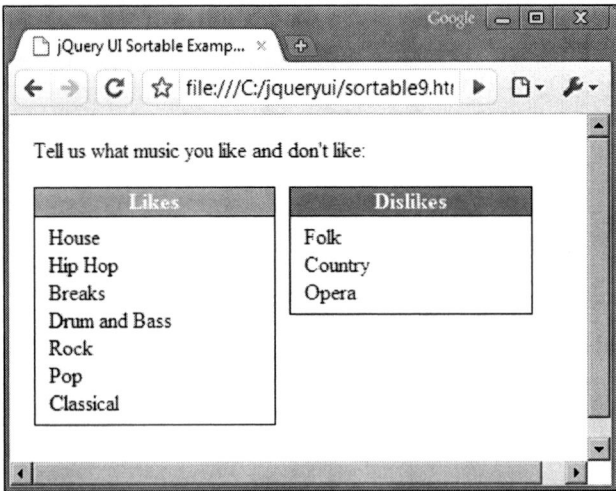

Reacting to sortable events

In addition to the already large list of configurable options defined in the sortables class, there are also a whole lot more in the form of event callbacks, which can be passed functions to execute at different points during a sortable interaction. These are listed in the following table:

Callback	Fired
activate	When sorting starts on a connected list.
beforeStop	When the sort has stopped but the original slot is still available.
change	During a sort, when the DOM position of the sortable has changed.
deactivate	When sorting stops on a connected list.
out	When a sortable is moved away from a connected list.
over	When a sortable is over a connected list. This is great for providing visual feedback while a sort is taking place.
receive	When a sortable is received from a connected list.
remove	When a sortable is moved from a connected list.
sort	When a sort is taking place.
start	When the sort starts.
stop	When the sort ends.
update	When the sort has ended and the DOM position has changed.

Event handlers such as these are important because they allow us as the programmers to react with code to specific things occurring. Each of the components that we've looked at in the preceding chapters has defined their own suite of custom events and the sortables component is certainly no exception.

Many of these events will fire during any single sort interaction. The following list shows the order in which they will fire:

- start
- sort
- change
- beforeStop
- stop
- update

As soon as one of the sortables is 'picked up', the start event is triggered. Following this, on *every single mouse move* the sort event will fire, making this event very intensive.

As soon as another item is displaced by the current sortable, the `change` event is fired. Once the sortable is 'dropped', the `beforeStop` and `stop` events fire and if the sortable is now at a different position, the `update` event is fired last of all.

For the next few examples, we'll work some of these event handling options into the previous example, starting with the `start` and `stop` events. Change the configuration object in `sortable9.html` so that it appears as follows:

```
var sortOpts = {
  items: "div",
  connectWith: ["#likes", "#dislikes"],
  start: function(e, ui) {
    $("<p>").text("The active sort item is " +
      ui.helper.text()).css({clear:"both"}).attr("id",
      "message").appendTo("body");
  },
  stop: function() {
    $("#message").remove();
  }
};
```

Save this as `sortable10.html`. Our event usage in this example is minimal. When the sort starts, we simply create a new paragraph element and add some text to it, including the text content of the element that is being sorted. The text message is then duly appended to the `<body>` of the page. When the sort stops, we remove the text.

Using the second object passed to the callback function is very easy as you can see. The object itself refers to the parent sortables container, and the `helper` property refers to the actual item being sorted (or its helper). As this is a jQuery object, we can call jQuery methods, like `text`, on it.

When we run the page, the message should appear briefly until the sort ends, at which point it's removed.

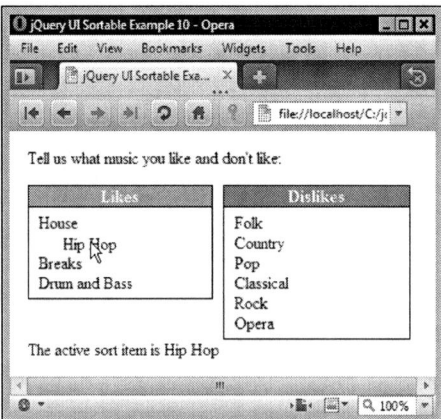

Let's look at one more of these simple callbacks before we move on to look at the additional callbacks used with connected sortables. Change the final `<script>` element in `sortable10.html` to this:

```
<script type="text/javascript">
  $(function() {

    var places = [
      "1st",
      "2nd",
      "3rd",
      "4th",
      "5th",
      "6th",
      "7th",
      "8th",
      "9th",
      "10th"
    ];
    var getPlaces = function(e, ui) {
      $("#message").remove();
      $(this).children().not("p").each(function(x, item) {
        if ($(item).text() === ui.item.text()) {
          $("<p>").text(ui.item.text() + " is now at " + places[x] +
            " place in the " + $(item).parent().find("p").text() +
            " list").css({clear: "both"}).attr("id",
            "message").appendTo("body");
        }
      });
    };
    var sortOpts = {
      items: "div",
      connectWith: ["#likes, #dislikes"],
      beforeStop: getPlaces,
      receive: getPlaces
    };
    $("#likes, #dislikes").sortable(sortOpts);
  });
</script>
```

Save this as `sortable11.html`. In this example, we work with the `receive` and `beforeStop` callbacks to provide a message indicating the position within the list that any sortable is moved to as well as which list it is in. We also make use of the `ui.item` property from the object, which is automatically passed to any callback functions used by the events.

We start by defining an array where each item is a string specifying any of the positions that any sortable may occupy. We then define our callback function `getPlaces()`; within this function. We first remove any message that may exist from previous sort operations.

We then cycle through each child in the active sortable (except for the heading paragraphs) and compare the text content of the current child to the text content of the element that was sorted. Note that `$(this)` is mapped to the list that the sorted element belongs to, not the element itself.

If they match then we know programmatically which item was sorted and can get the appropriate place label from our array using the first argument passed to the `each` function. We can then display a brief message indicating the new position of the sorted element.

In our configuration object, we specify that just the `<div>` elements should be sortable with the `items` option and connect the two lists using the `connectWith` option. We make use of both the `receive` and `beforeStop` options, which both point to our `getPlaces` function.

The `receive` event is fired whenever a sortable container receives a new sortable element from a connected list. The `beforeStop` event is fired just before the sort interaction ends. In terms of event order in this example the `beforeStop` event is fired first followed by the `receive` event.

The reason we need to hook into both events is for when a sortable is moved from one sortable to another. If we didn't use the `receive` callback as well, when the `beforeStop` event is fired, the sortable will not be part of the new sortable yet. Therefore, its text won't match any of the sortables in the new list, so the message will not be created.

The `receive` event will only be fired if a sortable element moves to a new sortable container. The following screenshot shows how the page should look following a sort interaction:

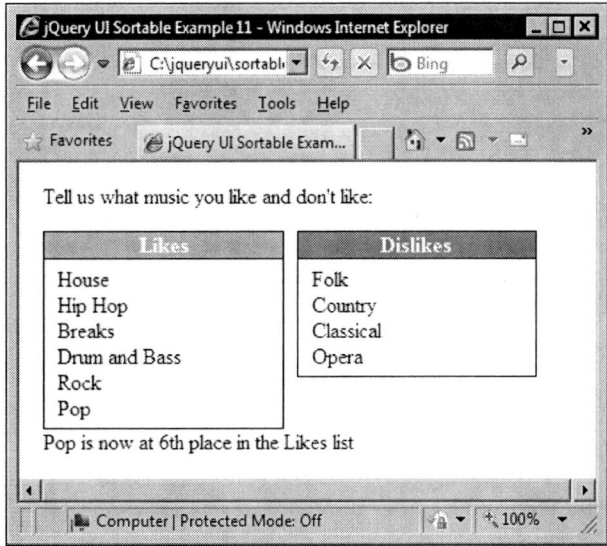

Connected callbacks

Six of the available callbacks can be used in conjunction with connected sortables. These events fire at different times during an interaction alongside the events that we have already looked at.

Like the standard unconnected events, not all of the connected events will fire in any single interaction. Some events, such as `over`, `off`, `remove`, and `receive` will only fire if a sort item moves to a new list.

Other events, such as the `activate` and `deactivate` events, will fire in all executions, whether any sort items change lists or not. Additionally, some connected events, such as `activate` and `deactivate`, will fire for each connected list on the page.

Provided at least one item is moved between lists, events will fire in the following order:

- `start`
- `activate`
- `sort`
- `change`

- beforeStop
- stop
- remove
- update
- receive
- deactivate

Let's now see some of these connected events in action. Change the configuration object in sortable11.html so that it appears as follows:

```
var sortOpts = {
   items: "div",
   connectWith: ["#likes", "#dislikes"],
   activate: function() {
      $("<p>").text($(this).attr("id") + " has been
         activated").css({clear:"both"}).appendTo("body");
   },
   deactivate: function() {
      $("<p>").text($(this).attr("id") + " has been
         deactivated").css({clear:"both"}).appendTo("body");
   },
   receive: function(e, ui) {
      $("<p>").text(ui.item.text() + " was moved out of " +
         ui.sender.attr("id") + " and into " +
         $(this).attr("id")).css({clear: "both"}).appendTo("body");
   }
};
```

Save this as sortable12.html. The activate and deactivate events are fired for each connected list at the start of any sort interaction. As these events are executed in the context of each sortable, we can again use $(this) to refer to each sortable container instead of using the second object that is automatically passed to each of our functions.

When we run the page in a browser we see that as soon as a sort begins, both of the sortables are activated, and when the sort ends, both of them are deactivated. If an item is moved between lists, the message generated by the receive callback is shown.

We can easily determine which sortable the item originated in using the `sender` property of the second object passed to our function. The following screenshot shows how the page should appear when an item is moved between sortables:

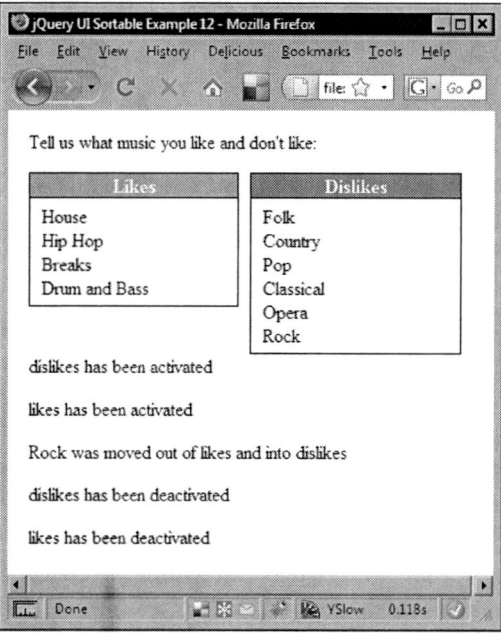

Sortable methods

The sortables component exposes the usual set of methods for making the component 'do things', and like the selectables component that we looked at before. It also defines a couple of unique methods not seen in any of the other components. The following table lists sortable's full unique methods:

Method	Use
cancel	Cancels the sort and causes elements to return to their original positions.
refresh	Triggers the reloading of the set of sortables.
refreshPositions	Triggers the cached refresh of the set of sortables.
serialize	Constructs a URL-appendable string for sending new sort order to the server.
toArray	Serializes the sortables into an array of strings.

The `serialize` and `toArray` methods are great for doing something useful with the resulting post-sort sortables, such as sending the list to a server app. Let's see this in action. In a new file in your text editor, create the following page:

```
<!DOCTYPE HTML PUBLIC "-//W3C//DTD HTML 4.01//EN"
  "http://www.w3.org/TR/html4/strict.dtd">
<html lang="en">
  <head>
    <link rel="stylesheet" type="text/css"
      href="css/sortableConnected.css">
    <meta http-equiv="Content-Type" content="text/html;
      charset=utf-8">
    <title>jQuery UI Sortable Example 13</title>
  </head>
  <body>
    <p>Put these in ascending order of your preference</p>
    <div id="likes">
      <p>Likes</p>
      <div id="likes_house">House</div>
      <div id="likes_hiphop">Hip Hop</div>
      <div id="likes_breaks">Breaks</div>
      <div id="likes_drumandbass">Drum and Bass</div>
      <div id="likes_rock">Rock</div>
    </div>
    <button id="serialize">Serialize it!</button>
    <script type="text/javascript"
      src="development-bundle/jquery-1.3.2.js"></script>
    <script type="text/javascript"
      src="development-bundle/ui/ui.core.js"></script>
    <script type="text/javascript"
      src="development-bundle/ui/ui.sortable.js"></script>
    <script type="text/javascript">
      $(function() {
        var sortOpts = {
          items: "div"
        };
        $("#likes").sortable(sortOpts);
        $("#serialize").click(function() {
          var serialized = $("#likes").sortable("serialize",
            { key:"likes"});
          $("#string").remove();
          $("<p>").attr("id",
            "string").text(serialized).appendTo("body");
        });
      });
    </script>
  </body>
</html>
```

Save this as `sortable13.html`. We've dropped the second set of sortables for this example and added a button to the page that triggers the serialization. We've also added `id` attributes to each of the sortable items in the format of the name of the parent sortable (likes) and the individual items, separated by an underscore.

The click handling function simply serializes the sortable elements by calling the `serialize` method and then removes any previous message that may exist on the page. Finally the serialized string is added to the page so that we can see the format it takes.

We use the `key` configuration property of the `serialize` method to set the list `id` as the first part of each item in the serialized string.

The following screenshot shows what you should see when you run the page in your browser and click the **Serialize it!** button (and, optionally perform an actual sort):

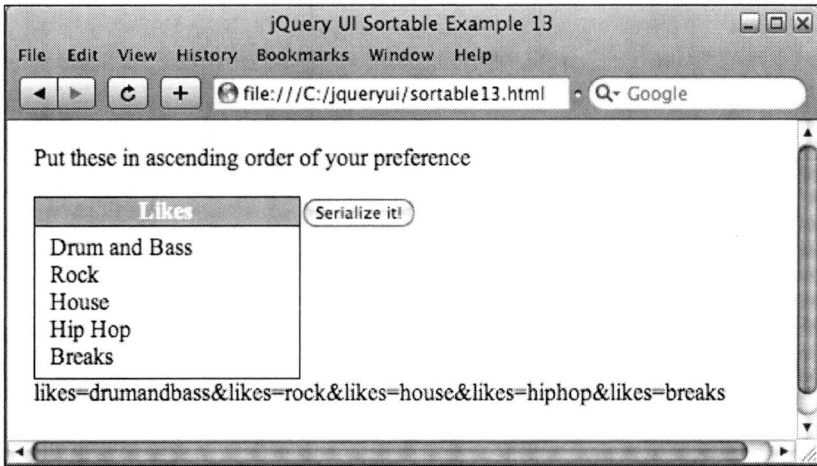

As you can see, the format of the serialized string is quite straight-forward. The sortable items appear in the order that the items appear on the page and are separated by an ampersand. Each serialized item is made up of two parts — the name of the sortable to which they belong and the individual item, separated (by default, but can be changed) by the `=` character.

If serialization is a term you've never come across before, and as no native serialization methods exist within JavaScript, this would be no surprise. Don't worry as you've probably used it before (or at least its opposite deserialization) without even realizing.

When data is converted into JSON so that you can download it and process it directly in the browser, it is serialized into a format suitable for transportation across the Internet. When you process the JSON object on the client-side to extract the data within it, you are in effect deserializing, or parsing it.

You might be wondering why the method doesn't serialize the sortable into a JSON object to pass back to the server. The main reason is because the output of the serialize method is in the format that backend code, such as PHP will most likely be expecting.

In the previous example, all we do is display the serialized string on the page, but the string is in the perfect format for use with jQuery's `ajax` method, or to append to a URL to pass the resulting string to a server for further processing.

The component uses a regular expression to read the `id` attributes of each sortable item and split them into the set name and item name format found in the outputted string. It is possible to supply an alternative expression using a literal configuration object passed to the `serialize` method. It is also possible to use an alternative attribute than `id` to build the serialized string.

The options available for use with this method are listed in the following table:

Option	Default value	Usage
attribute	id	Specifies the `id` to use as the item name in the parsed string.
connected	false	If set to `true` serialization will include all connected lists.
expression	`"(.+)[-=_](.+)"`	The expression used to parse the specified attribute of each sortable item.
key	The first result of expression	Specifies the key to be used as the property of each item in the serialized output.

The `toArray` method works in a similar way to serialize, except that with `toArray` the output is not a string but an array of strings. This gives us an object that can easily be passed to other widgets on the page.

Widget compatibility

In the previous chapter, we saw that both the resizables and the selectables component worked well with the tabs widget (and we already know how well the dialog and resizables components go together). The sortable component is also highly compatible with other widgets. Let's look at a basic example. In a new page in your text editor, add the following code:

```
<!DOCTYPE HTML PUBLIC "-//W3C//DTD HTML 4.01//EN"
  "http://www.w3.org/TR/html4/strict.dtd">
<html lang="en">
  <head>
    <link rel="stylesheet" type="text/css"
      href="development-bundle/themes/base/ui.core.css">
    <link rel="stylesheet" type="text/css"
      href="development-bundle/themes/base/ui.theme.css">
    <link rel="stylesheet" type="text/css"
      href="development-bundle/themes/base/ui.tabs.css">
    <link rel="stylesheet" type="text/css"
      href="css/sortableTabs.css">
    <meta http-equiv="Content-Type" content="text/html;
      charset=utf-8">
    <title>jQuery UI Sortable Tabs Example</title>
  </head>
  <body>
    <div id="tabs">
      <ul>
        <li><a href="#0"><span>Sort Tab 1</span></a></li>
        <li><a href="#1"><span>Sort Tab 2</span></a></li>
        <li><a href="#2"><span>Sort Tab 3</span></a></li>
      </ul>
      <div id="0">The first tab panel</div>
      <div id="1">The second tab panel</div>
      <div id="2">The third tab panel</div>
    </div>
    <script type="text/javascript"
      src="development-bundle/jquery-1.3.2.js"></script>
    <script type="text/javascript"
      src="development-bundle/ui/ui.core.js"></script>
    <script type="text/javascript"
      src="development-bundle/ui/ui.tabs.js"></script>
    <script type="text/javascript"
      src="development-bundle/ui/ui.sortable.js"></script>
    <script type="text/javascript">
      $(function() {

        $("#tabs").tabs();
        var sortOpts = {
          axis: "x",
          items: "li"
        };
        $("#tabs").sortable(sortOpts);
      });
    </script>
  </body>
</html>
```

Save this page as `sortableTabs.html`. There is nothing in the code that we haven't seen before, so we won't go into any great detail about it. Note that only the `tabs()` and `sortable()` methods are called on the same element — the outer container containing `<div>` element. We also need a little bit of CSS, so in another new file in your text editor add the following selectors and rules:

```
#tabs .ui-sortable-helper, #tabs .ui-sortable-placeholder {
  height:42px !important;
}
.ui-tabs .ui-tabs-nav li.ui-sortable-helper a {
  padding:10px 0 0 15px;
}
```

Save this file in the `css` folder as `sortableTabs.css`. The first rule overrides a fixed height that is given to the tab headings while a sort is in progress. The fixed height is added to the element directly as part of the `style` attribute, which is why we need to use the `!important` flag. The second rule is used to prevent the text in the tab heading overflowing on to the next line.

When we run the page in a browser, we should find that the components work in exactly the way that we want them to. The tabs can be sorted horizontally to any order, but as the tabs are linked to their panel by `href`, they will still refer to the correct panel.

Sorting the tabs works on the `mousedown` event and selecting the tabs works on the `mouseup` event, so there are no event collisions and no situations arising where you want to select a tab but end up sorting it. The next screenshot shows how the tabs may appear after sorting.

Adding draggables

When we looked at draggables and droppables earlier in the book, we saw that there was a configuration option for draggables called `connectToSortable`. Let's take a look at that option now that we've been introduced to the fundamentals of the sortables component. In this example we'll create a sortable task list that can have new tasks dragged into it. The resulting page will appear as follows:

In a new file in your text editor add the following code:

```
<!DOCTYPE HTML PUBLIC "-//W3C//DTD HTML 4.01//EN"
  "http://www.w3.org/TR/html4/strict.dtd">
<html lang="en">
  <head>
    <link rel="stylesheet" type="text/css"
      href="css/sortableDrag.css">
    <meta http-equiv="Content-Type" content="text/html;
      charset=utf-8">
    <title>jQuery UI Sortable Example 14</title>
  </head>
  <body>
    <ul id="drag">
      <li>Click to write new task...</li>
    </ul>
    <a id="add" href="#"></a>
    <div id="taskList">
      <ul id="tasks">
```

```
        <li>Design new site</li>
        <li>Call client</li>
        <li>Order pizza</li>
      </ul>
    </div>
    <script type="text/javascript"
      src="development-bundle/jquery-1.3.2.js"></script>
    <script type="text/javascript"
      src="development-bundle/ui/ui.core.js"></script>
    <script type="text/javascript"
      src="development-bundle/ui/ui.sortable.js"></script>
    <script type="text/javascript"
      src="development-bundle/ui/ui.draggable.js"></script>
    <script type="text/javascript">
      $(function() {
        var dragOpts = {
          connectToSortable: "#tasks",
          helper: "clone"
        };
        $("#drag li").draggable(dragOpts);

        var sortOpts = {
          stop: function() {
            $("#add").css("display", "none");
            $("#drag li").text("Click to write new task...");
          }
        };
        $("#tasks").sortable(sortOpts);
        $("#drag li").click(function() {
          if ($("#tasks").children().length > 7) {
            alert("too many tasks already!");
          } else {
            var input = $("<input>").attr("id", "newTask");
            $(this).text("").append(input);
            input.focus();

            $("#add").removeClass("down").css("display",
              "block").insertAfter("#drag");
          }
        });
        $("#add").live("click", function(e) {
          e.preventDefault();
          $("#drag li").text($("#newTask").val());
          $("#drag input").remove();
          $("#add").addClass("down").attr("title", "drag new task
            into the list");
        });
      });
    </script>
  </body>
</html>
```

Save this as `sortable14.html`. We first define the draggable configuration object, setting the `connectToSortable` to the `id` selector for the parent sortables container, and the `helper` option to `clone`. The `draggables()` method is then called on the draggable's container.

We then define the configuration object for the sortables, specifying a callback function for the `stop` event that resets the text that we enter into the draggable later in the script. Once this has been defined we simply add the constructor for the sortables.

Next we add a click handler to the draggable element, which when clicked, will show an input field and an add button. The visitor can enter a new task and make the new task draggable. The text-box and icon will appear like this:

We also add a click handler for the add button that we create. This function gets the text that has been entered into the text field, removes the text field, and adds the text to a draggable `<li>` element. The new task can then be dragged into the list.

We also use a new stylesheet for this example. Add the following code to a new page in your text editor:

```
#drag { margin:0; padding:0 0 0 56px; float:left; }
#drag li { font-style:italic; color:#999999; }
#taskList {
  width:250px; height:400px;
  background:url(../img/sortable/tasks/paper.jpg) no-repeat;
  clear:both;
}
#tasks {
  margin:0; padding:89px 0 0; width:170px; float:right;
}
#tasks li, #drag li {
  height:28px; padding-top:5px; list-style-type:none;
}
#add { width:24px; height:24px;
  background:url(../img/sortable/tasks/add.png) no-repeat;
  position:absolute; left:218px; top:13px; display:none;
}
#add.down {
  background:url(../img/sortable/tasks/down.png) no-repeat;
}
```

Save this as `sortableDrag.css` in the `css` folder. Mostly this is just decorative, superficial stuff for the purposes of the example.

Sortable page widgets

It's time for our final sortable example. We're going to put the component to good use by creating a page with content boxes on it that can be sorted into various positions to suit the visitor's personal preference, a little like **iGoogle**. The following screenshot shows what we're aiming for:

The markup for the page is minimal as most of the content will be added dynamically from various remote sources. You don't need to worry about having a full web server set up to complete this example. The code that returns the data makes use of JSON, which as you know can be interpreted directly in the browser (when used in conjunction with JSONP callbacks). We'll also be making use of cookies, which again can be used purely with JavaScript.

The underlying page

To begin, create the following basic HTML page:

```
<!DOCTYPE HTML PUBLIC "-//W3C//DTD HTML 4.01//EN"
  "http://www.w3.org/TR/html4/strict.dtd">
<html lang="en">
  <head>
    <link rel="stylesheet" type="text/css"
      href="css/smoothness/jquery-ui-1.7.1.custom.css">
    <link rel="stylesheet" type="text/css" href="css/jPage.css">
    <meta http-equiv="Content-Type" content="text/html;
      charset=utf-8">
    <title>jQuery UI Customizable Home Page Example</title>
  </head>
  <body>
    <div class="page">
      <h1>Customizable Home Page Example</h1>
      <p>Move the boxes around or close them completely. Your choices
        will be saved and the page will appear as it was when you
        left it.<p>
        <a id="restore" href="#"
          title="Restore Deleted Boxes">Restore Deleted Boxes</a>
      <div id="sortGrid" class="ui-helper-clearfix">
        <div id="col1" class="col"></div>
        <div id="col2" class="col"></div>
        <div id="col3" class="col"></div>
        <div id="hidden"></div>
      </div>
    </div>

    <script type="text/javascript"
      src="development-bundle/jquery-1.3.2.js"></script>
    <script type="text/javascript"
      src="development-bundle/ui/ui.core.js"></script>
    <script type="text/javascript"
      src="development-bundle/ui/ui.sortable.js"></script>
    <script type="text/javascript"
      src="development-bundle/external/cookie/jquery.cookie.js">
    </script>
  </body>
</html>
```

Save this as jPage.html. I said it would be simple, but let's just look at what the page contains. At the top, we've got a header, some explanatory text, and a link which will be used to reopen boxes that may have been closed.

The main part of the page contains three `<div>` elements that will be styled to float next to each other to represent columns, plus a hidden column that will be used to store closed boxes. That's it, the rest of the elements are the `<script>` resources that we'll be using for this example.

Working with cookies

The jQuery cookie plug-in by Klaus Hartl really helps us to avoid relying on backend PHP (or other generic server-side environment) to process the desired state of the boxes. It also makes working with cookies much less cumbersome and saves us a good deal of code.

Styling the page

Next, we can add the CSS that is needed to make the page work. Some of the selectors in our stylesheet will be matching elements that don't yet exist, but we'll add the styling for them now anyway so that we don't have to come back to the stylesheet later on. In a new page in your text editor, add the following code:

```
.page { width:936px; margin:auto; text-align:center; }
p {
    font-family:Verdana, Arial, Helvetica, sans-serif;
    font-size:0.8em;
}
#sortGrid { width:960px; padding:20px 0; }
a#restore {
    font-family:Arial, Helvetica, sans-serif; float:right;
    font-size:0.7em; color:#000;
}
.col {
    float:left; width:312px; min-height:700px;
    height:auto !important; height:700px;
}
.box {
    width:290px; margin:0 0 10px 10px; position:relative;
    border:1px solid #999999; text-align:left;
    padding:25px 5px 5px 5px; font-size:0.7em; overflow:hidden;
    background-color:#fff;
}
.title {
    width:100%; position:absolute; top:0; left:0; padding:4px 0;
    font-size:1.1em; cursor:move; border:0;
    border-bottom:1px solid #aaa; text-indent:10px;
}
.close {
```

```
      position:absolute; right:3px; top:3px; cursor:pointer;
   }
   #hidden { display:none; }
   .ui-widget-content { border:none; padding:5px; }
   .box a {
      text-decoration:none; font-weight:bold; color:#0000ee;
   }
   #video span, #video a { width:137px; display:block; }
   .box img { border:none; }
```

Save this as jPage.css in the css folder. We'll just skim over the CSS as there are only a couple of points worth raising here.

One of the most salient points is the fact that we're using min-height on our columns. The reason for this is that if we don't set some kind of height on our columns they will collapse down to nothing if all of the content boxes are moved out of them.

Using min-height prevents this from happening and allows the columns to grow if a large box is moved into them. IE6 of course doesn't support min-height, hence the crafty hack.

Minimum Height

We're using Dustin Diaz's celebrated Min-Height Fast Hack in our CSS for this example to improve the quality of the resulting page. For more information, visit Dustin's blog at http://www.dustindiaz.com/min-height-fast-hack/

Other than this, the CSS merely lays out the page in the way we want. We'll be making use of a few of the CSS framework classes in the example, so we will be able to use a lot of the automatic styling provided by the library, which can save the amount of CSS we need to write ourselves.

The main script

To bring the page to life, we now need to focus on the JavaScript required to turn this collection of elements into a usable interface. There's a good deal of code to cover. This is probably the biggest example in the book, so instead of looking at the whole script at once, we'll break it down and look at the different sections of code that cover each aspect of behavior. The page is pretty empty at the moment, so our first task is to get the data. Directly after the last <script> element in jPage.html add the following code:

```
<script type="text/javascript">
  $(function() {
    var processData = {
      twitter: {
        title: "Recent Tweets",
        defaultCol: 1,
        parser: $.getJSON("http://pipes.yahoo.com/danwellman/
          tweetstream?_render=JSON&_callback=?", function(data) {
            $.each(data.value.items, function(i, item) {
              $("<a />").attr("href", "http://twitter.com/" +
                item.user.screen_name).text("@" +
                item.user.screen_name).appendTo("#twitterContent");
$("<p>").text(item.text).appendTo("#twitterContent");
            });
        })},
      flickr: {
        title: "Latest Flickr Image",
        defaultCol: 1,
        parser: $.getJSON("http://api.flickr.com/services/feeds/
          photos_public.gne?format=json&jsoncallback=?",
          function(data){
        $("<a />").attr({"href": data.items[0].link,"id":
          "imgLink"}).appendTo($("#flickrTitle").parent());
        $("<img />").attr("src",
          data.items[0].media.m).appendTo("#imgLink");
        $("<p>").text("Image name: " +
          data.items[0].title).appendTo($(
          "#flickrTitle").parent());
        $("<p>").text("Author: " +
          data.items[0].author.split("(")[1].replace(")",
          "")).appendTo("#flickrContent");
      })},
      youtube: {
        title: "Today's Most Viewed YouTube Video",
        defaultCol: 2,
        parser: $.getJSON("http://pipes.yahoo.com/danwellman/
        mostpopularyoutube?_render=JSON&_callback=?", function(data) {
          $("<div>").attr("id",
            "video").html(data.value.items[0].description).appendTo("
            #youtubeContent");
      })},
      jquery: {
        title: "Latest Stories on Learning jQuery",
        defaultCol: 2,
        parser: $.getJSON("http://pipes.yahoo.com/danwellman/
          learningjquery?_render=JSON&_callback=?", function(data) {
            $.each(data.value.items, function(i, item) {
              $("<a />").attr({"id": "articleLink", "href":
                item.link}).text(item.title).appendTo("#jqueryContent");
```

```
            $("<p>").text(item.description.split("<")[0]).appendTo(
                "#jqueryContent");
            return (i > 3) ? false : null;
        });
    })},
    news: {
        title: "Current UK Headlines from BBC News",
        defaultCol: 3,
        parser: $.getJSON("http://pipes.yahoo.com/danwellman/
            ukbbcnews?_render=JSON&_callback=?", function(data) {
            $.each(data.value.items, function(i, item) {
                $("<div>").addClass("headline").attr("id", "headline" +
                    i).appendTo("#newsContent");
                ("<a />").attr("href",
                    item.link).text(item.title).appendTo("#headline" + i);
                $("<p>").text(item.description).appendTo("#headline" +
                    i);
                return (i > 3) ? false : null;
            });
        })},
    weather: {
        title: "Today's Weather for Southampton, UK",
        defaultCol: 3,
        parser: $.getJSON("http://pipes.yahoo.com/danwellman/
        southamptonweather?_render=JSON&_callback=?", function(data) {
            $("<div>").attr("id", "weatherData")
                .html(data.value.items[0].description)
                .appendTo ("#weatherContent");
            $("#weatherData img").remove();
            $("#weatherData br:first").remove();
        })}
    };
    });
</script>
```

We've defined an outer object literal in the variable processData. As the variable name indicates we'll be storing information to help us process the remote data within this object. Inside this object are six properties that represent the six content boxes that we'll create. Each of these properties has a key name that dictates which box it belongs to.

The value of each of these properties is another literal object. These inner objects each contain three properties, which are a text string to use as the title of the content box, an integer specifying which column the box belongs in by default, and a function that retrieves the actual content of the box.

Even though we're using **Yahoo! Pipes** to return most of the data in a format that can be used with jQuery's getJSON() method, the way that we need to create the content for the boxes still differs between each box.

For example, the news pipe returns lots of results, over twenty, which is way too many for our page. Therefore, we use jQuery's each() utility method to loop through the first five results and then discard the rest. Sometimes we don't need to use the loop and can just work with the first result like with the Youtube Function.

Building the content boxes

Next, we need to build the content boxes and insert them into the page. As I mentioned, the page uses cookies to store the state of each box—it's position, the column it's in, and whether it's open or hidden, therefore, we need to check for the presence of the cookie and do different things depending on whether it exists or not. Directly after our processData object add the following code:

```
      $("#weatherData br:first").remove();
    })}
  };
  if (!$.cookie("columnOrder")) {
    $.each(processData, function(i, item) {
      $("<div>").addClass("box ui-widget ui-corner-all").attr("id",
        "col" + processData[i].defaultCol + "_" + i).appendTo("#col" +
        processData[i].defaultCol);
      $("<div>").addClass("title ui-widget-header
        ui-corner-top").attr("id", i +
        "Title").text(processData[i].title).appendTo("#col" +
        processData[i].defaultCol + "_" + i);
      $("<div>").addClass("close ui-icon ui-icon-close").attr("title",
        "Close").appendTo("#" + i + "Title");
      $("<div>").addClass("ui-widget-content").attr("id", i +
        "Content").appendTo("#col" + processData[i].defaultCol + "_"
        + i);
    });
    $("#hidden").empty();
  } else {
    var cols = $.cookie("columnOrder").split("&");
    $.each(cols, function(i, item) {
      if(item != "") {
        var col = item.split("=")[0],
          box = item.split("=")[1];
        $("<div>").addClass("box ui-widget ui-corner-all").attr("id",
          col + "_" + box).appendTo("#" + col);
        $("<div>").addClass("title ui-widget-header
          ui-corner-top").attr("id", box +
```

```
            "Title").text(processData[box].title).appendTo("#" + col +
            "_" + box);
        $("<div>").addClass("close ui-icon
            ui-icon-close").attr("title", "Close").appendTo("#" + box +
            "Title");
        $("<div>").addClass("ui-widget-content").attr("id", box +
            "Content").appendTo("#" + col + "_" + box);
    }
    });
}
```

Our cookie will have the title `columnOrder`, so if this doesn't exist we know that a cookie has not been saved and we should use the default layout. The first branch of the `if` statement deals with this scenario.

We use jQuery's `each()` utility method to iterate over our `processData` object and on each of the (six) properties within it we execute a function. Within this function we create four `<div>` elements with each element making part of each content box—the outer container, the title, the close button, and the inner content container.

We use the different inner objects from each of the six properties to add the data to the content box. Each box is given an `id` based on the key or the current property, which is passed to our function as the `i` argument. We also use the `defaultCol` property from our object to append the content box to the correct column.

Each of these elements is given some custom class names, so that we can provide any styles not provided by the library, and some of the framework class names to pick up styling from the CSS framework. Using the framework classes like this is great because it means that our content boxes will be styled the same as any additional widgets we may decide to use on the page.

The last thing we do is empty the hidden column from any elements that may be inside it. There shouldn't be, but to be sure we call jQuery's `empty()` method on it.

The second branch of the `if` statement processes the cookie and uses the information from it to build the IDs of the boxes and append them to their respective columns. Note that we still use the `processData` object to obtain the title's of each box. Storing this information in the cookie as well as the column order would push up the size of the cookie and different browsers put different restrictions on cookie size. Therefore, it's best to keep it as minimal as possible.

We first split the cookie based on the `&` character, which is the separator we'll use when building the cookie (we'll come to that next). We then use jQuery's `each()` method once more to iterate over the items in the array created when we split the cookie.

We check that each item in the array does not equal an empty string, and provided it doesn't we split the array item again using the = character. The format of each item in the `cols` array will be in the format *columnName=boxId* , so we can get both the `id` of the column to append the box to and the `id` to give the box by splitting each array item.

Writing the cookie

Next we need to add a function that can write the current state of the page to a cookie when requested. Directly after the `processData` object add the following new function:

```
function cookieWriter() {
    var colOrders = $("#col1").sortable("serialize",
      {key:"col1"}) + "&" + $("#col2").sortable("serialize",
      {key:"col2"}) + "&" + $("#col3").sortable("serialize",
      {key:"col3"}) + "&" + $("#hidden").sortable("serialize",
      {key:"hidden"});

    $.cookie("columnOrder", colOrders, { path:"/", expires:365 });
}
```

All we do is build a text string containing the ID's of the boxes that appear in each column (including the hidden column) using the column name as the serialization key, and the order that the boxes appear in. The resulting string will look something like: **col1=twitter&col1=youtube&col2=news...**

We then call the `cookie()` method of the cookie plugin and pass in the title of the cookie, `columnOrder`, our serialized text string as the cookie data, and the `path` and `expires` properties that are required when the cookie is created.

Making the boxes sortable

Next we need to make the boxes sortable, which we can do with the following code:

```
var sortOpts = {
    handle: ".title",
    containment: "#sortGrid",
    dropOnEmpty: true,
    connectWith: ["#col1", "#col2", "#col3"],
    stop: cookieWriter
};

$("#col1, #col2, #col3").sortable(sortOpts);
$("#hidden").sortable();
```

We've seen each of these configuration options before so I won't go into too much detail in this section. The `title` option is used to ensure that boxes are only sorted when the title element is used. The boxes are confined to the `sortGrid` container to keep things tidy and the `dropOnEmpty` option ensures that empty columns can accept new boxes that may be sorted into them.

Each of the three visible lists is connected, so that the content boxes can be moved freely between them. We don't need to connect the hidden column because boxes won't be sorted into it — they can be moved there when closed by other means. The `cookieWriter` function we defined a moment ago is passed to the `stop` option, so a new cookie will be written each time a box is moved.

Closing and restoring boxes

Our final task is to deal with the close button in each box being clicked, and wiring up the link to restore closed boxes. Directly after the code we just looked at add the following two functions:

```
$(".close", "#sortGrid").click(function() {
  $(this).parent().parent().appendTo("#hidden");
  cookieWriter();
});
$("#restore").click(function() {
  $("#hidden").children().each(function() {
    var col = "",
      box = $(this);
    $(".col", "#sortGrid").each(function() {
      ($(this).children().length < 2) ? col = $(this).attr("id") :
        null ;
    });
    var boxId = box.attr("id").split("_")[1];
    box.attr("id", col + "_" + boxId).appendTo("#" + col);
    cookieWriter();
  });
});
```

Closing the boxes is easy. When a close button is clicked we move its box to the hidden column and as the state of the page has changed, we call our cookie writing function once more. That's all we need to do in our click handler.

We also use a click handler to restore closed boxes. We cycle through each box inside the hidden column and create a `col` variable and a `box` variable. The `col` variable will be used to determine which column to insert the box into when it is restored and the `box` variable is a cached reference to the current content box. We determine which column has the space to hold a new box which will be the first column the script encounters that has less than two boxes in it.

Boxes moved to the hidden column will automatically be renamed when the page loads so that they have the `id` hidden_*sortableName*. We need to change this so that the box's `id` is *columnName_sortableName* instead.

We then add the box to a column that has space, setting its `id` in the process, before finally serializing the new column order and calling the `cookieWriter` function once more. This brings us to the end of the example.

We should find when we run the page that we can move the boxes around, close the browser, run the page again and see the boxes retain the order and positions that we gave them.

 Please note that the example does not run correctly in Opera and exhibits the same unusual placement of sorted items that occurred in some of the earlier examples in the chapter. Also, Chrome does not seem to like the use of cookies in this example, which may or may not be related to the size restrictions that I mentioned earlier.

Summary

We've finished our tour of the interaction components of the library by looking at the sortables component. Like the other modules that we looked at before, it has a wide range of properties and methods that allow us to configure and control its behavior and appearance in both simple and more complex implementations.

We started off the chapter with a look at a simple, default implementation with no configuration to see the most basic level of functionality added by the component. We looked at some of the different elements that can be made sortable and added some basic styling to the page.

Following this, we looked at the range of configurable options that are exposed by the sortable API. The list is extensive and provides a wide range of functionality that can be enabled or disabled with ease.

We moved on to look at the extensive event model used by this component that gives us the ability to react to different events as they occur in any sort operation initiated by the visitor.

Connected lists offer the ability to be able to exchange sortable items between lists or collections of sortables. We saw the additional options and events that are used specifically with connected sortable lists.

In the last part of the chapter, we looked at the methods available for use with the sortables component and focused on the highly useful `serialize` method, and also had a quick look at its compatibility with other members of the jQuery UI library in the form of the sortable tabs example.

13
UI Effects

We've so far looked at a range of incredibly useful widgets and interaction helpers. All are easy to use but at the same time powerful and highly configurable. Some have had their subtle nuances which have required consideration and thought during their implementation.

The effects provided by the library on the other hand are for the most part, extremely compact, with very few options to learn and no methods at all. We can use these effects quickly and easily, with minimum configuration.

The effects that we'll be looking at in this chapter are listed below:

- blind
- bounce
- clip
- drop
- explode
- fold
- highlight
- pulsate
- scale
- shake
- slide
- transfer

The core effects file

Like the individual components themselves, the effects require the services of a separate core file. It provides essential functionality to the effects, such as creating wrapper elements and controlling the animations. Most, but not all, of the effects have their own source files, which build on the core foundation to add functionality specific to the effect.

All we need to do to use an effect is include the core file (`effects.core.js`) in the page before the effect's source file. Unlike the `ui.core.js` file however, the `effects.core.js` file has been designed to be used, in part, completely standalone.

When using the core effect file on its own we can take advantage of color animations. This includes changing the background color of an element into another color (and not just a snap change but a smooth morphing of one color into another), class transitions, and advanced easing animations.

Using color animations

Let's look at creating color animations. First; create the following new page:

```html
<!DOCTYPE HTML PUBLIC "-//W3C//DTD HTML 4.01//EN"
  "http://www.w3.org/TR/html4/strict.dtd">
<html lang="en">
  <head>
    <link rel="stylesheet" type="text/css"
      href="css/effectColor.css">
    <meta http-equiv="Content-Type" content="text/html;
      charset=utf-8">
    <title>jQuery UI Color Animation Example</title>
  </head>
  <body>
    <form action="#">
      <div><label>Name: </label><input type="text"></div>
      <div><label>Age: </label><input type="text"></div>
      <div><label>Email: </label><input type="text"></div>
      <button type="submit">Submit</button>
    </form>
    <script type="text/javascript"
      src="development-bundle/jquery-1.3.2.js"></script>
    <script type="text/javascript"
      src="development-bundle/ui/effects.core.js"></script>
    <script type="text/javascript">
      $(function() {

        $("form").submit(function() {
```

```
$("input").each(function() {
    ($(this).val().length == 0) ? $(this).animate({
        backgroundColor:"#ff9999",
        borderTopColor: "#ff0000",
        borderRightColor: "#ff0000",
        borderBottomColor: "#ff0000",
        borderLeftColor: "#ff0000"
    }) : $(this).animate({
        backgroundColor:"#ccffcc",
        borderTopColor: "#00ff00",
        borderRightColor: "#00ff00",
        borderBottomColor: "#00ff00",
        borderLeftColor: "#00ff00"
    });
});
    });
    });
        });
        </script>
    </body>
</html>
```

Save the page as `effectColor.html`. As you can see, all we need are jQuery and the `effects.core.js` file to create attractive color transitions. On the page we have a simple `<form>` element enclosing three container elements and three sets of `<label>` and `<input>` elements. The `animate` method is part of jQuery rather than jQuery UI specifically, but the `effects.core.js` file extends jQuery's `animate` method by allowing it to specifically work with colors and classes.

When the **Submit** button is clicked, we simply use the `animate` method to apply a series of new CSS properties to the target elements based on whether the text inputs have been filled out or not. If they have been completed we color them green, if not we color them red. We also use a basic stylesheet in this example. In another new page in your text editor, add the following basic selectors and rules:

```
div { margin-bottom:5px; }
label { display:block; width:100px; float:left; }
input { border:1px solid #000000; }
```

Save this as `effectColor.css` in the `css` folder. When we view this page in our browser, we should see that any fields left blank smoothly turn red when the **Submit** button is clicked, while fields that are not empty smoothly turn green. The most attractive however is when a field changes from red to green.

The following screenshot shows the page once the **Submit** button has been clicked:

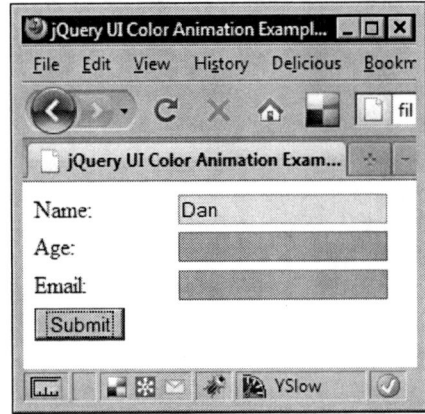

The style attributes that color animations can be used on are:

- `backgroundColor`
- `borderTopColor`
- `borderRightColor`
- `borderBottomColor`
- `borderLeftColor`
- `color`
- `outlineColor`

Colors may be specified using either RGB, hexadecimal (in the format #000000), or even standard color names. Although there can be cross-browser issues when using color names, so these are best avoided in most cases.

Using class transitions

In addition to animating individual color attributes, `effects.core.js` also gives us the powerful ability to animate between entire classes. This allows us to switch styles smoothly and seamlessly without sudden, jarring changes. Let's look at this aspect of the file's use in the following example. Change the `<link>` in the `<head>` of `effectColor.html` to point to a new stylesheet:

```
<link rel="stylesheet" type="text/css"
    href="css/effectClass.css">
```

Then change the final `<script>` element so that it appears like this:

```
<script type="text/javascript">
  $(function() {
    $("form").submit(function(e) {
          e.preventDefault();
      $("input").each(function() {

        if ($(this).hasClass("error")) {
        ($(this).val().length == 0) ? null :
          $(this).switchClass("error", "pass", 2000);
        } else if ($(this).hasClass("pass")) {
          ($(this).val().length != 0) ? null :
            $(this).switchClass("pass", "error", 2000);
        } else {
          ($(this).val().length == 0) ? $(this).addClass("error",
            2000) : $(this).addClass("pass", 2000);
        }
      });
    });
  });
</script>
```

Save this as `effectClass.html`. The `effects.core.js` file extends the jQuery class API by allowing us to specify a duration over which the new class name should be applied instead of just switching it instantly. We can also specify an easing effect.

The `switchClass` method of the `effects.core.js` file is used when the fields already have one of the class names and need to change to a different class name. The `switchClass` method requires several arguments, we specify the class name to remove, followed by the class name to add. We also specify a duration as the third argument.

Essentially, the page functions as it did before, although using this type of class transition allows us to use non-color-based style rules as well, so we can adjust widths, heights, or many other style properties if we wanted. Note that background images cannot be transitioned in this way.

As in the previous example, we have a stylesheet attached. This is essentially the same as in the previous example except with some styles for our two new classes. Add the following selectors and rules to the bottom of `effectColor.css`:

```
.error { border:1px solid #ff0000; background-color:#ff9999; }
.pass { border:1px solid #00ff00; background-color:#ccffcc; }
```

Save the updated file as `effectClass.css` in the `css` folder. In the next screenshot, we see the page after it has been interacted with:

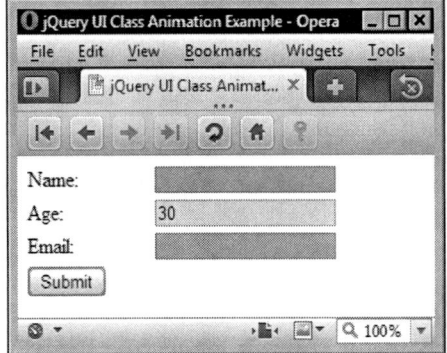

 Please note that at the time of writing, this example does not work correctly in IE. It will only apply the class to one of the `<input>` elements per click and it will throw errors as well. As of jQuery UI 1.8 the class transitions will work in Webkit-based browsers such as Safari or Chrome.

Advanced easing

The `animate` method found in standard jQuery has some basic easing capabilities built-in, but for more advanced easing, you have to include an additional easing plugin (ported to jQuery by GSGD).

However, the `effect.core.js` file has all of these advanced easing options built right in, so there is no need to include additional plugins. We won't be looking at them in any real detail in this section, however, we will be using them in some of the examples later on in the chapter.

Highlighting specified elements

The highlight effect temporarily applies a light yellow coloring to any element that it's called on. Let's put a simple example together so we can see the effect in action. In `effectClass.html` change the link to the stylesheet in the `<head>` of the page as follows:

```
<link rel="stylesheet" type="text/css"
  href="css/effectHighlight.css">
```

The `<script>` element that refers to the effect's source file so that it uses the
`effect.highlight.js` file:

```
<script type="text/javascript"
  src="development-bundle/ui/effects.highlight.js"></script>
```

Then remove the `<form>` from the `<body>` of the page and replace it with the
following markup:

```
<h1>Choose the correct download below:</h1>
<div id="win" class="download-link">
  <a title="Download windows installer"
    href="#"><span>Windows</span></a>
</div>
<div id="mac" class="download-link">
  <a title="Download mac dmg" href="#"><span>Mac</span></a>
</div>
<div id="linux" class="download-link">
  <a title="Download linux tarbal" href="#"><span>Linux</span></a>
</div>
<button id="hint">Hint</button>
```

Lastly, change the final `<script>` element so that ends up like this:

```
<script type="text/javascript">
  $(function() {
    $("#hint").click(function() {

      $("#win").effect("highlight");
    });
  });
</script>
```

Save this page as `effectHighlight.html`. The code that invokes the highlight effect
takes the same familiar form as other library components. The `effect` method is
called and the actual effect is specified as a string argument to the method. We also
need to create the new stylesheet, in a new page in your text editor add the following
selectors and rules:

```
.download-link {
  float:left; border:1px solid #000; width:120px;
  height:120px; position:relative; margin:0 10px 10px 0;
}
.download-link a {
  display:block; width:100%; height:100%; position:aboslute;
  left:0; top:0;
}
.download-link a span {
```

```
    display:block; width:100%; position:absolute; bottom:0;
    text-align:center;
}
#win {
    background:url(../img/effects/windows.jpg) no-repeat 50% 0;
}
#mac {
    background:url(../img/effects/osx.jpg) no-repeat 50% 0;
}
#linux {
    background:url(../img/effects/linux.jpg) no-repeat 50% 0;
}
button { display:block; clear:both; }
```

Save this file as `effectHighlight.css` in the `css` folder.

View the example and click the **Hint** button. The first `<div>` should be highlighted:

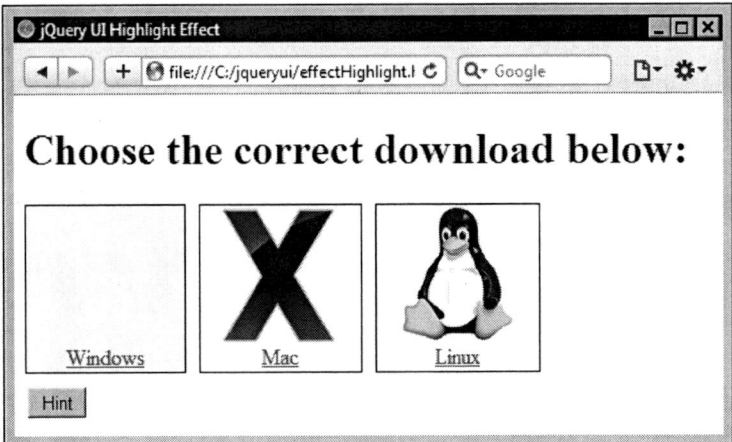

The library files we needed for this example are listed below:

- `jquery-1.3.2.js`
- `effects.core.js`
- `effects.highlight.js`

While our example may seem a little contrived, it is easy to see the potential for this effect as an assistance tool on the frontend. Whenever there is a sequence of actions that needs to be completed in a specific order, the `highlight` effect can instantly give the visitor a visual cue as to the step that needs to be completed next.

Additional effect arguments

Each of the `effect` methods, as well as the argument that dictates which effect is actually applied, can take up three additional arguments, which control how the effect functions. All are optional, and consist of the following (in the listed order):

- An object containing additional configuration options
- An integer representing in milliseconds, the duration of the effect, or a string specifying one of `slow`, `normal`, or `fast`
- A callback function that is executed when the effect ends

The `highlight` effect has only one configurable option that can be used in the object passed as the second argument and that is the highlight color.

Let's add these additional arguments into our highlight example to clarify their usage. Change the final `<script>` element in `effectHighlight.html` so that it appears as follows:

```
<script type="text/javascript">
  $(function() {
    $("#hint").click(function() {
      $("#win").effect("highlight", {}, 2000, function() {
        $("<p>").text("That was the
          highlight").appendTo("body");
      });
    });
  });
</script>
```

Save this as `effectHighlightParameter.html`. Perhaps the most striking feature of our new code is the empty object passed as the second argument. In this example, we don't use any additional configurable options, but we still need to pass in the empty object in order to access the third and fourth arguments.

The animation should now proceed much slower as we have set the duration to `2000` milliseconds (2 seconds). Note that this third argument may also take a string representing the speed of the animation.

Our callback function, passed as the fourth and final argument, is perhaps the least useful callback in the history of JavaScript, but it does serve to illustrate how easy it is to arrange additional post-animation code execution.

Bouncing

Another simple effect we can use with little configuration is the bounce effect. To see this effect in action create the following page:

```html
<!DOCTYPE HTML PUBLIC "-//W3C//DTD HTML 4.01//EN"
  "http://www.w3.org/TR/html4/strict.dtd">
<html lang="en">
  <head>
    <link rel="stylesheet" type="text/css"
      href="css/effectBounce.css">
    <meta http-equiv="Content-Type" content="text/html;
      charset=utf-8">
    <title>jQuery UI Bounce Effect</title>
  </head>
  <body>
    <div id="ball"></div>
    <script type="text/javascript"
      src="development-bundle/jquery-1.3.2.js"></script>
    <script type="text/javascript"
      src="development-bundle/ui/effects.core.js"></script>
    <script type="text/javascript"
      src="development-bundle/ui/effects.bounce.js"></script>
    <script type="text/javascript">
      $(function() {

        $("#ball").click(function() {
          $(this).effect("bounce", { distance: 140 });
        });
      });
    </script>
  </body>
</html>
```

Save this as `effectBounce.html`. Using the bounce effect in this example shows how easy it is to add this simple but attractive effect. We configure the `distance` option to set how far the element travels. Other options that can be configured are listed below:

Option	Default	Usage
direction	up	Sets the direction of the bounce.
distance	20	Sets the distance in pixels of the first bounce.
times	5	Sets the number of times the element should bounce.

You'll notice when you run the example that the bounce effect has an ease-out easing feature built into it, so the distance of the bounce will automatically decrease as the animation transpires. We also need a little CSS for this example. Add the following styles in a new page:

```
#ball {
  width:48px; height:48px;
  background:url(../img/effects/ball.png) no-repeat;
  position:relative; top:200px;
}
```

Save this as effectBounce.css in the css folder. Here's how the page should look:

One thing to note is that with most of the different effects, including the bounce effect (but not the highlight effect we just looked at), the effect is not actually applied to the specified element. Instead a wrapper element is created and the element targeted by the effect is appended to the inside of the wrapper. The actual effect is then applied to the wrapper.

This is an important detail to be aware of because if you need to manipulate the element that has the effect applied to it in mid-animation, the wrapper will need to be targeted instead of the original element. Once the effect's animation has completed, the wrapper is removed.

Shaking an element

The shake effect is very similar to the bounce effect but with the crucial difference of not having any built-in easing. So, the targeted element will shake the same distance for the specified number of times instead of lessening each time (although it will come to a smooth stop at the end of the animation).

Let's change the previous example so that it uses the shake effect instead of the bounce effect. Change effectBounce.html so that it uses the shake source file instead of the bounce source file:

```
<script type="text/javascript"
  src="development-bundle/ui/effects.shake.js"></script>
```

Then change the final <script> appears like this:

```
<script type="text/javascript">
  $(function() {

    $("#ball").click(function() {
      $(this).effect("shake", {direction:"up"}, 100);
    });
  });
</script>
```

Save this as effectShake.html. This time, as well as changing the effect, we've also made use of one of the configuration options, direction. This option controls the direction of the shake. This is to override the default setting for this option which is left.

This effect shares the same options as the bounce effect, although the defaults are set slightly differently. The options are listed in the following table:

Option	Default	Usage
direction	left	Sets the direction of the shake.
distance	20	Sets the distance of the shake in pixels.
times	3	Sets the number of times the element should shake.

Transferring an element's outline

The transfer effect is different from others in that it doesn't directly affect the targeted element. Instead, it transfers the outline of a specified element to another specified element. To see this effect in action, create the following page:

```html
<!DOCTYPE HTML PUBLIC "-//W3C//DTD HTML 4.01//EN"
  "http://www.w3.org/TR/html4/strict.dtd">
<html lang="en">
  <head>
    <link rel="stylesheet" type="text/css"
      href="css/effectTransfer.css">
    <meta http-equiv="Content-Type" content="text/html;
      charset=utf-8">
    <title>jQuery UI Transfer Effect</title>
  </head>
  <body>
    <div id="container">
      <div id="productContainer">
        <img alt="GTX 280" src="img/effects/gcard.jpg"></img>
        <p>BFG GTX 280 OC 1GB GDDR3 Dual DVI HDTV Out PCI-E
            Graphics Card</p><p id="price">Cost: $350</p>
        <div id="purchase"><button id="buy">Buy</button></div>
      </div>
      <div id="basketContainer">
        <div id="basket"></div>
        <p>Basket total: <span id="total">0</span></p>
      </div>
    </div>
    <script type="text/javascript"
      src="development-bundle/jquery-1.3.2.js"></script>
    <script type="text/javascript"
      src="development-bundle/ui/effects.core.js"></script>
    <script type="text/javascript"
      src="development-bundle/ui/effects.transfer.js"></script>
    <script type="text/javascript">
      $(function() {

        $("#buy").click(function() {
          $("#productContainer img").effect("transfer",
            { to:"#basket" }, 750, function() {
            var currentTotal = $("#total").text();
            numeric = parseInt(currentTotal);
            $("#total").text(numeric + 1);
          });
        });
      });
    </script>
  </body>
</html>
```

Save this as `effectTransfer.html`. We've created a basic product listing for an imaginary hardware retailer. When the **Buy** button is clicked, the transfer effect will give the impression of the product being moved into the basket.

Of course, a proper shopping cart application would be exponentially more complex than this, but we do get to see the transfer effect in all its glory. We also get to use the built-in callback function to do a little post-animation processing, so the exercise should still be beneficial.

We also need some CSS for this example, so create the following new stylesheet:

```
#container { width:607px; margin:0 auto; }
#productContainer img {
  width:92px; height:60px;
  border:2px solid #000000;
  float:left; position:relative;
}
#productContainer p {
  width:340px; height:50px;
  font-family:Verdana; font-size:11px; font-weight:bold;
  float:left;
  margin:0; padding:5px;
  border-top:2px solid #000000;
  border-right:2px solid #000000;
  border-bottom:2px solid #000000;
}
p#price {
  height:35px; width:70px;
  padding-top:20px; float:left;
}
#purchase {
  height:44px; width:75px;
  border-top:2px solid #000000;
  border-right:2px solid #000000;
  border-bottom:2px solid #000000;
  padding-top:16px; float:left;
  text-align:center;
}
#basketContainer {
  float:right; width:90px; margin-top:100px;
}
#basket {
  width:65px; height:31px;
  position:relative; left:13px;
  background:url(../img/effects/basket.gif) no-repeat;
}
.ui-effects-transfer { border:2px solid #66ff66; }
```

Save this as `effectTransfer.css` in the `css` folder. The key rule in our stylesheet is the one that targets the element which has a `class` of `ui-effects-transfer`. This element is created by the effect and together with our styling produces the green outline that is transferred from the product to the basket.

Run the file in your browser. I think you'll agree that it's a nice effect which would add value to any page that it was used on. Here's how it should look while the transfer is occurring.

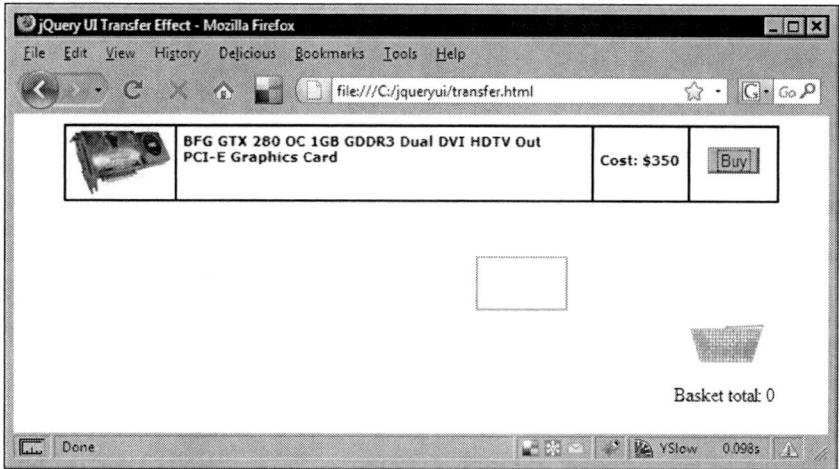

The transfer effect has just two configurable options, one of which is required and that we have already seen. For reference, both are listed in the following table:

Option	Default	Usage
`className`	`ui-effects-transfer`	A new class to apply to effect helper element.
`to`	*none*	Sets the element the effect will be transferred to. This property is mandatory.

The four effects that we've looked at so far all have one thing in common—they can only be used with the `effect` method. The remaining effects can be used not only with the `effect` method, but also with the `toggle` and the `show`/`hide` methods. Let's take a look.

Element scaling

The next effect that we'll look at is scaling, which allows us to shrink or grow any specified element. At the end of the last chapter, we created a page that had a series of boxes on it that could be reordered or closed. When they were closed, they simply vanished instantly from the page.

Let's use the `scale` effect to make them gracefully shrink to nothing instead. First add the required `<script>` elements for the effect directly after the `<script>` element for the cookie plugin:

```
<script type="text/javascript"
    src="development-bundle/ui/effects.core.js"></script>
<script type="text/javascript"
    src="development-bundle/ui/effects.scale.js"></script>
```

Next change the click handler for the close buttons so that it appears as follows:

```
$(".close", "#sortGrid").click(function() {
    $(this).parent().parent().effect("scale", { percent:0 }, "slow",
        function() {
            $(this).appendTo("#hidden").height("").width("").css({
                fontSize:"", borderWidth: "", padding: "" }).find("img").
                height("").width("");
            cookieWriter();
        });
});
```

Save this file as `effectScaling.html`. The `percent` option indicates the ending size of the element the effect is applied to. We need to tidy up the element after the effect has been applied to it as the style attributes that are manipulated to produce the effect (a wrapper is not used with this effect) remain on the element. Our content boxes should smoothly disappear when the close button is clicked as shown in the following screenshot (part way through the closing animation):

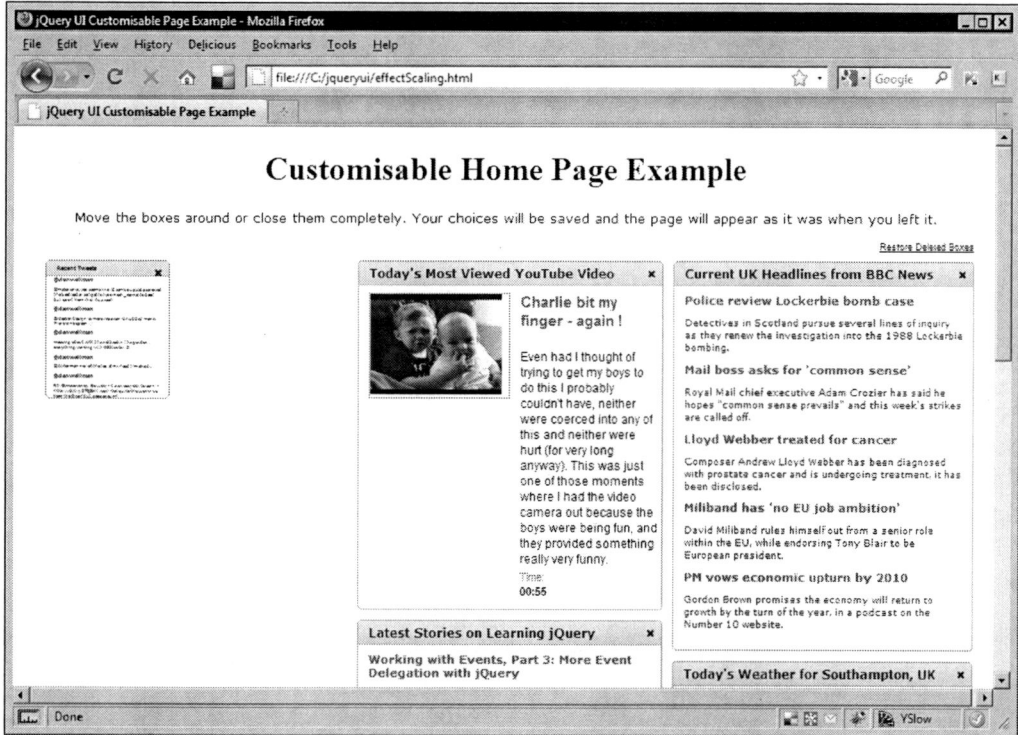

There are several more options that can be used with `scale`, which are as follows:

Option	Default	Usage
direction	both	Sets the direction to scale the element in. May be a string specifying either both, vertical, or horizontal.
from	{}	Sets the starting height and width of the element to be scaled.
origin	["middle","center"]	Sets the vanishing point, used with show/hide animations.
percent	0	Sets the end size of the scaled element.

I mentioned a little while ago that the effects that we're looking at now can be used with other methods. The file in our previous example could be reconstructed to use the `hide` method instead of the `effect` method:

```
$(".close").click(function() {
  $(this).parent().parent().hide("scale", { }, "slow",
    function() {
    $(this).appendTo("#hidden").height("").width("").css({
      fontSize:"", borderWidth: "", padding: "" }).find("img").
      height("").width("");
    cookieWriter();
  });
});
```

Save this variation as `effectScalingHide.html`. We've gotten away with a slightly lighter method as we don't have to configure the `percent` option in our configuration object, but other than this, the effects are very similar code-wise. Visually, the only difference in the execution of this version of the file is that the boxes now vanish to the center instead of the top-left:

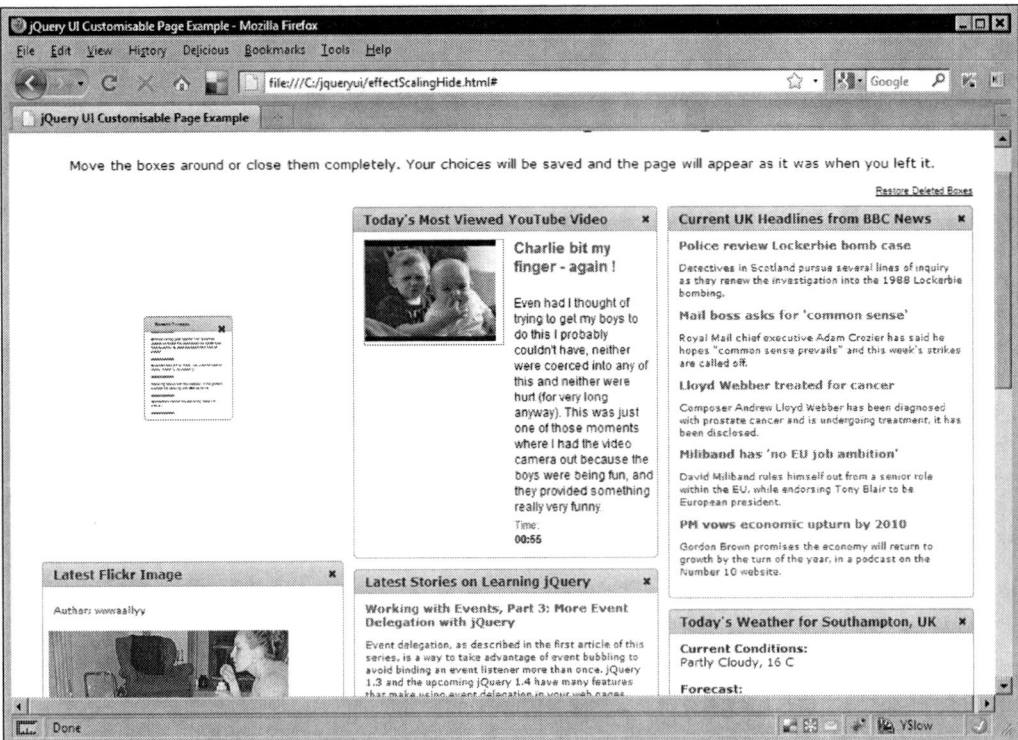

One thing to note with this example is that the elements within whichever box we apply the effect to (by closing it) will have various properties (such as their widths, heights, and their borders) set to 0. Therefore, when we add the box we closed back again by clicking the restore link, the contents of the box is not visible. We would need to cycle through each child element and reset the style properties.

Element explosion

The explosion effect is truly awesome. The targeted element is literally exploded into a specified number of pieces before disappearing completely. It's an easy effect to use and has few configuration properties, but the visual impact of this effect is huge, giving you a lot of effect in return for very little code. Let's see a basic example. Create the following new page:

```
<!DOCTYPE HTML PUBLIC "-//W3C//DTD HTML 4.01//EN"
   "http://www.w3.org/TR/html4/strict.dtd">
<html lang="en">
  <head>
    <link rel="stylesheet" type="text/css"
      href="css/effectExplode.css">
    <meta http-equiv="Content-Type" content="text/html;
      charset=utf-8">
    <title>jQuery UI Explode Effect</title>
  </head>
  <body>
    <p>Click the grenade to pull the pin!</p>
    <div id="theBomb"></div>
    <script type="text/javascript"
      src="development-bundle/jquery-1.3.2.js"></script>
    <script type="text/javascript"
      src="development-bundle/ui/effects.core.js"></script>
    <script type="text/javascript"
      src="development-bundle/ui/effects.explode.js"></script>
    <script type="text/javascript">
      $(function() {

        $("#theBomb").click(function() {
          $(this).effect("explode");
        });
      });
    </script>
  </body>
</html>
```

Save this as `effectExplode.html`. We also need a little CSS, so create the following stylesheet:

```css
#theBomb {
   width:69px; height:100px;
   background:url(../img/effects/nade.jpg) no-repeat;
   position:absolute;
   top:50px; left:50px;
}
```

Save this as `effectExplode.css` in the `css` folder. As you can see, the code is extremely simple and can be used completely out of the box with no additional configuration. This effect has only one configurable property, which is the `pieces` property and determines how many pieces the element is exploded into. The default is `9`.

Once the specified element has been exploded it will be hidden from view by having its style attribute set to `display:none`. This is the default behavior. However, it will still remain in the DOM of the page.

As our example shows, the effect can be used with either simple CSS properties like colored backgrounds and borders, or more complex implementations involving proper images.

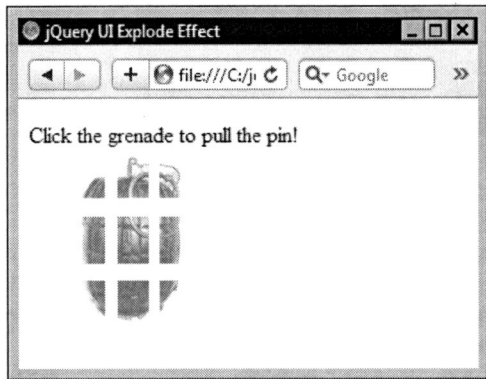

Physicists sometimes speculate as to why the arrow of time seems to only point forwards. They invariably ask themselves philosophical questions like 'why do we not see grenades spontaneously forming from a large cloud of debris?' (actually the object is usually an egg but I don't think an egg-based example would have had quite the same impact!)

jQuery UI cannot help our understanding of entropy, but it can show us what a grenade spontaneously reassembling might look like. Change the click-handler in the previous function so that it appears as follows:

```
$("#detonate").click(function() {
  $("#theBomb").show("explode");
});
```

Save this variant as `effectExplodeShow.html`. This time we use the `show` method instead of the `effect` method to trigger the animation. The animation is the same except that it is shown in reverse and this time, the grenade is not hidden from view once the animation ends. Like the other effects, explode can also make use of specific timings and callback functions.

The puff effect

Similar to the explode effect but slightly more subtle is the puff effect, which causes an element to grow slightly before fading away. Like explode, there are few configuration options to concern ourselves with.

Consider a page that has AJAX operations occurring on it. It's useful to provide a loading image that shows the visitor that something is happening. Instead of just hiding an image like this when the operation has completed, we can puff it out of existence instead. Create the following page:

```
<!DOCTYPE HTML PUBLIC "-//W3C//DTD HTML 4.01//EN"
  "http://www.w3.org/TR/html4/strict.dtd">
<html lang="en">
  <head>
    <link rel="stylesheet" type="text/css"
      href="css/effectPuff.css">
    <meta http-equiv="Content-Type" content="text/html;
      charset=utf-8">
    <title>jQuery UI Puff Effect</title>
  </head>
  <body>
    <img id="loading" alt="Loading" src="img/effects/loading.gif">
    <script type="text/javascript"
      src="development-bundle/jquery-1.3.2.js"></script>
    <script type="text/javascript"
      src="development-bundle/ui/effects.core.js"></script>
    <script type="text/javascript"
      src="development-bundle/ui/effects.scale.js"></script>
    <script type="text/javascript">
      $(function() {
```

```
        $("#loading").click(function() {
          $(this).hide("puff");
        });
      });
    </script>
  </body>
</html>
```

Save this as effectPuff.html. The stylesheet used in this example is purely to position the image slightly so that we can see the full effect of the, well, the effect. For reference, it is comprised of the following styles:

```
#loading { position:relative; top:100px; left:100px; }
```

Save this as effectPuff.css in the css folder. We're actually not detecting whether a given process has finished loading in this example. It would require much too much work just to see the effect we're looking at. Instead we tie the execution of the effect into a simple click-handler as we did with several examples earlier on.

You'll notice that we used the effect.scale.js source file for this effect. The puff effect is the only effect that does not have its own source file and is instead part of the very closely related scaling effect's source file.

Like the explode effect that we looked at in the last section, this effect has just one configuration option that can be passed in an object as the second argument of the effect constructor. This is the percent option and controls how big the image is scaled up to. The default value is 150%. Like the explode effect, the target element is hidden from view once the animation ends.

The effect stretches the targeted element (and its children), while at the same time reducing its opacity. It works well on proper images, background colors, and borders, but you should note that it does not work so well with background images specified by CSS. Nevertheless, it's a great effect. The following screenshot shows it in action:

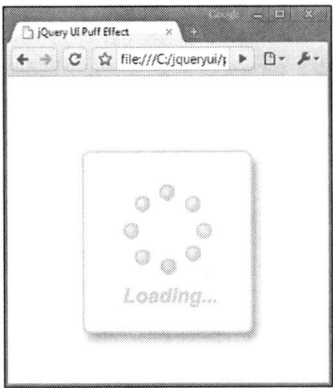

The pulsate effect

The pulsate effect is another effect that works with the opacity of a specified element. This effect reduces the opacity temporarily a specified number of times, making the element appear to pulsate.

In the following basic example, we'll create a simple countdown time that counts down from 15. When the display reaches 10 seconds, it will begin to flash red. In `effectPuff.html` change the link in the `<head>` of the page to point to a new stylesheet:

```
<link rel="stylesheet" type="text/css"
   href="css/effectPulsate.css">
```

Then remove the loading `<img>` from the page and add the following element in its place:

```
<div id="countdown">15</div>
```

Next change the source file of the effect so that the `effects.pulsate.js` file is used:

```
<script type="text/javascript"
   src="development-bundle/ui/effects.pulsate.js"></script>
```

Finally, change the final `<script>` element so that it appears as follows:

```
<script type="text/javascript">
  $(function() {
    var age = 15;
    adjustAge = function() {
      $("#countdown").text(age - 1);
      (age < 11) ? $(
        "#countdown").css({backgroundColor:"#ff0000"}).effect("
        pulsate", { times:1 }) : null ;
      (age == 1) ? clearInterval(timer) : age -= 1;
    }

    timer = setInterval("adjustAge()", 1000);
  });
</script>
```

Save this as `effectPulsate.html`. Both the page and the script for this example are simple, but the goal is to show off the effect after all. The page itself contains just a simple `<div>` element with the number (as a text string) 15 inside it.

The code first sets a variable equal to the text within the `<div>`. It then defines the global `adjustAge()` function. Unfortunately, this function must be global so that it is visible to the `setInterval` method, which is automatically executed in the context of the browser window.

This function first changes the text content of the specified element to one less than the current `age` variable. It then checks whether `age` has reached `10` yet and if so, applies a background color of red to the element and starts the pulsate effect. It then checks whether the `age` variable has reached `1` yet. If it has, it clears the interval so that it doesn't keep counting down past `0`.

We use the `times` property to specify how many times the element should pulsate. As we'll be executing the method once every second, we can set this to just pulsate once on each call.

After our `adjustAge` function, we start the interval using JavaScript's `setInterval` function. This function will repetitively execute the specified function after the specified interval, which in this example is `1000` milliseconds, or 1 second.

So every second the number in the countdown `<div>` will decrement by `1` until it gets to `10` when the pulsate effect kicks in. Once the timer reaches `0`, the pulsating stops. The new stylesheet is very simple and consists of the following code:

```
#countdown {
   width:100px; font-size:60px; margin:10px auto 0;
   border:1px solid #000000; text-align:center;
}
```

Save this in the `css` folder as `effectPulsate.css`. The following screenshot shows how the page should appear once the countdown has crossed the 10 second barrier:

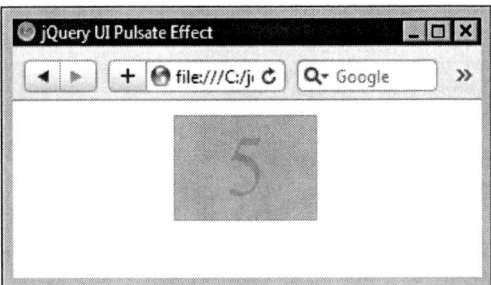

Dropping elements onto the page

The drop effect is simple. Elements appear to drop off of (or onto) the page, which is simulated by adjusting the element's height and opacity. There are many situations in which this would be useful but one that instantly springs to mind is when creating custom tooltips.

We can easily create a tooltip that appears when an element is hovered over, but instead of just showing the tooltip after a specified period of time has elapsed, we can drop it on to the page instead. Add a link to the CSS framework file and change the stylesheet link in the `<head>` of `effectPulsate.html`:

```
<link rel="stylesheet" type="text/css"
  href="development-bundle/themes/smoothness/ui.all.css">
<link rel="stylesheet" type="text/css" href="css/effectDrop.css">
```

Remove the countdown `<div>` from the page and add the following markup instead:

```
<div id="container" class="ui-widget-content" >
  <p>Lorem <a id="link1" href="#" title="This is a link">ipsum</a>
    dolor sit amet, consectetuer adipiscing elit. Sed dapibus libero
    non lacus. Morbi <a id="link2" href="#" title="This is another
    link">sagittis</a> ante vitae tortor. Quisque quis neque vel
    augue laoreet consectetuer. Vestibulum tempor. Morbi non
    <a id="link3" href="#" title="This is the third link">justo</a>.
    Aliquam ullamcorper, enim sed ultricies accumsan, ipsum mauris
    eleifend urna, in ullamcorper nisl urna at erat.</p>
</div>
```

Now we need to change the effect's source file.

```
<script type="text/javascript"
  src=" development-bundle/ui/effects.drop.js"></script>
```

Lastly change the final `<script>` element so that it appears as follows:

```
<script type="text/javascript">
  $(function() {

    $("#container a").mouseover(function(e) {

      $("<div>").text($(this).attr("title")).addClass("tooltip
        ui-widget-header ui-corner-all").css({left:e.pageX,
        top:(e.pageY - 40)}).appendTo($("body"));

      tip = setTimeout("$('.tooltip').show('drop', { direction:'up'
        }); ", 750);

      $(this).attr("title", "");

    });
```

```
    $("#container a").mousemove(function(e) {
        $(".tooltip").css({'left':e.pageX, 'top':e.pageY - 35});
    });

    $("#container a").mouseout(function(e) {

        clearTimeout(tip);

        $("#" + e.target.id).attr("title", $(".tooltip").text());

        $(".tooltip").remove();
    });
  });
</script>
```

Save this as effectDrop.html. The page itself is simple. We've got a container <div> and a paragraph with three links inside it. The links are the elements that will trigger our tooltips.

Within our outer document.ready function, we have three distinct anonymous functions. The first is executed when one of the trigger elements fires the mouseover event, another is executed on mousemove, and the last works with the mouseout event.

In the first function, a new <div> element is created and its contents are set to the contents of the title attribute of the element that fired the mouseover event. The new element is given a class of tooltip and has its left and top style properties set to 35 pixels above the mouse pointer at the time of the event.

Next, a timer is started using JavaScript's setTimeout method, which will show the new tooltip using the drop effect after 750 milliseconds have passed. The title attribute of the element that was hovered over is then set to an empty string to prevent the OS default tooltip from appearing.

Our next anonymous function is attached to the mousemove event of whichever element fired the initial mouseover. Every time the mouse pointer moves our tooltip, <div> will be repositioned. This means that if the pointer is moved before the tooltip is shown, the tooltip will still appear in the correct location, and while the tooltip is open, it will follow the mouse pointer.

The final function basically tidies up after the tooltip. It clears the timeout (if it is still present) and retrieves the text content of the tooltip to put back as the element's title attribute. Finally, it removes the tooltip and the effect wrapper from the DOM, putting everything back as it was.

There is also some minimal CSS required for this example in addition to the styles provided by the CSS framework, mostly to style the new tooltip. Create the following stylesheet:

```css
#container {
  width:500px; margin:20px auto; padding:0 20px;
  font-family:Verdana; font-size:14px;
}
.tooltip {
  font-family:Georgia; font-weight:bold; font-size:16px;
  position:absolute; padding:2px 5px 3px; display:none;
  z-index:1000;
}
```

Save this in the `css` folder as `effectDrop.css`. When you run the file in your browser, you should see how the drop effect shows our tooltip, as in the following screenshot:

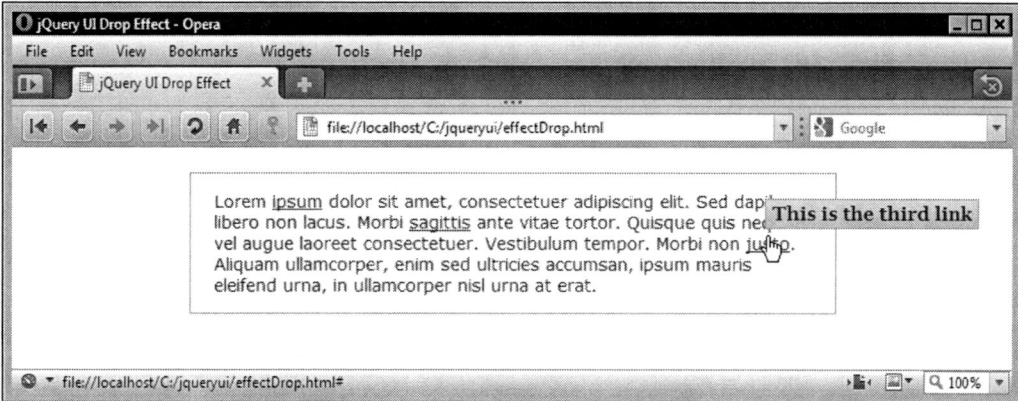

Sliding elements open or closed

The remaining effects of the jQuery UI library all work by showing and hiding elements in different ways rather than using opacity like most of the effects we have already looked at.

The `slide` effect is no exception and shows (or hides) an element by sliding it into (or out of) view. It is similar to the drop effect that we just looked. Its main difference is that it does not use opacity. This is a very common effect on things like login forms that slide out from the headers of websites.

For our next example, we can create exactly this kind of functionality. In `effectDrop.html` add a link to the CSS framework file and change the link to `effectDrop.css` to `effectSlide.css`:

```
<link rel="stylesheet" type="text/css"
  href="development-bundle/themes/smoothness/ui.all.css">
<link rel="stylesheet" type="text/css" href="css/effectSlide.css">
```

Then remove the container `<div>` from the `<body>` of the page and add the following HTML in its place:

```
<div id="loginBar" class="ui-corner-bottom">
  <form id="login" action="#"
    class="ui-corner-bottom ui-helper-clearfix">
    <label for="user">Username:</label><input type="text" id="user">
    <label for="pass">Password:</label><input type="text" id="pass">
    <button type="submit">Submit</button>
    <button id="cancel">Cancel</button>
  </form>
  <a href="#" id="showForm" title="Show login form"
    class="ui-corner-bottom">Login</a>
</div>
```

Don't forget to change the `<script>` element for the effect's source file to use `effects.slide.js`:

```
<script type="text/javascript"
  src="development-bundle/ui/effects.slide.js"></script>
```

The final `<script>` element will need to be changed to the following code:

```
<script type="text/javascript">
  $(function() {

    $("#showForm").click(function() {
      $(this).hide();
      $("#login").toggle("slide", { direction:"up" }, 1000,
        function() {
          $("#loginBar").removeClass("ui-corner-bottom").addClass(
            "ui-corner-bl");
        });
    });

    $("#cancel").click(function(e) {
      e.preventDefault();
      $("#login").toggle("slide", { direction:"up" }, 1000,
        function() {
```

```
        $("#loginBar").removeClass("ui-corner-bl").addClass(
            "ui-corner-bottom").find("a").show();
        });
    });
    });
</script>
```

Save this as `slide.html`. The page contains an outer container `<div>` element with a `<form>` element and a hyperlink inside it. The form contains a couple of labels, a couple of text inputs and a couple of buttons. The **Cancel** button will be used to close the login form, while the link in the container will be used to open it.

In the JavaScript, we have two event handling functions — the first catches the click event of the link and second hides the link along with executing the slide effect on the form using the `toggle` method. The default value for the `direction` option is `left`, so we override this and specify `up` as the value instead. Unintuitively, this will cause the form to slide *down*.

We use a callback function as the third argument to the slide method. Within this function we remove the class name that gives rounded edges to the bottom of the container element, and add the class name to give just the bottom-left corner a radius. This is to tidy up the appearance of the container with the form open.

The next function catches the click event of the **Cancel** button. Some browsers (IE) treat any button inside a form as a **Submit** button. So, to smooth out the closing animation in a cross-browser way we can use the `preventDefault()` method on the event object that is passed to our callback automatically.

We call the `toggle` method once again to slide the form back up and use the same arguments that we did in the first function. In the callback function for the effect we swap the class names back again so that both bottom corners of the container element are rounded. We also show the hyperlink again so that the form can be reopened.

We also use a little CSS in this example. Create the following stylesheet:

```
#loginBar {
  width:600px; height:20px; margin:auto;
  border:2px solid #aaa; background-color:#eee;
  position:relative;
}
#loginBar form {
  display:none; width:300px; background-color:#eee;
  border:2px solid #aaa; border-top:none; position:relative;
  left:298px; top:20px;
}
```

```
#loginBar form label {
  float:left; width:70px; margin:0 12px; padding-top:3px;
  color:#000; font-family:Verdana; font-size:12px;
  font-weight:bold;
}
#loginBar form input {
  float:left; width:190px; color:#000; margin-bottom:12px;
}
#loginBar form button { float:right; margin:0 12px 12px 0; }
#loginBar a {
  position:relative; left:520px; top:20px;
  padding:2px 10px 6px; color:#000; border:2px solid #aaa;
  border-top:none; background-color:#eee;
  text-decoration:none; text-align:center;
  font-family:Verdana; font-size:14px; font-weight:bold;
}
```

Save this as `effectSlide.css` in the `css` folder. The effect in progress should appear as in the following screenshot:

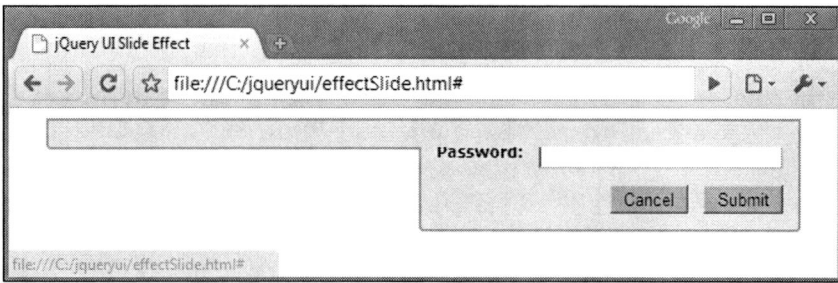

I said earlier that the `effects.core.js` file had the built-in ability to seamlessly use easing with the effects. Let's see how easy this is to achieve. Change the last `<script>` element in `slide.html` so that it appears as follows (new code shown in bold):

```
$(function() {
  $("#showForm").click(function() {
    $(this).hide();
      $("#login").toggle("slide", { direction:"up",
        easing: "easeOutBounce" }, 1000, function() {
      $("#loginBar").removeClass("ui-corner-bottom").addClass(
        "ui-corner-bl");
    });
  });
```

```
$("#cancel").click(function(e) {
  e.preventDefault();
  $("#login").toggle("slide", { direction:"up",
    easing: "easeOutQuad" }, 1000, function() {
    $("#loginBar").removeClass("ui-corner-bl").addClass(
      "ui-corner-bottom").find("a").show();
  });
});
});
```

Save this as `slideEasing.html`. See how easy that was. All we need to do is add the `easing` option within the effect's configuration object and define one, or more, of the easing methods as the option value. In this example, we specify a different easing method for each toggle state. When the form slides down, it bounces slightly at the end of the animation. When it slides back up, it will gradually slow down over the course of the animation.

The full range of easing methods we can make use of with the effects are as follows:

swing	easeInQuad	easeInCubic
linear	easeOutQuad	easeOutCubic
	easeInOutQuad	easeInOutCubic
easeInQuart	easeInQuint	easeInSine
easeOutQuart	easeOutQuint	easeOutSine
easeInOutQuart	easeInOutQuint	easeInOutSine
easeInExpo	easeInCirc	easeInElastic
easeOutExpo	easeOutCirc	easeOutElastic
easeInOutExpo	easeInOutCirc	easeInOutElastic
easeInBack	easeInBounce	
easeOutBack	easeOutBounce	
easeInOutBack	easeInOutBounce	

The window-blind effect

The blind effect is practically the same as the slide effect. Visually the element appears to do the same thing, and the two effects' code files are also extremely similar. The main difference between the two effects that we need worry about is that with this effect we can only specify the axis of the effect, not the actual direction.

The `direction` option that this effect uses for configuration only accepts the values `horizontal` or `vertical`. We'll build on the last example to see the blind effect in action. Add the `<script>` resource for the blind effect directly after the `<script>` that refers to the `effects.slide.js` file:

```
<script type="text/javascript"
  src="development-bundle/ui/effects.blind.js"></script>
```

Now change the handler function attached to the **Cancel** button, so that it appears as follows:

```
$("#cancel").click(function(e) {
  e.preventDefault();
  $("#login").effect("blind", { direction:"vertical" }, 1000,
    function() {
      $("#loginBar").removeClass("ui-corner-bl").addClass(
        "ui-corner-bottom").find("a").show();
    });
});
```

Save this as `effectBlind.html`. Literally, all we've changed is the string specifying the effect, in this case to `blind`, and the value of the `direction` property from `up` to `vertical`. Notice the subtle difference when we view the file between sliding the element and blinding it up?

When the login form slides up, the bottom of the element remains visible at all times, as if the whole form is moving up into the login bar. With blinding however, the element is hidden from view starting with the bottom first.

Clipping elements

The clip effect is very similar to the slide effect. The main difference is that instead of moving one edge of the targeted element towards the other, to give the effect of the element sliding out of view, the clip effect moves both edges of the targeted element in towards the center.

At the end of *Chapter 5*, we created an AJAX dialog example that showed a full-size image in a dialog when a thumbnail image was clicked. When the close button on the dialog was pressed, the dialog was simply removed from the page instantly. We could easily use the clip effect to close our dialog instead. In `ajaxDialog.html`, add the source files for the clip effect:

```
<script type="text/javascript"
  src="development-bundle/ui/effects.core.js"></script>
<script type="text/javascript"
  src="development-bundle/ui/effects.clip.js"></script>
```

Then change the dialog configuration object so that it appears as follows:

```
var dialogOpts = {
  modal: true,
  width: 388,
  height: 470,
  autoOpen: false,
  open: function() {
    $("#ajaxDialog").empty();
      $("<img>").attr("src", filename).appendTo("#ajaxDialog");
    $("#ajaxDialog").dialog("option", "title", titleText);
  },
  close: function() {
    $(this).parent().hide("clip");
  }
};
```

Save this as `effectClip.html`. In this simple addition to the existing file, we use the clip effect in conjunction with the `close` event callback to hide the dialog from view. The default configuration value of `vertical` for the `direction` option and the default speed of `normal` are both fine, so we just call the `hide` method specifying clip with no additional arguments.

The next screenshot shows the dialog being clipped:

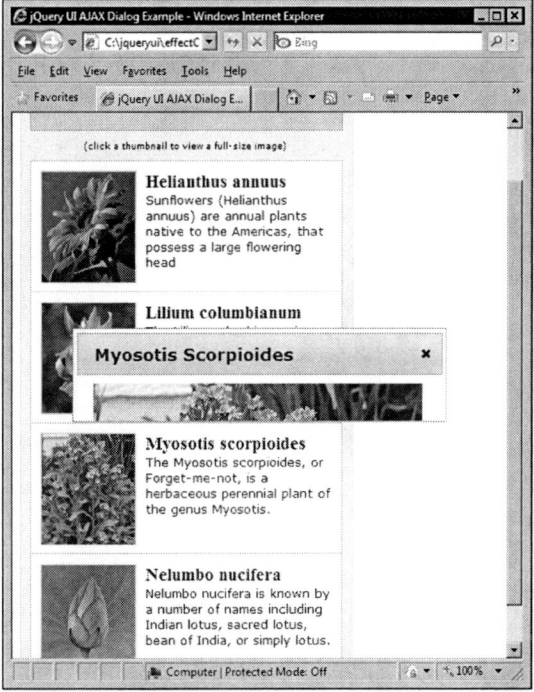

The clip effect also has just a single native configuration property. This is the `direction` property that we already saw in the drop and slide effects, but this time the property may take just one of two values, instead of four. The values that the clip effect's `direction` property accepts are `horizontal` or `vertical`, with `vertical` being the default.

Folding elements

Folding is a neat effect that gives the appearance that the element it's applied to is being folded up like a piece of paper. It achieves this by moving the bottom edge of the specified element up to 15 pixels from the top, then moving the right edge completely over towards the left edge.

The distance from the top that the element is shrunk to in the first part of this effect is exposed as a configurable property by the effect's API. So, this is something that we can adjust to suit the needs of our implementation. This property is an integer. We can see this in action by modifying our last example. In `ajaxDialog.html` once again, link to the fold source file:

```
<script type="text/javascript"
    src="development-bundle/ui/effects.fold.js"></script>
```

Then change the `close` event callback to this:

```
close: function() {
    $(this).parent().hide("fold", { size:200 }, 1000);
}
```

Save this as `effectFold.html`. This time we make use of the `size` configuration option to make the effect stop the first fold 200 pixels before the top of the dialog. We also slow the animation down a little by setting the duration to 1000 milliseconds. It's a really nice effect, the following screenshot shows the second part of the animation:

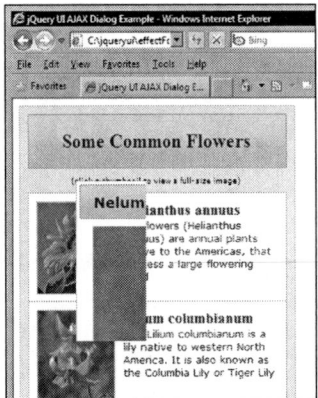

Summary

In this chapter, we've covered the complete range of UI effects available in the jQuery UI library. We've seen how easy it is to use the `effects.core.js` base component to construct attractive color animations and smooth class transitions.

We also saw that the following effects can be used in conjunction with the simple effect API:

- bounce
- highlight
- shake
- transfer

An important point is that most of the individual effects can be used not only with the effect API but can also make use of `show`/`hide` and `toggle` logic, making them incredibly flexible and robust. The following effects can be used with this advanced API:

- blind
- clip
- drop
- explode
- fold
- puff
- pulsate
- scale
- slide

This now brings us to not only the end of this chapter, but also the end of the book. There is a saying, I'm sure that almost all of you will have heard it before. It's the "give a man a fish..." saying. I hope that during the course of this book, I've taught you how to fish instead of just giving you a fish.

The aim of the examples that we've worked through over the chapters has not been just to show you how to use the library, but also to show you that it is powerful enough and flexible enough to be limited only by your imagination. The world class interfaces of tomorrow are made possible today with jQuery UI.

Index

Symbols

A

V

value option 130
values option 130

W

widget compatibility
  draggables, adding 306-310
  example 304, 306
width property 101
window-blind effect
  about 353, 354
  direction option 354

Y

Yahoo! Pipes
  using 317
yearRange option 153

Z

zIndex option
  using 111
zIndex property 198, 283

Thank you for buying
jQuery UI 1.7: The User Interface Library for jQuery

Packt Open Source Project Royalties

When we sell a book written on an Open Source project, we pay a royalty directly to that project. Therefore by purchasing jQuery UI 1.7: The User Interface Library for jQuery, Packt will have given some of the money received to the jQuery UI project.

In the long term, we see ourselves and you—customers and readers of our books—as part of the Open Source ecosystem, providing sustainable revenue for the projects we publish on. Our aim at Packt is to establish publishing royalties as an essential part of the service and support a business model that sustains Open Source.

If you're working with an Open Source project that you would like us to publish on, and subsequently pay royalties to, please get in touch with us.

Writing for Packt

We welcome all inquiries from people who are interested in authoring. Book proposals should be sent to author@packtpub.com. If your book idea is still at an early stage and you would like to discuss it first before writing a formal book proposal, contact us; one of our commissioning editors will get in touch with you.

We're not just looking for published authors; if you have strong technical skills but no writing experience, our experienced editors can help you develop a writing career, or simply get some additional reward for your expertise.

About Packt Publishing

Packt, pronounced 'packed', published its first book "Mastering phpMyAdmin for Effective MySQL Management" in April 2004 and subsequently continued to specialize in publishing highly focused books on specific technologies and solutions.

Our books and publications share the experiences of your fellow IT professionals in adapting and customizing today's systems, applications, and frameworks. Our solution-based books give you the knowledge and power to customize the software and technologies you're using to get the job done. Packt books are more specific and less general than the IT books you have seen in the past. Our unique business model allows us to bring you more focused information, giving you more of what you need to know, and less of what you don't.

Packt is a modern, yet unique publishing company, which focuses on producing quality, cutting-edge books for communities of developers, administrators, and newbies alike. For more information, please visit our website: www.PacktPub.com.

Learning jQuery 1.3

ISBN: 978-1-847196-70-5   Paperback: 444 pages

Better Interaction Design and Web Development with
Simple JavaScript Techniques

1. An introduction to jQuery that requires
    minimal programming experience

2. Detailed solutions to specific client-side
    problems

3. For web designers to create interactive elements
    for their designs

4. For developers to create the best user interface
    for their web applications

5. Packed with great examples, code, and clear
    explanations

jQuery Reference Guide

ISBN: 978-1-847193-81-0   Paperback: 268 pages

A Comprehensive Exploration of the Popular
JavaScript Library

1. Organized menu to every method, function,
    and selector in the jQuery library

2. Quickly look up features of the jQuery library

3. Understand the anatomy of a jQuery script

4. Extend jQuery's built-in capabilities with
    plug-ins, and even write your own

Please check **www.PacktPub.com** for information on our titles

Object-Oriented JavaScript

ISBN: 978-1-847194-14-5   Paperback: 356 pages

Create scalable, reusable high-quality JavaScript applications and libraries

1. Learn to think in JavaScript, the language of the web browser

2. Object-oriented programming made accessible and understandable to web developers

3. Do it yourself: experiment with examples that can be used in your own scripts

4. Write better, more maintainable JavaScript code

Learning Ext JS

ISBN: 978-1-847195-14-2   Paperback: 324 pages

Build dynamic, desktop-style user interfaces for your data-driven web applications

1. Learn to build consistent, attractive web interfaces with the framework components

2. Integrate your existing data and web services with Ext JS data support

3. Enhance your JavaScript skills by using Ext's DOM and AJAX helpers

4. Extend Ext JS through custom components

Please check **www.PacktPub.com** for information on our titles

LaVergne, TN USA
23 April 2010
180236LV00006B/22/P